4th Fighter Intcp. Gp.
Home Of The Mig Killers
4th Ftr. Intcp. Group
Combat Operations

112976
FU-976

Motorbooks International

WARBIRD HISTORY

F-86 SABRE

Robert F. Dorr

Motorbooks International
Publishers & Wholesalers

First published in 1993 by Motorbooks International Publishers & Wholesalers, PO Box 2, 729 Prospect Avenue, Osceola, WI 54020 USA

Library of Congress Cataloging-in-Publication Data

Dorr, Robert F.
F-86 Sabre/Robert F. Dorr.
p. cm. — (Warbird history series)
Includes index.
ISBN 0-87938-748-3
1. Sabre (Jet fighter plane) I. Title.
II. Series.
UG1242.F5D58 1993
358.4'383—dc20 93-1157

Printed and bound in Hong Kong

On the front cover: An F-86 Sabre over Korea, circa 1954–1955. *John Wilson.* Inset, FJ-3 Furys of VF-191 Satan's Kittens on the USS Yorktown. *Richard E. White*

On the back cover: Top, two Sabres from the 335th FIS. Bottom, Sabre pilots Marty Bambrick and Hank Crescibene pose beside Bambrick's Sabre. *Martin Bambrick*

On the title page: Sabres on the sand. The island of Paengyongdo, known to Americans as P. Y.-do, lay north of the 38th Parallel and offered its hard-packed Yellow Sea beach as an emergency landing spot for battle-damaged Sabres. In this previously unpublished view taken between January and May 1953, two NAA F-86F Sabres of the 336th FIS, part of the 4th FIW, have just made the perilous landing without damage. Marines of the West Coast Islands Defense Unit (WCIDU) scrutinize the ship. Not seen is a Sikorsky H-19 helicopter that hovered watchfully while F-86F-1-NA (s/n 51-2863; farthest from camera) and F-86F-15-NA (s/n 51-12976) touched down. The island, incidentally, remained part of South Korea after the 1953 armistice. *Richard I. Sudhoff*

On the frontispiece: In 1953, it was routine to spell the Soviet ship Mig rather than MiG. The 4th Fighter-Interceptor Group was the first F-86 Sabre outfit to reach the Korean peninsula and the first to kill a MiG. The real Sabres represented by these caricatures wore red stars all over their fuselages as the number of MiG kills grew and grew. The 51st, 18th, and 8th wings joined the 4th in Korea, but those who served in the 4th Wing (and its group, announced by this sign) went to some length to make it clear that MiG kill numbers put them at the top of the chart. *Richard B. Keener*

Contents

PU597
PU-597

CHAPTER ONE

Design and Development of the F-86

In 1944, America's aircraft industry reached its wartime peak, producing nearly 100,000 warplanes annually. The heroic machinery of the American heartland demonstrated how true, how prophetic, was the warning Japan's Adm. Isoroku Yamamoto uttered. Rather than claiming a victory at Pearl Harbor, Yamamoto had warned his fellow officers that the attack had merely "awakened a sleeping giant."

World War II air ace and manufacturer's test pilot George Welch pushes the silvery prototype XP-86 (45-59597) through glassy skies over Muroc, California. This portrait was snapped during, or not long after, the first flight of the XP-86 on 1 October 1947. The appearance of NAA's jet-powered pursuit ship was now fixed, and was to change little in years ahead, but the aircraft did not yet have a popular name. PU-597, inscribed beneath the left wing and on both sides of the rear fuselage, was a buzz number to enable groundlings to report any overzealous pilot who flew too low. The P in the airplane designation and buzz number reminds us that in 1947, the USAAF had not yet adopted the F for fighter designation. NAA via Steve Pace

In Dearborn, Michigan, the Ford company was turning out a new B-24 Liberator bomber every 51min. In Bethpage, New York, Grumman was in the midst of delivering 12,275 F6F Hellcat fighters in just 30 months. In Inglewood, California, the North American Aviation (NAA) plant produced B-25 Mitchell bombers and P-51 Mustang fighters so rapidly that the aircraft sat waiting, row after row, while US Army Air Forces (USAAF) personnel worked in a frenzy to get them delivered. American factories, workers, and products set a standard for all the world.

While World War II was being won, American leadership in science (the word technology did not exist then) brought astounding change. It was rumored that a time machine was being developed at the Philadelphia Navy Yard. It was true that a new bomb of incredible power was being assembled in a remote village in New Mexico. Radical new warplanes were taking shape with both propeller and jet-engine power.

So dominant was American industry that it could afford a luxury: more experimental planes were built and tested than were needed to win the war. In the California desert at a bleak, sandy outpost called Muroc, bizarre pursuit ships flew with strange wing shapes and different engines. The Curtiss XP-55 Ascender was pushed, rather than pulled, through the air (by a propeller) and boasted a swept-back wing. The Bell P-59A Airacomet was trucked to the desert with a fake propeller glued to its nose (to fool watching gophers and rattlesnakes) but flew without one. It was a time of miracles. American know-how dominated the world.

But science advanced elsewhere, too; in some disciplines, others were ahead. The Germans flew the first true jet aircraft and fielded the first operational jet fighter. The British pressed close behind. The world's most powerful nation, soon to unleash the fury of the atomic bomb, was merely third among those producing jet airplanes. And as we shall soon learn, the Soviet Union—a backward nation in so many other ways—was advancing at about the Americans' pace.

At the NAA facility in Inglewood, California, the company's Confidential Design Group, under Edgar Schmued, was pondering radically new versions of the P-51 Mustang, which had established itself as one of the most important fighters of World War II. Some of the impetus for Schmued's design effort came from the US Navy, which test-flew a P-51D Mustang from the carrier USS *Shangri-la* (CV-38) in 1944. Looking for a new carrier-based fighter that would exploit the Mustang's proven qualities, Schmued and his colleagues studied several advanced concepts, including a Mustang with swept-forward wings and both turboprop and turbojet power.

In great secrecy, the Navy turned down these advanced Mustang concepts. Instead, the Navy pressured NAA's engineers for a wholly new, but far from radical jet fighter, the XFJ-1.

The XFJ-1, later nicknamed the Fury, was radical only in introducing jet power. Otherwise, it was a conventional and straightforward design. To maintain full advantage of its very thin, high-speed wing, the aircraft was to have a circular nose engine air intake and straight-through ducting, rather than the side or wing air inlets chosen for the Lockheed P-80 Shooting Star, McDonnell XFD-1 Phantom, Vought XF6U-1 Pirate, and other new jet designs of the period. Only one American jet under development, the Republic XP-84 Thunderjet, had a circular nose air intake.

In 1945, USAAF selected a design nearly identical to the Navy's yet-unbuilt XFJ-1, including the latter's thin, straight wing. The USAAF gave its aircraft the designation XP-86. Because this fighter did not require the structural strength of a carrier-based craft, the XP-86 fuselage was thinner. Compared with the XFJ-1 Fury, the XP-86 also had slightly different air intake and empennage shapes.

But the XP-86, as it developed in the form of a drawing-board design, was unremarkable. In some flight regimes, it could not outperform the Mustang. In a few, the XP-86 offered no improvement whatsoever over the P-80 Shooting Star, which was already entering service, or the XP-84 Thunderjet, which was soon to fly.

Surprisingly, several NAA engineers from the period insist that no full-scale mock-up of this straight-wing XP-86 was ever completed. They are wrong. NAA did fabricate a mock-up of the straight-wing XP-86 and showed it to visiting USAAF officers, although no photo of the mock-up seems to have survived.

XP-86 Contract

On 18 May 1945, NAA received a contract for three XP-86 prototypes (45-59597, -59598, and -59599). Long after the XP-86's straight wing was being reconsidered (below), on 20 June 1945 the USAAF's formal Mock-Up Board approved the design. The approval seems to have been less than enthusiastic, however. USAAF officers pointedly argued that performance of the XP-86 would offer no improvement over Republic's XP-84, which was by now the recipient of a production contract.

In early 1945, the NAA designers at Inglewood came into possession of captured German wind-tunnel data that had been obtained by US technical intelligence experts. By then, Schmued's engineers were also aware of an operational German jet fighter, the Messerschmitt Me-262.

The Messerschmitt had almost nothing in common with US designs (it was a twin jet, with engines hung under the wings and a slight sweepback on the leading edge of its wing, roughly 15deg). Furthermore, it wasn't as if the Germans had thought up this innovation all by themselves. American designers had long ago proposed swept wings for some aircraft but had been run up against a total lack of interest at the newly-completed Pentagon building in the days prior to the Axis surrender.

Larry Green, NAA's head of Design Aerodynamics, attended night school to sharpen his fluency in the German language so he could pore through the wind-tunnel reports. Green also studied interrogations of captured German scientists and engineers.

Finally, a captured Me-262 became available for rigorous study by Schmued's Inglewood team. A pile of documents, a real Me-262, and Green's fast-improving German proficiency all added up to a dramatic change at NAA. Engineers, military officers, and corporate decision makers alike came to the realization, as if struck by a bolt from above, that the lackluster performance of the XP-86 could be improved strikingly with a swept wing.

A 35deg sweep 5.0 aspect ratio wing with full span leading slats was quickly built and tested in September 1945 on the XP-86 model in NAA's low-speed wind tunnel. It had been expected that the wing would show instability at high lift coefficients, and it did; but engineers determined that satisfactory stalling characteristics could be achieved with the slats. They could not have guessed that removing the very same slats, nearly a decade later, would help Americans at war in a country most had never heard of.

The proposal to overhaul the XP-86 design and install a swept wing was prepared under the watchful eye of USAAF Project Engineer Capt. Roy Mann. NAA's Raymond H. Rice discussed the concept with Gen. William Craigie, head of research and development at Wright Field. Told that installing a new wing would cause a six-month delay in the first flight of what had seemed, so far, a mediocre performer, Craigie said, "Go ahead." The swept wing was officially approved on 1 November 1945.

Even then, the swept-wing XP-86 was to have straight tail surfaces. Details of the leading-edge slat design were debated intensely.

Eventually, vertical and horizontal tail surfaces were also swept. During this period, high-speed wind tunnel tests were being conducted on a model of the revised XP-86 at the National Advisory Committee for Aeronautics (NACA), Ames Laboratory. Considerable difficulty was encountered with tunnel wall corrections in trying to reach the required high-subsonic Mach numbers. Tests showed that the relatively large trailing-edge angle of the airfoil had to be changed, so a constant 4in (10cm) chord extension was added over the full span to reduce the trailing edge angle. This was the final change to the wing planform and was used on all F-86s until introduction of the 6-3 hard wing seven years later on the F-86F.

As of 1 November 1945, when many projects were being cancelled after war's end and USAAF were "chopping off" on a swept-wing XP-86, the only warplane with fully swept wings that had proven successful was the

Probably with Maj. Ken Chilstrom at the controls, the second NAA XP-86, not yet named the Sabre (45-59598), flies over the desert expanses near Muroc. Note the extended speed brakes. The early XP-86 had to be flown with a J35 engine because the more powerful J47 was not available. Long before Chilstrom signed off on successful Phase II flight tests with the XP-86, USAAF handed NAA a contract for F-86A fighters. via Larry Davis

Me163 rocket fighter. Schmued, Rice, Green, and others could not possibly know that in a remote corner of the Union of Soviet Socialist Republics, similar research was very close to producing a fighter called the MiG-15.

In January 1946, 445 full-time engineers were on the project. On 28 January 1946, the USAAF approved a cockpit mock-up. Designed for air-to-air combat, the XP-86 was being built to specifications calling for empty weight of 9,243lb (4,192kg), a normal gross weight of 13,311lb (6,037kg), and a maximum gross weight of 16,438lb (7,456kg). The thin shape of the new fighter's wing imposed some weight penalties elsewhere and the XP-86, long before its first flight, was already 40 percent heavier than the P-51H Mustang.

The XP-86, or company model NA-140, was to be powered by a Chevrolet-built, General Electric-designed J35-C-3 or Allison J35-A-5 with 4,000lb (1,814kg) thrust (originally designated TG-180). This was an unhappy compromise, since plans called for a more powerful engine to become known as the J47. The first three XP-86 aircraft were unarmed.

Test pilot for the new fighter, as on many NAA aircraft of the period, was George (Wheaties) Welch. At Pearl Harbor, Welch, then a USAAF lieutenant, had gotten aloft in a Curtiss P-40 and had shot down four of the Japanese attackers. He'd become an air ace in the Pacific theater, raising his total to 16 kills, before joining NAA in 1944. Welch was following a tradition of achievement set by Bob Chilton, who'd made the first flights of most versions of the P-51 Mustang.

Welch began to rack up his own series of first flights. He drew the honors when it was time for the maiden flight of NAA's P-82B Twin Mustang on 31 October 1945, and the P-82E Twin Mustang on 17 April 1947. The Twin Mustang was an attempt to achieve long range in a fighter by joining two modified Mustang fuselages to a single wing structure, and the B and E models flown by Welch proved successful. The type was the final propeller-driven fighter for the USAAF. On 18 September 1947, the US Army Air Forces became an independent branch of service as the US Air Force (USAF); we will use the latter term from this point onward.

Test pilot George Welch also made the first flight of the Navy's XSN2J-1 trainer on 10 February 1947. Two prototypes of the XSN2J-1 were tested, but the type was not adopted, although it later evolved into the T-28 used by both the Navy and Air Force.

XP-86 Flight-Testing

The first XP-86 (45-59597) was completed on 8 August 1947. On 10 September 1947, NAA trucked this prototype from Inglewood to the Air Force's remote desert installation at Muroc Dry Lake, California.

Some of what went on at Muroc was secretive. Much was not. Used for training and check-out of P-38 Lightning pilots and initial flying of other hazardous aircraft from 1941 on, the base was quite primitive. P-38 transition was accomplished here so that Los Angeles' congested areas would be spared the frequent crashes by newly-graduated fighter pilots.

Muroc had been a secluded hideaway for secret tests of weird and mys-

Test pilot George (Wheaties) Welch confers with a ground technician while sitting in the very first XP-86. It's interesting to note that when the 9,823rd and last aircraft in the Sabre series was manufactured, making the Sabre the most numerous jet fighter outside the Soviet Union, the external appearance of the aircraft had changed very little. Pitot tubes at the leading edge of both wings and absence of gunports help to identify this ship as a prototype. NAA via Ed Davies

terious airplanes, among them the previously mentioned Curtiss XP-55 Ascender pusher-prop fighter with swept wings developed years before German data on wing sweep was available. Over time, as Americans' perception of distance changed, Muroc was to become merely a commute from the Los Angeles megapolis, but in 1947, Muroc was near the end of the earth. The hundreds of P-38 pilots who had transitioned there knew about a place that was almost entirely unknown to the civilian populace.

Welch made the first flight of the first XP-86 on 1 October 1947 at Muroc. After a few trial taxying runs, he lifted off for what was supposed to be a 10min familiarization hop around the pattern. As Welch turned final to land, however, his nose gear jammed in the half-extended position. The test pilot aborted his landing and began a series of gentle maneuvers aimed at freeing the nose gear.

More than 40min elapsed, tensions building. It became apparent that the nose wheel wasn't going to lock into place successfully, so Welch chose to land anyway. As he touched down, the impact locked down the nose leg correctly and the number one XP-86 came to a stop, undamaged.

It has been speculated, ever since, that Welch may have exceeded Mach 1 on that first flight, or on an early flight that followed.

The sound barrier was an evil, invisible enemy in Hollywood films and some of the earliest TV dramas. The myth of the era was that a solid wall, or barrier, was waiting to be cracked open by a fearless and reckless jock in a fast jet.

The truth was, pilots had encountered compressibility near the speed of sound for years, and the phenomenon was well understood. Sonic speed is 763mph (1,228km/h) at sea level and decreases with altitude. Every fast plane from the P-38 Lightning onward had certainly poked up against the barrier and some may have gone through it. Though some have denied it, including test pilot Charles E. (Chuck) Yeager, it is not impossible that the first supersonic flight may have been attained by the Republic XP-47J Thunderbolt (43-46952) of 1944, which is thought to have attained 504mph (811km/h) while in a dive at the relatively high altitude of 34,300ft (10,454m).

In the same way we know that Christopher Columbus discovered America, those of us who grew up in the era know that mankind's first supersonic flight was made on 14 October 1947 by Captain Yeager in the number one Bell XS-1, later designated X-1 (46-0062). Evidence suggests that long before the Admiral of the Ocean Sea, however, explorers from China and the Nordic countries discovered America (if anyone can discover a nation already populated by natives), but there is no proof of it. Though they, too, lack proof, very few people connected with the XP-86 believe that Yeager went supersonic before Welch did. Many years later, it can only be speculated that the XP-86 could have flown at supersonic speed before the XS-1, although the XP-86 did not officially penetrate the sound barrier until 26 April 1948, with Welch at the controls. Most accounts have it that the XP-86 was the second supersonic aircraft.

Interestingly, the XP-86 was not revealed to the world until 24 November 1947, fully eight weeks after its maiden flight. An NAA press release disclosed that it had "successfully completed its initial flight tests." Whoever drafted the release was hyper-sensitive to the issue of supersonic flight, for the release asserted only that the XP-86 was "designed and built to come nearer the speed of sound than any other American fighter."

Apart from the question of its speed, the early flight trials of the XP-86 at Muroc were aimed at determining whether it could meet the USAF's requirements for a fighter. In its handling qualities, the XP-86 proved remarkably docile. Stall characteristics were good, with a positive warning buffet about 6 knots above the stall and immediate recovery when speed was regained.

The first USAF officer to fly the XP-86 was Maj. Ken Chilstrom. Once Welch had completed Phase I of the test program with about 30hr of flight time, it was time to begin Phase II test flying that required USAF direction. Despite rains and flooding of the dry lake bed, Chilstrom convinced the chief of the Flight Test Division, Col. Al Boyd, that Phase II could proceed. On 2 December 1947, Chilstrom went aloft in the first XP-86 (still powered by a J35 engine because the planned J47 was as yet available). After a get acquainted flight, Chilstrom flew a second sortie the same day, with no serious problems.

Chilstrom had extensive experience with the straight-wing Republic YP-84 Thunderjet, which was not his favorite aircraft, and was delighted to find the XP-86 faster and easier to handle. He made the Phase II follow-on flights in six days, logging 10hr 17min in 11 flights. He checked out the new fighter's performance up to Mach 0.9 and up to 45,000ft (13,716m). One glitch: the cabin pressurization system was inoperative. Chilstrom concluded many years later that oxygen systems in use at the time did not provide the safety margins needed to fly in an unpressurized cockpit.

In 1947, the P for pursuit designation became F for fighter. It was fitting, then, that early Sabres went to the First Fighter, the 1st Fighter Group at March Field, California. Among the first Sabres in service were these NAA F-86A-5-NA Sabres (48-210, in foreground) of the group's 71st Fighter Squadron. An aircraft with markings identical to this one (48-214) set a world speed record on 20 May 1950, piloted by Capt. Richard D. Creighton who subsequently became a Korean War ace. USAF

USAF deliveries

A series of flight tests continued into 1948 and ultimately the aircraft was officially handed over to the USAF on 30 November 1948. The USAF had already ordered 33 fighters known to the manufacturer as the NA-151 and to the USAF as the F-86A-1 (47-0605/0637). These were expected to have improved performance with the 5,200lb (2,358kg) thrust General Electric J47-GE-13 turbojet.

Welch made the first flight of the first F-86A-1 (47-0605) on 20 May 1948. The first two F-86A-1s, the manufacturer's model NA-151, were accepted by the USAF on 28 May 1948.

The early production aircraft now had an increased empty weight of 10,077lb (4,571kg), or some 347lb (157kg) more than the prototype. With its more powerful engine, the fighter seemed for the first time realistically able to challenge the world air speed record, 650.796mph (1,047.352km/h), set by the straight-wing Douglas D-558 Skystreak on 25 August 1947. Both the Skystreak and the previous record holder, a Lockheed P-80R Shooting Star, were specialized aircraft optimized for the high-speed effort. The F-86A-1, in contrast, was very close to a fully operational warplane.

The speed record attempt was made 5 September 1948 by Maj. Robert L. Johnson in an early F-86A-1 (47-0611).

With an audience of no fewer than 80,000 (the only time a vast public gathering observed such an effort), Johnson flew his fully-loaded F-86A-1 on six passes over the measured course. The audience saw the new fighter fly faster than ever before, reaching an average speed of 669.480mph (1,077.420km/h). Unfortunately, technical glitches prevented the effort from being properly recorded and registered.

Another attempt was mounted in the privacy of Muroc air base (AB), and on 15 September 1948, Johnson was able to achieve a record of 670.981mph (1,079.836km/h). This time, the achievement was fully sanctioned, but it was not as difficult as it might have appeared. At the time, NAA was beginning to turn out the F-86A-5 version (company model NA-161) with slightly more powerful J47-GE-7 and J47-GE-13 engines. Though early deliveries were delayed by engine shortages, the production airplanes coming from the factory routinely exceeded the speed Johnson had attained.

Unfortunately, Sabres were also routinely falling out of the sky. The 1st Fighter Group under Col. Frank Perego at March Field, California—operating the Lockheed F-80B Shooting Star—was chosen as the first unit in the newly-independent USAF to receive the new NAA fighter. The group's 94th Hat in the Ring Fighter Squadron headed up by Maj. Jim Lemon took delivery of its first aircraft in February 1949. The group's 71st Fighter Squadron under Lt. Col.

USAF dependents Jim Prebbanow and Jean Abay pose on 28 February 1950 in front of one of the first F-86A-5-NA Sabres (48-159) seen at Williams Field, Arizona, while visiting from March Field, California. Note the doors covering the .50cal machine gunports, a cantankerous feature that was unique to F-86A-1 and F-86A-5 airplanes. The previous month, the USAF changed the names of all its fighter groups and made them fighter wings. This ship belongs to the pioneer 1st Fighter Wing's 94th Hat in the Ring Squadron. The previous year, the Soviet Union had exploded its first atomic bomb, so all of these F-86As were assigned to the Air Defense Command (ADC) to defend the North American continent. Jim, Jean, and other Americans could have had no clue that five months hence they would be at war on a little-known Asian peninsula.
Joseph A. Buebe

Robert Petit, soon commanded by Lt. Col. Loren McCollum, followed. But it was happening too fast. The bugs had not been exterminated from the Sabre design.

World War II air ace Maj. Robin Olds was operations officer of the 94th FS when the first Sabres arrived. "About 35 F-86A-1s were delivered to the 1st Fighter Group then stationed at March Field," recalls Olds. "It was *not* a good machine [Olds' emphasis]! I can't remember how many we wrecked, or how many pilots were injured or killed in the damned things. There was too much of both. Sometimes being on the sharp end of the sword ain't all that much fun."

The sharp end? As Capt. James J. Hagenback describes it, "We in the 1st Fighter Group were considered the avant-garde in USAF fighter operations because we'd been first with the F-80 and first into the F-86. There was an abundance of WW II pilots around. When the 1st Group was reactivated at March, the group commander, Col. Gilbert Meyers [later replaced by Perego] personally interviewed all fighter pilots to determine if they had satisfactory qualifications. Only pilots with several hundred hours of fighter time were accepted. This paid off transitioning into the F-86 [where] the principal problem was the inherent bugs in the introduction of a new aircraft and the fact that almost weekly a new problem was discovered in the engineering and maintenance areas."

Robin Olds: "I imagine you are already aware of the emotions that played upon those of us who flew the 86s in those early days, but think of this: We so distrusted the brand-new ejection seats, we flew with the safety pins in the handles. And they weren't that easy to remove. The brand-new leading edge slats were so flimsy we often faced no slats on one wing and full or partial slats on the other. I won't go into wheels that refused to come down, elevators that tore off in high-speed dives, engines that caught fire or exploded, stick grips that melted in your hands...all those little things made you happy just to last until Friday beer call."

It was considered a historic moment when, on 18 October 1949, the 1st Fighter Group put 16 F-86As into the air for a ceremonial flyover at NAA's Inglewood factory.

Even before fighter pilots at March Field began risking their lives in as-yet-unperfected Sabres, the US Navy placed the straight-wing FJ-1 Fury into service. The Navy was not contemplating a swept-wing version—though one was to come much, much later. The Navy's Fury fighters, including the FJ-2 which came on the scene nearly a decade after the FJ-1, will reappear in Chapter 3.

Service Trials

Accelerated service tests officially began on the F-86A at Muroc in January 1949 and continued at nearby March Field. As Hagenback recalls, "We were officially performing field testing in our daily operations and tactics applications and maneuvers." Maj. Frank Everest set an unofficial speed record from Dayton, Ohio, to Washington, D.C., in February 1949 at 33min and 3sec.

Every man who served at March Field remembers the day Lt. Dick O'Leary used a Sabre to prove the old maxim that, in aviation, 99 percent of all accidents occur upon contact with the ground.

Hagenback: "One day, one flight was practicing aerobatics such as one might encounter in combat. The flight leader performed a few rolls and [a] normal loop when a wingman stated he had an engine problem or had lost his aileron boost. This was O'Leary, a rather new problem, who couldn't seem to control his altitude for the controls seemed locked and he could only do a series of chandelles all the while he was losing altitude.

"He was told to bail out if he didn't think he could get back to March Field and, being about 30mi [48km] from the base, he tried to bail. His next radio transmission was that he couldn't eject because the canopy wouldn't come off.

"The rest of the flight watched [O'Leary] descend in the hilly area east of the base and saw him doing these crazy pitch-ups until he was seen to strike the earth on the side of a hill as he descended. Naturally, the others thought O'Leary had received fatal injuries judging from the dust and appearance of the crash so they returned to base and directed the search and recovery effort immediately.

"When the medics arrived by helicopter, they found Lieutenant O'Leary outside the aircraft with relatively minor injuries. He had hit the hillside much as a skier lands after a jump. Because the aircraft had just straightened out at the correct angle to hit the hill with least impact, it wasn't demolished but rather slid to a stop in the valley below. A local farmer who had been plowing nearby saw the plane impact and rushed to the rescue of the pilot.

O'Leary meanwhile managed to open the canopy and jumped out onto the ground just as the farmer rushed up. The farmer asked if he was injured and if he needed anything. O'Leary said, 'Yeah, I could use a cigarette.' O'Leary, of course, was hospitalized with back and leg injury, but wasn't nearly the catastrophe it could have been." Other pilots who flew Sabres in early days were not so lucky. Indeed, as we shall see, in the 1950s Sabres and other jets fell to earth far more often than they do today.

By March 1949, the last of 33 F-86A-1s (not 35, as Olds remembered) was completed. Delivery began of the first F-86A-5 (48-0129). The F-86A-1 supposedly had a distinctive recognition feature: numerous sources say that it was the only version delivered with flush-fitting gun muzzle doors that maintained the smooth flow of air around the nose. When the pilot thumbed the trigger, the doors opened in less than 0.05sec, then closed automatically after each burst. In fact, at least some F-86A-5s were also delivered with the gun doors that were replaced by open troughs very slowly. The protective doors over the gunports were an unnecessary frill that involved maintenance problems: they froze up at the most inopportune times so crew chiefs wired them in the open position. Belatedly, they were dispensed with.

The armament of six .50cal machine guns was to be standard on nearly all F-86s built for the USAF (initially, six M-3 guns with a rate of fire of 1,100 rounds per minute and ammunition supply of 1,602 rounds or 267 rounds per gun).

In the 1949 Thompson Trophy Race, Capt. Bruce Cunningham won the Jet Division of the contest flying a F-86A-5 in what can only be described as an incredibly difficult event. The planes flew 10 laps of a 15mi (25km) circular course around seven pylons for 150mi (241km). Cunningham was credited with an elapsed time of 15:21.23min, or an average speed of 586.173mph (943.352km/h).

Test program

As more and more of the new fighters became available, one was dispatched to Eglin Air Force Base (AFB), Florida, for indoor climatic testing and several others served as test ships. NACA obtained an early F-86A-1 (47-0609) which was unarmed but heavily instrumented for in-flight experiments and for evaluation of low-speed performance in the pattern.

The F-86A-5 model introduced a V-shaped bulletproof windscreen and heated gun compartments. The F-86A-5 could carry 206gal drop tanks, rockets, and bombs. One F-86A-5 (49-1172) was fitted with an aerial refueling receptacle in its upper forward fuselage where its radar had been, but air refueling was never adopted on operational F-86s.

During deliveries to March Field, a name for the fighter was chosen.

Aircraft 48-0184, an F-86A-5, appeared at Muroc and later at March Field with a knife painted on its rudder that might have been a cutlass or a scimitar. It was, of course, a sabre. The name was chosen by a board of officers and became official on 4 March 1949. In later years, popular literature wanted to call NAA's ferocious fighter the Sabrejet or the Sabre Jet. But the proper name of the F-86 was always simply Sabre.

A few months after the name was chosen, in September 1949, Secretary of State Dean Acheson gave a speech proclaiming that in the postwar era, with the growing threat of communism, the United States was willing and ready to protect its interests abroad. Acheson ticked off a roster of countries that qualified as close allies, and which Americans would shed blood to defend, if necessary, rather than allow them to be swallowed up by the Red Scourge. In one of those catastrophic mistakes that alter history, Acheson left newly-independent South Korea, also known as the Republic of Korea (ROK) off his list, even though he never intended to. In Pyongyang, the secretary's words were interpreted as an invitation.

At this critical juncture, a few men came together at March Field to replace the F-80B, bring up the F-86A, and develop the means to wield the newly-named Sabre like a terrible swift sword.

Just as Americans failed to grasp Acheson's blunder (in later years, North Korean Foreign Minister Ho Dam said that the speech made South Korea "fair game"), they failed to realize that others, too, were playing at the cutting edge of scientific progress.

Two key aircraft designers in the Soviet Union, Artem I. Mikoyan and Mikhail I. Gurevich, lent their names to the Mikoyan-Gurevich OKB (design bureau), which was surfacing as a leader in the development of jet fighters.

Almost as important, the Mikoyan-Gurevich OKB gave birth to a new term in the vocabulary of men who fly and fight. The one-syllable term actually dated to the recent world war, but was not yet well known in the West. Soon it would take on a meaning rich with dread; the term would keep its horrific meaning for half a century. Like the Sabre's name, the Soviet bureau's three-letter abbreviation is often published incorrectly. It is not Mig or MIG. The proper name for the Sabre's adversary is, and always was, MiG.

The MiG-9 had been a successful straight-wing jet fighter. The MiG-15 was the result of a program launched by a Kremlin meeting of March 1946. The design of the MiG-15 was well advanced in September 1946 when, in an inexplicable error nearly as cataclysmic as Acheson's, Great Britain sold 25 Rolls-Royce Nene turbojet engines to the Soviet Union. Maj. Gen. V. Klimov headed a team that transformed the Nene into the fully operational RD-45/VK-1 engine which powered the MiG-15.

Because the United States had sought no monopoly on captured German scientific data, the MiG OKB's engineers exploited the same data on swept-back wings that had occupied the attention of NAA's Larry Green and others. Still, Russian ingenuity had as much to do with creating the new fighter as did British or German engineering work. The first MiG-15 was taken for its maiden flight by Viktor N. Yuganov on 30 December 1947, precisely 90 days after George Welch's first flight in the XP-86. The MiG-15 was unknown outside the secretive Soviet Union; but thanks to the German data on wing sweep, the British Nene sale, Acheson, and North Korea's Premier Kim Il Sung who peered toward the south with lust in his heart, the Sabre and the MiG were destined to meet.

In early days at March Field, it didn't immediately look like the F-86A Sabre was going to be a giant success. World War II ace Maj. Robin Olds, operations officer for the 94th, remembered, "We were dropping them out of the sky like flies."

Sq. Ldr. William (Paddy) Harbison, a Royal Air Force (RAF) pilot on an exchange posting at March Field, says that the first F-86A-1s posed "terrible difficulties." Remembers Harbison, "We lost a lot of people. We got the airplanes very quickly and were doing accelerated service tests, trying to fly a lot of hours."

Early Operations

The flaps on the F-86A-1 were not interconnected, making it possible for an asymmetrical condition to occur on takeoff. This, combined with a hydraulic failure, killed at least one 1st Fighter Group pilot. Harbison found that the F-86A-1, with power boost instead of the fully reversible ailerons that came later, could not go supersonic without dropping the left wing, making it difficult for the pilot to maintain stability. Worse, early J47 turbojets had a very short engine life, far less than 50hr. When the 1st Fighter Group's pilots began delivering Sabres to the USAF's second user of the aircraft, the 4th Fighter Group at Langley AFB, Virginia, it was not unusual during a delivery flight to need an engine change on the way. Pilots were also frustrated by the protective doors on the F-86A-1's gunports. Sometimes, Harbison remembers, "When you fired the guns, you had malfunctions with those [doors]. The guns would fire when the doors were not open and you'd be ricocheting all over the place."

Many of the problems were resolved with the F-86A-5 variant and by the time the 81st Fighter Group at Kirtland AFB, New Mexico, began receiving Sabres in 1950, things were looking much better. Furthermore, the F-86A-5 had a decisive edge in performance over other fighters of the era: It was substantially faster than the F-84E Thunderjet or F9F-5 Panther and at least as maneuverable. It was as well armed and, with the introduction of the Mark 18 lead-computing gunsight followed by the A-1CM gunsight on later models, its armament was more effective.

The A-1CM gunsight was coupled with an AN/APG-30 radar installed in the upper lip of the nose intake. Although almost useless at low altitude because of ground clutter, the radar could be slaved to the sight for effective tracking of an aerial target. F-86A-5 airplanes retrofitted with A-1CM sight were redesignated F-86A-6 when they retained AN/APG-5C radar, and F-86A-7 when retrofitted with AN/APG-30.

While development of the MiG-15 continued and North Korea's leaders rejoiced that the southern half of their peninsula was ripe for the picking, F-86 Sabre deliveries continued in 1950 with few significant problems or delays. Beginning with the 100th Sabre, an improved canopy defrost system was installed to eliminate frosting problems encountered above 37,000ft (11,277m). Beginning with the 160th F-86A, a new wing slat eliminated the lock and provided fully automatic operation.

F-86As were built in batches that occupied serial numbers (s/n) 47-0605/0637, 48-0139/0316, and 49-1007/1339. Long before the 554th and last F-86A model was delivered in December 1950, the Sabre proved itself a fully operational and important part of the USAF's arsenal. A flight demonstration team, the Sabre Dancers, headed by the 1st Fighter Group's Capt. Dwight S. Beckham, gave public demonstrations of the Sabre's maneuverability. At a fighter meet at Kirtland in May 1950, F-86A Sabre pilots of the 1st, 4th, and 81st groups demonstrated their capabilities. Next to acquire the Sabre were the 33rd Fighter Group at Otis AFB, Massachusetts, and the 56th Fighter Group at Selfridge AFB, Michigan.

The first F-86As sent to Europe were with the 81st Fighter Wing (after wings replaced groups as the standard USAF unit) sent to RAF Bentwaters, England, in August 1951.

As this narrative will relate when we reach the Asian conflict awaiting early Sabres, a number of F-86A Sabres were converted to RF-86A reconnaissance aircraft (variously reported as six to 11 airplanes). The first six were modified at Tachikawa, Japan, under Project Honeybucket. The full total (apparently 11) was later referred to as Project Ashtray airplanes. There were different Ashtray conversions for different RF-86A missions.

The F-86B designation was temporarily assigned to a planned version that would have met a USAF requirement for bigger tires on the Sabre. On the drawing board, the F-86B would have had a fuselage fully 7in (17.8cm) wider, just to accommodate the new undercarriage. Because of improvements in tire and brake technology, the USAF decided that the Sabre could keep its original tire size. In place of 190 F-86B Sabres that were to have been delivered, 188 airframes became part of the F-86A-5 purchase, and two became F-86Cs.

The F-86C (manufacturer's model NA-157) was NAA's response to the USAF's request for a penetration fighter to escort Strategic Air Command (SAC) bombers to targets deep in the Soviet Union. Work on the design was begun on 17 December 1947. In place of the open nose intake, this much-redesigned aircraft had a bullet-shaped nose with scooped air intakes on its fuselage sides. The penetration fighter model was powered by an 8,000lb (3,628kg) thrust Pratt & Whitney J48-P-1 centrifugal-flow turbojet engine, itself a license-built version of the British Rolls-Royce Tay. Although an improved version later produced satisfactory results with the Lockheed F-94C Starfire, the J48 engine was never a big success in American service and was an Achilles' heel to the

Flown by George Welch on 24 April 1950, this NAA YF-93A (48-317), originally designated F-86C, had side-mounted air intakes and a 6,250lb (2,834kg) thrust Pratt & Whitney J48-P-1 centrifugal-flow turbojet. The overweight YF-93A made a dismal last-place showing in a penetration fighter competition with the McDonnell XF-88 Voodoo and Lockheed XF-90, none of which was ever ordered into production. The two YF-93A test ships were turned over to the National Advisory Committee for Aeronautics (NACA) where they were employed in various tests until being retired and scrapped.

Over the years, a number of Sabres flew in research projects for NACA and its successor, the National Air and Space Administration (NASA). The first was this F-86A-1-NA (47-609), the eighth Sabre built. With a nose sensor boom, an unusual gray finish, and the number NACA 135 (not yet applied here), this early Sabre performed early explorations into compressibility and trans-sonic maneuverability. NACA via Robert L. Burns

At first designated F-95A, the NAA F-86D Sabre was an interim, one-man interceptor armed with 24 2.75in (6.98cm) folding fin aircraft rockets (FFAR) in a ventral tray. First flight of this service-test YF-86D Sabre (50-0577) was made on 22 December 1949 by Joseph Lynch. This proof-of-concept vehicle lacked the intended radar fire-control system and had a very crude after-burner fed by external pipes, which are visible beneath the tail. NAA via Ed Davies

NAA penetration fighter. Indeed, no centrifuged-flow engine was to prove especially successful after the early 1950s.

Because the F-86C was radically redesigned to accommodate this "fat" engine, it was redesignated YF-93A in 1950. Compared with production Sabres, this aircraft was bigger and heavier requiring dual main wheels and a larger internal fuel supply. The F-86C/YF-93A competed with the McDonnell XF-88 Voodoo and Lockheed XF-90 in an intense competition that was held not once but twice—and came in dead last, both times.

The second time, the YF-93A was seriously considered but found deficient in the penetration fighter contest. First flown no sooner than 24 January 1950 with George Welch as pilot, and with no justifiable reason for its Y service-test prefix, the YF-93A simply proved that the best way to develop a big fighter was not to enlarge the Sabre. Two were built (47-0317/0318) and even before the YF-93A flunked in competition with the two other types, plans existed to purchase 188 of them. In the end, none of the penetration fighter candidates was produced. Gen. Curtis E. LeMay, SAC boss, despised a bureaucracy that wanted to shackle him with fighters; LeMay coined the expression, "Fighters are fun, but bombers are important." The USAF ordered more bombers instead, and NACA used the two YF-93As to test lateral air intakes.

Dog Sabre

North Korea invaded across the 38th Parallel on 25 June 1950 and President Harry S. Truman made his courageous decision—despite the Acheson speech—to send American forces to defend South Korea. It took only months to defeat North Korea and to open a new war with China, which introduced the Sabre and the MiG (covered in Chapter 2). But the threat of communism had greater poignancy when it was closer to home.

In the 1950s, Americans built fallout shelters in their basements. Children practiced taking cover from a nuclear flash in the sky. Nikita Khrushchev detonated a bigger hydrogen bomb than the United States possessed. Serious thinkers predicted that the human race would not make it to 1960. The air defense of North America became a challenge, having a national priority second to none. Way down in a distant second place came American troops fighting and dying in a faraway spot. Lt. Gen. John R. Hodge used a one-liner to deflate the morale of newly-arriving servicemen. "Men," Almond warned newcomers, "nobody back home can even find you on the map. Now that you're here, I've got three items of bad news for you. They're gonorrhea, diarrhea, and Korea."

In 1950, the State Department estimated the number of ethnic Koreans residing in the United States at 3,275. Television was in its infancy. Newspaper and radio reports often were delayed, and even urgent intelligence found its way to the Pentagon slowly. Neither the brass nor the public learned about events in Korea until many hours, often many days, later.

Air Defense Command (ADC) with no fewer than 60 fighter squadrons became the showcase of the USAF, siphoning off the service's best people and equipment, ADC got the best of everything, including the first F-86As and F-86Es. ADC got the cream of the World War II fighter aces, some of whom, like Maj. Robin Olds of the 71st Fighter Squadron, could find no way to break the command's shackles and get to Asia where the fighting was taking place. ADC was also the moving force behind the F-86D all-weather interceptor, itself merely an interim solution to the air defense challenge.

Work on the F-86D began in March 1949. The idea was to add radar and afterburner to the Sabre, giving it all-weather capability and faster climb. Other aircraft being developed to confront attacking Soviet bombers (Northrop F-89 Scorpion, Lockheed F-94) required a second crew member to operate the radar, but the F-86D remained a single seater. In place of guns, the F-86D was armed with 24 2.75in (6.98cm) Mighty Mouse FFAR (folding fin aircraft rockets) in a tray that extended from the bottom of the fuselage for firing. A barrage of these unguided projectiles would bracket an approaching bomber and blow it out of the sky.

Early on, it was determined that the all-weather interceptor Sabre was a new aircraft, having in common only the wing and landing gear of the day fighter racking up MiG kills in Korea. An order was placed for two service-test planes and 153 operational interceptors (company model NA-164 and NA-165), and the USAF dubbed them YF-95A and F-95A. In July 1950, partly to avoid Congressional scrutiny of a new warplane, the designation reverted to F-86D. Pilots called it the Dog Sabre, not always happily.

The first flight of a service-test YF-86D (50-0577), or company model NA-164, was made on 22 December 1949 by Joseph Lynch. First flight of an F-86D (50-0455), fully equipped with electronic fire-control system and known to the company as the NA-165, was made on 8 June 1951 by George Welch.

To ease the pilot's work load, the Dog Sabre's 7,500lb (3,402kg) thrust J47-GE-17 turbojet with afterburner was fitted with an electronically controlled fuel-scheduling system. A single throttle level determined the amount of fuel fed to the engine, and matched the engine and afterburner for optimum efficiency. This system increased the response of the engine to changes of throttle setting and, by relieving the pilot of the need to constantly monitor engine behavior, simplified flight operations.

To carry out its mission, the F-86D relied upon navigation and fire-control systems that were more advanced than anything previously developed—and more trouble prone.

In November 1949, a decision was made to tailor the system to rocket attacks from a lead collision course instead of the traditional pursuit curve. Intercepting a bomber on a frontal collision course simplified the pilot's task and increased the chances that his burst of rockets would kill the enemy bomber. The system, however, depended on hundreds of fragile and temperamental vacuum tubes, all assembled selectively. The E-4 fire-control system was complex and difficult to perfect, resulting in F-86Ds sitting forlorn in front of NAA's Inglewood plant, unable to fly because radar had not been installed.

Another problem with the F-86D led to what pilots called the Jesus Christ maneuver. By itself, the early F-86Ds would go into a pitch-down mode. When the pilot pulled back to compensate, the aircraft would start to pitch up, then begin to porpoise. "Guys would be bouncing off their cockpits,"

In early days, unexpected delays with the radar fire-control system and a variety of other teething troubles kept newly built F-86D Sabres idle at NAA's Inglewood facility, unable to fly or fight. These factory-fresh F-86Ds lack several key components, including ejection seats, and will be delayed in reaching the ADC. NAA via Steve Pace

About the only feature of the F-86D Sabre that did not cause frustration and delay was its rocket armament, the unusual ventral tray containing 24 2.75in (6.98cm) Mighty Mouse FFARs. This study of a NAA employee installing a Mighty Mouse provides a good view of both the retractable tray and the casual attire of the early 1950s. NAA via Steve Pace

The F-86E version of the Sabre introduced the all-flying tail, which belatedly gave the Sabre maneuverability on a par with the MiG-15. This F-86E-15-NA Sabre (51-13019) knifes through clear southwestern skies near Nellis AFB, Nevada, where lead-in gunnery training was provided to new fighter pilots destined to Sabre assignments. In the 1950s, this was less a rite of passage than a question of survival, with fatal flying mishaps occurring as often as several times per month. Gene Sommerich

an engineer recalls. Adjustments to the size and shape of control surfaces eventually solved the problem.

The F-86D did not come into service easily. When NAA's Fred C. Wise left his duties on earlier Sabres to perform quality control work for the F-86D program, he concluded that, "[the F-86D] was an airplane that could make you quit and find another job."

"I had ship no. 7 on the flight line," Wise recalls, "and it sat there a month with the Radar Group trying to get it to work. I spent my time fixing fuel leaks. We also had a problem with the afterburner fuel pump. During engine run-up, you'd select afterburner and it wouldn't light. Then it was back to your parking area, drain the fuel, pull the belly pan with a million and a half screws, and change the high-speed pump." When Wise shifted to another program, F-86Ds were parked on the NAA ramp "from the east end to the west end" waiting for engines.

After years of frustrating development, the F-86D Sabre matured as a capable one-man all-weather interceptor, made in larger numbers (2,504, plus two prototypes) than any other Sabre version. Considerably heavier with gross weight of 19,975lb (9,061kg), and packed with complicated electronics in a wider and longer fuselage, the Dog Sabre eventually had a J47-GE-33C rated at 7,650lb (3,470kg) thrust.

Problems with the F-86D were to persist long after day-fighter Sabres went to war. A number of F-86Ds sent to the Far East in 1953 developed structural problems and mechanical failures, and forced the grounding of the entire F-86D fleet. The USAF ordered the return of the aircraft to the United States for modification and overhaul at the Sacramento Air Materiel Area (SMAMA), manager of F-86 maintenance from July 1952 onward.

SMAMA began modifying the aircraft in Project Pull Out. This project, one of the largest modification efforts in USAF history, required improvements to the fire-control system, automatic pilot, engine, and drag chute. SMAMA coordinated efforts by other Air Materiel Areas in completing the project. SMAMA processed 648 F-86Ds through its assembly lines while NAA

In a glimpse ahead to the next chapter and the war in Korea, this Canadair F-86E-6-CAN Sabre (52-2875) sits beside its auxiliary power unit at K-14 Kimpo AB, Korea, in 1952. The leading-edge slats used on F-86A, F-86E, and early F-86F models are amply illustrated here. This Sabre was assigned to Sq. Ldr. Eric G. Smith, a veteran of World War II combat in Mosquitos, who flew on an exchange tour with the 335th FIS/4th FIW. Eric G. Smith

processed 480 at a plant in Fresno, California.

Engine Failures

After these modifications were completed, the F-86 began to experience engine failures with tragic consequences. It was determined that these failures resulted from a combination of turbine-wheel failure and engine-control malfunction. USAF investigators discovered that the turbine experienced sudden stress and high temperatures resulting in failure of the turbine wheel. In mid-1955, replacement of the turbine wheel required an additional $20 million. At this time, the fire-control system proved a disappointment. USAF leaders determined that projects designed to modify and update the F-86D were not economical and phaseout of the aircraft began in 1957. In April 1958, the ADC ceased using the aircraft. The Air National Guard continued using two squadrons until the last F-86Ds were retired in June 1961.

While the F-86D's problems continued, production of Sabre day fighters shifted to the F-86E with an all-flying tail. The tailplane became a primary control surface, the elevators merely increasing its effect. An artificial feel was added for the first time on an operational fighter.

In 1955, a one-of-a-kind F-86D-60-NA Sabre (53-4061) was modified with underwing racks for four Hughes Falcon air-to-air missiles. An interesting sideline is that the Falcon itself was originally a fighter, designated XF-98 (Boeing's Bomarc surface-to-air mis-

sile was the XF-99), although it had been renamed the GAR-1B by the time the Sabre took it aloft. The Falcon had been deemed too heavy even before flight tests took place, and actual flying confirmed that it would seriously degrade the rate of climb, speed, and combat radius of the F-86D.

The first flight of the F-86E-1 Sabre (50-0579), or company model NA-170, was made by George Welch on 23 September 1950. Following evaluation of the new control system, it was accepted by the USAF on 9 February 1951.

The all-flying tail and the irreversible hydraulic systems introduced in the F-86E are considered one of the most important advances of the era. At Wright Field, Ohio, World War II ace and test pilot Maj. Clarence E. (Bud) Anderson flew the early version of the all-flying tail and discovered that it didn't feel right. The maneuverability and artificial feel were sluggish, awkward, perhaps dangerous. NAA and the USAF worked together to change and improve the F-86E's key features until the problems were resolved and the F-86E became, in Anderson's words, "a world-beater."

Sixty F-86E-1 models were followed by 51 F-86E-5s that differed only in minor panel switches. The designation F-86E-6 went to a batch of 60 Canadair-built CL-13 Sabre Mark 2 fighters built in Canada to fill the urgent need for Sabres in Korea. The designation F-86E-10 went to the first 132 examples of the company model NA-172, which were powered by J47-GE-13 engines only because planned J47-GE-27 models were not yet available—in short, the aircraft was an F-86F with an F-86E engine. The F-86E-10 also introduced a new flat windscreen and modified instrument panel. The total for the F-86E series, then, is 336 aircraft, or 396 when the Canadian-built Sabres are included in the count.

Subsequently, out of this order, 93 aircraft that were to have been delivered on the NA-172 contract as F-86F-

The F-86F was the definitive version of the Sabre, the version that decisively wrested control of MiG Alley from a determined enemy, and the version that was exported in the largest numbers. The author, a 19-year-old airman, snapped this portrait of a slat-wing Republic of Korea Air Force (ROKAF) F-86F-30-NA (52-4847) at K-55 Osan AB, Korea, on 20 May 1958.

15s reverted to the J47-GE-27 engine because of further powerplant delays and were given the out-of-order designation F-86E-15. These were assigned to Air Training Command instead of to combat wings, and brought the total of American-built fighters in the F-86E series to 340 aircraft.

Canada also manufactured F-86Es, as part of its impressive total of 1,815 Sabres. These began with an indigenous aircraft that was simply a hand-crafted F-86A-5, and ended with the final CL-13B Sabre Mark 6, delivered to Pakistan. The full story of Canada's aircraft, including introduction of the 6-3 wing on later Canadian versions, is covered in Chapter 4.

The 6-3 wing (so named because the wing's leading edge was extended 6in [15.24cm] at the root and 3in [7.62cm] at the tip) has appeared on several Sabre versions but is associated with the definitive F-86F Sabre, or company model NA-172, the first of which (51-2850) was flown on 19 March 1952 by James Pearce (although early F-86Fs lacked the wing). As we shall see, the combination of all-flying tail and 6-3 wing were absolutely vital to the outcome of that distant Asian war.

Korean demands led to NAA reopening the former Curtiss plant in Columbus, Ohio, where F-86Fs were manufactured. These aircraft, combined with those manufactured in Los Angeles, totaled 1,539.

The F-86F became the premier air-to-air fighter of the Korean War. But it was also the first version of the Sabre to be widely used in the fighter-bomber role. Limited tests were conducted with an F-86F as a fighter-bomber by the Air Proving Ground Command (Eglin AFB, Florida), the Aberdeen Proving Ground (Aberdeen, Maryland), and Fifth Air Force (Tokyo). The capabilities of the F-86F in this role were praised, but some drawbacks were noted, too. USAF officers noted a strong need for a new family of streamlined, lower-drag bombs, though that didn't happen until after the Sabre's time in service.

A report from a South African Air Force (SAAF) pilot who flew the F-86F commented favorably on this new mission: "The flight characteristics of the F-86F are excellent for the fighter-bomber role. It is a stable bombing platform and permits any dive angle up to vertical without danger of control difficulties or effects from compressibility. The speed brakes have proved effective and necessary for tactics that are desired. It is believed that use of steeper dive angles and higher entry altitudes will decrease vulnerability to AAA fire."

Early fighter-bomber operations in Korea were carried out with F-86F-30 aircraft with slatted leading edge, carrying 500lb (227kg) and 1,000lb (454kg) general purpose (GP) bombs with conical fins and 120gal Class I fuel tanks. Another variation on the F-86F was an experimental version equipped to fire a family of small 1.5in and 2.5in solid- or liquid-fuel air-to-air rockets. Named in part after two of the leading figures in the manufacturer's headquarters, these rocket projectiles were named NAKA rockets, which stood for NAA Kindelberger Atwood ("Dutch" Kindelberger and Lee Atwood approved and implemented the test, development, and limited production of the rockets).

Under the NA-210 company designation, two F-86Fs were modified for the NAKA rocket tests, 52-5143 and 52-5163. Apparently, one NAA B-45C Tornado was also modified for the tests. NAA's Bob Louden claims that only one of the two Sabres flew with the rockets (52-5143) and that no records of the program exist today. Capt. James O. Roberts, who will reappear in this narrative, was test pilot on the project. Until this book, no photo of a NAKA-configured F-86F has been published.

The one-of-a-kind F-86F(R) (52-4608) flew mostly at Edwards AFB, California, carrying twin GAR-8A Sidewinder missiles like those Chinese Nationalist F-86F Sabres had used in combat in 1958. The F-86F(R) was fitted with a Rocketdyne AR 2-3 rocket engine in the ventral fuselage and two large (200gal) hydrogen peroxide tanks on the wings and could climb to 30,000ft (9,144m) in just 24sec! J. O. Roberts was the engineering test pilot.
NAA via Larry Davis

Rocket-Boosted F-86F(R)

During the Korean War, a bizarre experiment was carried out in which JATO (jet-assisted takeoff) battles were mounted internally in the F-86F fuselage. Six aircraft were so modified, three with slotted wings and three without. At high altitude in combat, the JATO was fired to give the F-86F a sudden burst of speed and improve its closure rate against the MiG-15. The experiment by the 335th Fighter-

Perhaps least-known among Sabre versions was the Project Ashtray RF-86A reconnaissance aircraft, identified by the fuselage bulge just forward of the wing root. Some RF-86As were armed with four .50cal machine guns rather than the customary six, and carried downward-aiming cameras inside the bulge. Seen in the late 1950s with the California Air National Guard (ANG) commanded by Brig. Gen. Roy Santin, this RF-86A retains the bulge but appears to have had cameras removed and the full armament of six guns restored.
Warren M. Bodie

Interceptor Squadron(FIS), part of the 4th Fighter-Interceptor Group at Kimpo AB, Korea, is little known and produced mixed results. At least one MiG-15 kill was racked up and at least one F-86F Sabre was lost in combat using the JATO installation.

Efforts were resumed almost a decade later to give the Sabre extra boost. NAA saw the rocket mod as the answer to MiGs that were reported to be overflying Western Europe at an altitude that the NATO countries' F-86s could not reach.

The one-of-a-kind F-86F(R), s/n 52-4608, was an F-86F-30, one of 858 aircraft built on contract NA-191 (52-4305/5015) and flew mostly at Edwards AFB, California (as Muroc airfield was renamed in 1951). The F-86F(R) carried twin heat-seeking GAR-8A Sidewinder missiles (later designated AIM-9B). In 1957–1958, Chinese Nationalist F-86F Sabres had used Sabre and Sidewinder in combat against mainland Chinese MiGs.

The F-86F(R) was fitted with a Rocketdyne AR 2-3 rocket engine in the ventral fuselage and two large (200gal) hydrogen peroxide tanks on the wings. Surviving records show that with this "kick in the pants," the F-86F(R) could climb to 30,000ft (9,144m) in just 24sec!

NAA engineering test pilot J. O. Roberts flew the F-86F(R) wearing a specially made Canadian pressure helmet, pressure vest, and normal G-suit pants that were automatically inflated with loss of cabin pressure. Roberts' surviving notes indicate that the F-86F(R) "made the heaviest takeoff of any [version of the] F-86 at approximately 20,000lb [9,072kg]" and could "out-run an F-100 in afterburner."

The F-86F(R)'s Rocketdyne AR 2-3 motor weighed 225lb (102kg) and was controlled by a throttle that allowed

the pilot to "run up" thrust from 3,000 to 6,000lb (1,360 to 2,721kg). The requisite mix of fuel for the rocket motor came from JP-4 in the forward fuselage tank and twin external tanks modified to carry 165gal of hydrogen peroxide each. The system proved reliable and could be stopped and restarted, providing up to 2.8min of augmented boost. Roberts, however, noted that "logistics (primarily the volatility and storage problems associated with the hydrogen peroxide) defeated our efforts to sell this modification."

With twin Sidewinders, the F-86F(R) weighed 20,940lb (9,498kg) for the short-range, point-defense mission. With a pair of 120gal fuel tanks for longer-range intercept, the F-86F(R) weighed 22,850lb (10,365kg). Tests were carried out at Edwards and at Palmdale, California; the latter in November 1960 when the F-86F(R) reached 40,000ft (12,192m) in 1min, 6sec. Without the wing tanks, the F-86F(R) could reach Mach 1.22 at 60,000ft (18,288m). In the heavier configuration, a still-impressive Mach 0.96 at 55,000ft (16,764m) was possible.

A number of F-86F Sabre fighters were modified to RF-86F reconnais-

Of more than 9,000 Sabre variants manufactured in five countries, only a pair of airplanes were built as two-seaters. The first TF-86F Sabre (52-5016) with two men aboard is wrung out over the California mountains. The attempt to sell a two-seat tandem trainer to Air Training Command was too late in the Sabre's career and suffered an insurmountable setback when this first ship was destroyed in a crash. NAA

George Welch, Pearl Harbor hero, World War II ace, and pilot who made the first flight of the XP-86 (as well as the F-86A, YF-93A, and F-86E), poses in front of the unarmed first prototype of the ultimate Sabre, the re-engined F-86H (52-1975). The first two F-86Hs were tested with both leading-edge slats (shown) and the 6-3 wing. 1954 was to be a painful year, with three test pilots essential to early testing of the F-86H model losing their lives in crashes: Welch (in an F-100A), Lynch (in a TF-86F), and Capt. Joseph McConnell (in an F-86H). NAA

Like every Sabre version, the F-86H Sabre served late in its career as a stalwart in ANG squadrons. This F-86 is of the 121st TFS/113th TFW, District of Columbia ANG, normally stationed at Andrews AFB, Maryland, but seen here during a 1961 exercise in Savannah, Georgia. Harold L. Shank

sance aircraft under Project Haymaker, a latter-day version of the Ashtray effort that had produced earlier RF-86As. Haymaker aircraft were factory-built RF-86F-30-NAs. Like their predecessors in the reconnaissance world, the RF-86Fs were configured for various photo-gathering missions. Some later flew for Japan and Korea.

There was always talk of a two-seat Sabre, but only two were ever built. The first TF-86F, or company model NA-204 (52-5016) was flown on 5 August 1954 by Ray Morris. A considerable amount of the early TF-86F flying was done by Bob Hoover. The TF-86F had a 63in (160cm) fuselage stretch, wing slats, and tandem cockpits under a giant clamshell canopy. Interestingly, antispin tests with this ship were carried out with a JATO unit on the left wing tip rather than a spin parachute, as is customary.

The first TF-86F crashed on its ninth flight on 17 March 1954. Joe Lynch, NAA test pilot who had been assigned to demonstrate the aircraft to various USAF command organizations (and who had pioneered flying in the F-86H version), lost control of the aircraft while doing a slow roll on takeoff and was killed. A second TF-86F aircraft was authorized (53-1228). The second ship differed from the first, which was unarmed, by having two .50cal machine guns with 100 rounds per gun and underwing racks for practice bombs. This second aircraft made

A few early Sabres were camouflaged in an experiment during the Korean War. Otherwise, the only American Sabres to wear camouflage paint in service were the F-86H models that remained in service long enough to be adorned in Vietnam-era T.O. 1-1-4 colors. This F-86H-10-NH Sabre (52-1298) belongs to the 104th TFS/175th TFG, Maryland ANG, and is seen at Baltimore on 22 September 1967. Joseph G. Handelman, DDS

Following on the heels of two service-test prototypes, the first operational F-86K Sabre (54-1231) makes its maiden flight on 8 March 1955, piloted by Ray Morris. An all-weather interceptor was badly needed by NATO allies but (at first) the troublesome E-4 fire-control system of the F-86D was considered too secret to export. Italy's Fiat company rejected plans to manufacture the Gloster Meteor N.F.Mk14 or De Havilland Venom N.F.Mk3, both of which had straight wings, but Fiat was ready and eager to build the cannon-armed F-86K. NAA via Steve Pace

its first flight on 5 August 1954. The number two TF-86F flew as a chase plane at Edwards for many years before being scrapped.

Test pilot Roger Monroe remembers that, "as a step in obtaining USAF acceptance and approval for the purchase of this training version of the Sabre, flight demonstrations were provided to various command organizations." The demonstration tour began on 2 September 1954. As Monroe recalls:

"Bob Hoover was the point for these demonstrations, affording pilots a ride in this stretched version, affording the evaluating pilot an opportunity to fly the aircraft through the Mach 1.0 barrier and to feel the aircraft stick control pressures and flying characteristics changes."

Monroe was one of the lucky few to get aloft in the two-seater. "In September 1954, while stationed at ARDC (Air Research and Development Command) in Baltimore, Maryland, and having had some experience as a test pilot at Wright Field in the late 1940s, I, among others, was selected to help evaluate this aircraft, which was to be used as a trainer to acclimate student or new pilots in this aspect of our transitional training program.

"The demonstration flight Hoover allowed me to perform lasted less than an hour, and consisted of a rollover at 25,000ft [7,620m], into a fairly steep dive, to exceed Mach 1. Negligible stick force change was encountered and although I was advised that a moderate wing roll might occur, it did not. Probably the most noted event was the boom sounded over the Chesapeake Bay, and possibly a few small sailboats noted a mild breeze increase."

Fighter-Bomber F-86H

The ultimate Sabre, apart from those made in Australia and Canada, was the F-86H. With an 8,920lb (4,406kg) thrust General Electric J73 engine, the F-86H was by far the most powerful American version. Optimized as a fighter-bomber for Tactical Air Command (TAC), it also introduced a completely redesigned structure, and (from the 113th airplane onward) four 20mm M39 (T160) cannons. The F-86H also introduced the clamshell canopy in place of the sliding type previously found on all versions except the F-86D/K/L.

Maiden flight of the first F-86H, or company model NA-187 (52-1975), was made 9 May 1953 by Joe Lynch. The first two aircraft were built in California and were unarmed. Early test flying at Edwards was performed by Lynch and George Welch, both of whom were to lose their lives within a year (Lynch in the TF-86F, Welch in an F-100A Super Sabre). Early testing of the F-86H was set back with a third loss of a pilot's life in 1954 when, on 26 August, top Korean War ace Capt. Joseph McConnell was killed in a crash of one of the first H models.

The third and subsequent F-86H Sabres came from Columbus. The first Columbus-built F-86H, which eschewed the 6-3 wing tested on prototypes in favor of leading-edge slats, made its first flight on 4 September 1953.

As a stopgap measure, the first 112 F-86H-1-NH airplanes had six .50cal M3 machine guns with 300 rounds per gun. The company model NA-203 applied to Columbus-built H models.

Eventually, the F-86H reverted to the 6-3 wing and was equipped with the A-4 gunsight with AN/APG-30 radar-ranging set. The A-4 gunsight had also replaced the A-1 on other Sabres from the F-86F-30 onward.

The F-86H Sabre was given heavy responsibility for the Cold War nuclear mission. The Sabre's tactical nuclear bomb, weighing 1,200lb (544kg), was to be carried under the port wing with drop tanks under the starboard wing as a counterbalance. The method of delivery was to release the weapon when the aircraft was just over the vertical position in an Immelmann turn, so that the bomb would carry on in an upward trajectory allowing the Sabre time to exit the area before the explosion.

In time, the USAF operated five F-86H Sabre wings, the 50th Fighter-Bomber Wing (FBW) in Europe and the TAC's 83rd, 312th, 413rd, and 474th wings.

Numerous F-86Hs were used at Nellis AFB, Nevada, as target tugs. In later years, F-86Hs bulwarked the Air National Guard and equipped stateside units well after the United States went to war in Vietnam. Four hundred seventy-five F-86H aircraft were manufactured. By the late 1970s, a few of these had been relegated to the US Navy as QF-86H target drones.

Export Interceptor

Development of interceptor Sabres continued with the F-86K, intended for foreign use, which dispensed with advanced avionics and reverted to four 20mm cannons. First flight of a service-test YF-86K (52-3630) or company model NA-205, itself a modified F-86D, was made on 7 July 1954 by Ray Morris.

A second YF-86K (52-3804) was converted from F-86D standard. The first production F-86K, or company model NA-213 (54-1231), was flown on 8 March 1955. NAA produced 120 production F-86Ks (54-1231/1350), also known as the company model NA-214. Fiat, in Italy, built another 121.

The ultimate interceptor was the long-span F-86L rebuilt from the F-86D with the combined 6-3 wing and leading edge slats. F-86L rebuilds were upgraded with onboard computer and a data-link to tie the aircraft with the Semi-Automatic Ground Environment (SAGE) defense network. Like other versions, the F-86L was transferred to the Air National Guard in large numbers in the late 1950s.

FU-660

CHAPTER TWO

F-86 Sabre at War (Part I)

On 1 November 1950, Americans were celebrating their victory in Korea. The holiday season was within sight. The troops would be home for Christmas. They'd shown a thing or two to the Commies. After four months, the Korean "police action" was near its end. The Reds, as everybody called them, were near total defeat.

North Korea's invasion of South Korea had failed. Allied forces had landed at Inchon, retaken Seoul, and driven the North Korean invaders back where they came from—and farther. In just weeks, the United Nations (UN) Allies seized the northern capital of Pyongyang, kept going, and overran North Korea.

American soldiers stood on the banks of the Yalu River, peering into China. Rarely had Americans defeated an enemy so soundly. It was over.

On 1 November a flight of F-51 Mustangs reported being engaged by six swept-wing jet fighters from across the Yalu.

The USAF's Far East Air Forces (FEAF) had a hard-working intelligence shop where experts knew of huge airfields at Antung, Tatangkou, Fen Cheng, and other locations on the north side of the Yalu. Or did they? Today, it's not clear how much FEAF—or Gen. Douglas MacArthur, or anybody—actually knew about the swept-wing jet fighters reported by the Mustang pilots. At least one skeptic is supposed to have debriefed the Mustang pilots by telling them they couldn't have spotted swept-wing jets because there weren't any in the region. Besides, what difference could it make, since the war was over anyway?

When the existence of the swept-wing jets became indisputable, it was not immediately obvious that they were going to spoil the holidays. With six words, an American pilot engaged one of the them and achieved history's first jet-versus-jet aerial victory.

"Damn, I'm going to get him," uttered Lt. Russell J. Brown at the controls of a Lockheed F-80C Shooting Star (49-0737) of the 16th FIS, 51st Fighter-Interceptor Wing (FIW), when he found himself closing in on the new aircraft during a hectic engagement on 8 November 1950. In USAF jargon, Brown's outfit was the 16th FIS/51st FIW, a shorthand that will recur throughout this narrative.

Moments earlier, Brown and other F-80 pilots had come upon half a dozen of the swept wing, Soviet-built jets and had split them up, sending five scurrying back across the Yalu River toward Antung. The sixth MiG had broken in the wrong direction on this frigid winter afternoon and was now below Brown's F-80—a bad place to be.

Brown pushed down his nose and went into a dive behind the plummeting MiG-15 fighter. The MiG was being touted in the press as invincible and Brown knew it. Though all but one of his guns was jammed, Brown

Heading for MiG Alley. Sabre pilots had to travel 200mi (320km) into enemy territory before they could even begin to engage the MiG-15s, which could take off from protected sanctuaries north of the Yalu River, enter the fight at the time and place of their choosing, and strike from higher altitude. This takeoff was photographed in April 1952 when K-14 Kimpo AB, near Seoul, was securely in American hands and the 4th FIW was firmly settled. But when the Sabres first arrived in December 1950, the situation was far less certain and China's sudden entry into the Korean War was a devastating blow to the American psyche. Martin Bambrick

The 4th FIW arrived in December 1950 to confront the MiG-15 and the Chinese in Korea. Distinctive markings appeared on the F-86 Sabre to prevent Americans from mistaking each other for their enemy. The 4th Wing adopted the black-and-white stripes shown here. Later in the war, Sabres of all units flew with yellow bands on fuselage, wings, and tail. Lt. Col. Bob Moore is shown with his F-86A-5-NA Sabre (49-1227). via David W. Menard

unleashed bursts of fire that struck the MiG, set it afire, and sent it spinning in, engulfed in flames.

Brown's aerial victory might have been a crowning moment in a war ending in victory for Americans and their UN allies. But the pilot of the MiG was not one of the defeated North Koreans. The airfields on the forbidden north side of the Yalu were not North Korean. It was almost irrelevant that the North Koreans had been turned around, pushed back, and overwhelmed. Everything had just changed. There was to be no victory and no Christmas.

In one of the most dramatic moves in the history of warfare, undetected by the Allies, the Chinese inserted more than half a million troops into North Korea. American soldiers had captured Chinese volunteers as early as mid-November but did not know that they were now confronted by up to 50 divisions.

A massive force of Soviet-built MiG-15 fighters was forming at bases on the north side of the Yalu, flown by Chinese and a few Soviet pilots. The Allies had no fighter in theater that could even begin to cope with the MiG-15. Used properly, the MiGs had the performance to wrest air supremacy over the Korean peninsula and pick off American B-26s and B-29s like targets at a skeet shoot. The MiGs could easily clear the way for a major attack on UN air installations in South Korea, which were inadequately defended by Lockheed F-80C Shooting Stars.

The abrupt reversal came in late November 1950 when China entered the war. In a surprise as swift and stunning as Pearl Harbor, the Chinese struck. Conservative in the air, holding back their MiGs, China's troops attacked with incredible boldness on the ground.

Commanded by Marshal Peng Tehuai, these Chinese soldiers were tough battle veterans, accustomed to a tradition of success. They had seized all of mainland China from Chiang Kai-shek's armies the year before. They expected to take Korea easily.

China's Assault

Near the top of the map in central North Korea at an obscure hamlet called Kunu-ri, the US Army's 2nd Infantry Division was slaughtered. American soldiers were so stunned by China's attack that they wandered about in the snow, dazed, many unable to shoot back as they were overrun and killed.

In teeming hordes, the Chinese People's Third Field Route Army swarmed down on the 1st Marine Division at the Chosin Reservoir, deep inside North Korea near the west coast. The three-day battle was the costliest and bloodiest defeat in American history. The 5th and 7th Marine Regiments were outnumbered 50:1 by a tidal wave of Chinese troops.

The Chinese had picked a fiendish time to strike—the coldest Korean winter in 177 years. Frostbite took a bitter toll. Blood plasma froze and was useless. Carbine stocks became brittle and cracked in soldiers' hands. M-1 rifles could not be oiled, for the lubricant clogged the mechanism like glue. Marines tried everything from antifreeze to urine to save their water-cooled machine guns. Surrounded, outnumbered, the Marines fought their way south to the port of Hamhung while Chinese troops swarmed on the high ground above their route. "Retreat, hell. We're just attacking in another direction." Such was the quote affixed by lore to the shining moment of courage in the annals of American arms. But it was a misquote. The Marines' commander, Gen. Oliver P. Smith, was devout and had never voiced the word *hell* outside its Biblical context.

In the air, hell meant being a crew member of a B-29 Superfortress at the mercy of the MiGs. As early as 9 November 1950, MiGs shot up an RB-29 and sent it to a crash landing in which five crewmen died. The following day, MiG-15s shot down a B-29 near the Yalu.

Three more B-29s were damaged by cannon fire from MiGs even before the ground war was altered forever by China's entry into the Korean conflict. The Chinese now had as many as 650 MiGs at the air bases in and around Antung.

Surprisingly, the Chinese remained conservative in the air. Their burgeoning force of factory-fresh MiG-15s was kept north of the Yalu in sanctuaries around Antung. Still, they posed a new and deadly threat.

Even before the significance of the new war was understood, on 8 November 1950, the USAF ordered the 4th FIW with NAA F-86A Sabres to Korea. The 4th FIW, or 4th Wing, went to Korea amid a period of confusion and uncertainty. China's entry into the war had created doubt, and Americans did not know how to handle doubt.

The 4th Fighter Group was a proud outfit that had destroyed more than a thousand Luftwaffe aircraft in combat during World War II, flying the P-47 Thunderbolt and P-51 Mustang and commanded by Col. Donald Blakeslee, among others. The 4th had taken delivery of the F-86A-5 Sabre as its primary fighter on 27 March 1949 and with several changes of its home—from Andrews AFB, Maryland, to Langley AFB, Virginia, on 30 April 1949, and then to Wilmington County, Delaware, on 27 July 1950—was able to boast some of the best jet fighter pilots in the USAF, most of them wartime veterans. Like many USAF units, the 4th had become a wing on 20 January 1950: the 4th Wing was commanded by Col. George F. Smith. The term *group* now described a component of the wing, tapped for Korean duty. The wing's 4th Fighter-Interceptor Group was headed by Lt. Col. John C. Meyer, a World War II ace. Its squadrons were the 334th, 335th, and 336th FISs.

On 11 November 1950, Sabres of the 4th Wing launched from Wilmington, Delaware, and were flown to NAS North Island, California, where they were loaded aboard the escort carrier USS *Cape Esperance* (CVE-88) and a tanker to travel to Korea by sea. By this time, the USAF had some experience with air refueling, including limited fighter experience with two EF-84E Thunderjets taken to Europe by Col. Dave Schilling, but the F-86 Sabre was never to be fitted operationally for aerial tanking. The capability did not exist to deploy the 4th Wing by air. Ground crews and support personnel of the wing's 334th, 335th, and 336th squadrons headed for Korea by sea.

Cape Esperance arrived at Yokosuka, Japan, on 1 December 1950 with the 4th Wing's Sabres. On 13 December 1950, Meyer took an advance detachment of Sabres from Johnson AB, Japan, to Kimpo AB, Korea. Also known as K-14 under a numbering system created by Americans who could not handle Korean names, Kimpo was a sprawling natural airfield some 18mi (29km) west of Seoul and was, just as it is today, the aerial gateway to the South Korean capital. When Meyer began orientation flying at Kimpo, the Allies' predicament could hardly have seemed more bleak. By now, it was a war with China, the MiGs were in the fight, and the weather was terrible.

The skies cleared north of snow-covered Kimpo on 17 December 1950. Lt. Col. Bruce Hinton, commander of the 336th FIS and pilot of an F-86A-5 (49-1236), led BAKER Flight of four Sabres along the Yalu.

The Chinese may initially have mistaken Hinton's Sabres for slower F-80s. Warned by his wingman that MiGs were coming their way, Hinton turned his flight to engage four of the Soviet-built jets as they crossed his flight path a mile ahead. Hinton ordered his flight to jettison drop tanks, only to find that his radio was malfunctioning. Some confusion followed: Hinton dropped his tanks but became separated from his flight.

Hinton turned behind an element of two MiGs. The enemy pilot apparently thought he could outrun the fighter on his tail. Hinton dived after the MiG flight leader and was able to get on his six o'clock position. He fired a short burst and saw what looked like debris and leaks from damage.

When the Chinese struck and the MiG-15 made its debut, the best-performing American jet fighter in Korea was the F-80. This F-80C-10-LO Shooting Star (49-501) of the 25th FIS/51st FIW at Suwon, flown by 2nd Lt. Bill Atkinson is bombed up for the mission it performed best, hitting enemy forces on the ground. Though it scored history's first jet-versus-jet kill, the F-80 was not a match for the MiG-15. More to the point, it could not perform its air-to-ground mission until and unless the MiG-15 could be kept at bay. John Nossick

Hinton then took on the no. 2 MiG and found himself bucking in the MiG's jet wash. Hinton adjusted his position and fired a long burst that sent .50cal bullets into the MiG's engine. Hinton stayed in a left turn behind his opponent and had a spectacular view of the MiG. He closed in and fired again. In fact, Hinton kept firing. The rear section of the MiG was consumed by flames and the enemy fighter rolled on its back and went plummeting to earth. The MiG crashed 10mi (16km) southeast of the Yalu. There was no parachute. Bruce Hinton had just scored the first aerial victory to be credited to the F-86 Sabre.

It had not been easy. Hinton had nearly exhausted his Sabre's full load of 1,802 rounds. He'd fought aggressively and he'd shown that American pilots, generally, were more skilled than their Chinese adversaries. But Hinton also had shown that the MiG-15 was damnably difficult to bring down out of the sky.

Sabre Battles

Again on 19 December 1950, Hinton and company engaged MiGs. Lt. Col. Glenn T. Eagleston, 334th FIS commander, damaged a MiG-15. Two days later, Eagleston scored a probable kill. At this juncture, the MiG pilots had not yet shown how vigorously they intended to challenge the newly arrived Sabres, even though Chinese troops were fighting aggressively on the ground. But on 22 December 1950, MiGs bounced a flight of eight Sabres and shot down Capt. Lawrence V. Bach's F-86A, which took cannon hits in the wing roots and was seen to spin away in flames.

The enemy's first Sabre kill was made possible by the one advantage the Chinese would enjoy throughout most of the war—the MiG could fly higher than the Sabre. This meant the Chinese could strike at a time and place of their choosing.

Also on 22 December, Navy exchange pilot LCdr. Paul E. Pugh led a four-plane flight in company with four other Sabres. Pugh heard MiGs called while cruising 20mi (32km) south of the Yalu at 32,000ft (9,753m). Pugh turned his flight into the threat just in time to see a MiG-15 close aboard, too close to shoot. The two fighters passed canopy-to-canopy and Pugh wracked his Sabre into a hard reversal, picking up the bandit diving for the undercast. Pugh later told historian Barrett Tillman, "I cut across his turn and fired. I hit him pretty good. Then he disappeared into the cloud deck."

In pursuit, Pugh broke into the clear and found the MiG straight and level at about 500ft (152m). "I just dove up behind him," Pugh says—and got the MiG kill.

This was part of an eight-Sabre prolonged fray with 15 MiGs in a twisting, close-quarters dogfight. Aerial victories were scored by Eagleston, Meyer, 1st Lt. John Odinorne, Capt. James O. Roberts, 2nd Lt. Arthur O'Connor, and Pugh. Six kills in a single fight was a powerful achievement. It also defined the magnitude of this conflict: in days ahead, there were to be vast numbers of jet fighters, sometimes hundreds of them, battling along the slice of land bordering the Yalu that came to be known as "MiG Alley."

The holidays brought continuing, low-level fighting in the air while UN troops continued to be pushed back on the ground. On 30 December 1950, Pugh became the first F-86 Sabre pilot to rack up a second MiG kill. Since he was in the Navy, this achievement was chalked up with some embarrassment by the USAF. Capt. James Jabara claimed a probable kill. The 4th Wing could now claim eight kills and two probables with just one air-to-air loss.

This did not mean that the Americans were doing well. The F-86A version of the Sabre was still trouble prone, more than two years after the first examples had become operational at March Field. Pilots of the 4th Wing encountered problems with everything from the unreliable gun chargers to the Sabre's weak nosewheel. At times, MiG pilots thumbed their noses at the Americans. Any time the numbers looked equal, the Chinese pilots and their handful of Russian colleagues could simply stay on the ground, or continue to fly north of the Yalu. Even

when they entered Korean air space, the MiG pilots could look down at the Sabres from higher altitudes and scoff. If they chose to remain at maximum height, no Sabre could get near them. The MiGs controlled the time and place of every fight. And when they could break through Sabre patrols along the Yalu to attack other Allied warplanes, they seemed unbeatable.

Wing commander Col. George F. Smith became the first of many to notify 5th Air Force, and FEAF, that the 4th Wing was confronted with intolerable supply and maintenance problems. The smallest, simplest parts needed to keep the F-86A Sabre in the air were almost impossible for crew chiefs to obtain. The supply line, and the bureaucracy for handling supply requests, was as efficient as a clogged artery. As for badly-needed information that would help them to hone their fighting edge, Sabre pilots found that they were learning more from their NAA field representative than from their own USAF leaders. It is unclear whether Smith ever complained to Washington—as we shall see, one of his successors did—but an infuriating array of support problems were keeping Sabres grounded, eroding morale,

Two F-86A Sabres break ground at Kimpo and head north for the fighting in MiG Alley. These Sabres wear the black-and-white bands on fuselage and wings (with just a single black stripe on the tail, paralleling the rudder line) used by the 4th FIW after its December 1950 arrival in Korea. Though the Sabre immediately proved itself a serious rival to the MiG, months of frustration lay ahead as the USAF struggled with maintenance and supply issues while also working to improve the Sabre design. USAF via Warren M. Bodie

The MiG-15. When it first appeared in Korean skies, only a handful of intelligence experts had ever heard of it. The MiG could fly considerably higher than early models of the F-86 Sabre. Though American pilots had more experience and almost immediately began shooting down far more enemy airplanes than they lost, the Americans had to cope with supply and maintenance nightmares and with being vastly outnumbered, while fighting 200mi (320km) behind enemy lines. William H. Myers

and giving the upper hand to the MiGs by default.

Not that the MiGs weren't scoring their own points. Lt. John Frey, a pilot in the 4th Wing, wrote in his personal journal that, "We are not doing as well as we should. We are not winning. The MiGs are playing with us, while on the ground our guys are being pushed back all along the front...."

China's intervention had turned the ground struggle into a one-sided route. Chinese hordes swarmed down the Korean peninsula. The Marines came out with all of their wounded and dead when they evacuated North Korea at Hamhung but their "attack in another direction" was a retreat no matter how courageously it was carried out. UN forces fell back all along the line.

By 2 January 1951, the F-86A Sabres of the 4th Wing had to be evacuated from Kimpo. By the end of January, Chinese troops had pushed UN forces south of the 38th Parallel. For the second time in the war, Seoul fell. Again, air refueling would have been a boon: the 4th Wing's Sabres had to be withdrawn to Japan and did not have the range to fly missions up to MiG Alley along the Yalu.

Enemy Push

The Chinese now threatened to do what the North Koreans had almost done earlier in the conflict—overrun the Korean peninsula and push Allied troops into the sea. So desperate was the situation that the 4th Wing was challenged to try out the F-86A Sabre as a fighter-bomber, a role for which it had never been intended. Beginning 14 January 1951, an F-86 Sabre detachment returned to Korea at Taegu, far in the south, to begin flying air-to-ground missions. In this first attempt to use the Sabre as a fighter-bomber, 158 sorties were flown. The F-86A was sorely limited in this role, not just by a paucity of experience but by limited range, load-carrying capability, and accurate means of delivery.

In February 1951, the Chinese onslaught came to a halt before a Dunkirk-style debacle could push the Allies into the sea. The halt occurred for diverse reasons—none of them having much to do with the appearance of Sabres with bombs—and the Chinese still held the initiative.

It was remarkable, then, that the Chinese lacked imagination in employing the superb MiG-15. Perhaps they feared retaliation against their sanctuaries north of the Yalu. Perhaps the Chinese simply lacked experience using their air force to support their ground troops. For whatever reason, the MiG-15 continued to dominate the fighting in MiG Alley, but never deigned to enter the skies over the battlefield.

The situation on the ground appeared to stabilize, at least for a time. In fact, the Chinese were planning a spring offensive. Sabres returned to the war when the 4th Wing moved back to Korea, this time to Suwon, also known as K-13, on 6 March 1951. A few days earlier, a slashing attack by MiGs had damaged ten B-29 Superfortresses, three of which had to make emergency landings at Taegu. The reappearance of the F-86A Sabres blunted this threat somewhat. Air-to-air fighting persisted but at a modest level. On 31 March 1951, Fl. Lt. Omer Levesque of the Royal Canadian Air Force (RCAF), serving an exchange tour with the 4th Wing's 334th FIS, claimed a MiG-15.

Flying an F-86A-5 (49-1111), Levesque pursued a MiG-15 flight leader in a downward spiral. Attempting to evade the Canadian, the MiG pulled up into the sun. As the MiG came out of the sun, Levesque made a deflection shot at 2,000ft (609m) and observed hits on the left side of the fuselage. Levesque then fired a one-second burst at closer range and saw the left flap of the MiG-15 split along the trailing edge. The MiG snapped violently to the right, paused in an inverted position, and glided toward

Sinanju along the Yalu. The Sabre pilot saw the MiG crash and explode.

By now, the principal characteristics of the Sabre versus MiG confrontation were becoming well known. The MiG-15 had the important advantage of a much higher service ceiling. While a clean F-86A could barely struggle along at 42,000ft (12,800m), the MiG-15 cruised at 50,000ft (15,240m) and higher. Since the Sabres had to travel north from 200mi (320km) south of MiG Alley, they had to spend most of their fuel commuting and had little time to spend in the combat arena. Unlike the MiGs, the Sabres had no ground control intercept (GCI) operators to give them radar support. All of the advantages seemed to lie with the enemy.

Too, the MiG force included several Soviet fighter divisions with very skilled pilots—including some of their top World War II aces, according to the recently published book *MiG-15* by Yefim Gordon and Vladimir Rigmant, also published by Motorbooks International. MiG formations were called bandit trains in Allied radio jargon. It followed, naturally, that the real or mythical fighter wing commander leading the MiGs into battle was dubbed Casey Jones. If the typical Chinese MiG pilot (and the few North Korean pilots who belatedly flew MiGs toward the end of the war) lacked the skills and experience of his American challenger, it was true nevertheless that some Chinese, and apparently all of the Russians, were among the best fighter pilots in the world.

But so, too, were the Americans. The first batch of Sabre pilots in Korea were nearly all World War II veterans. Many were aces. All belonged to a disciplined, spirited force and had hundreds of hours more jet flying experience than their opponents. Some, it was to turn out, were MiG happy—more interested in getting kills than in using common sense—but most were, simply, men who commanded respect. They did not yet, however, command the skies. Far from it. Although claimed aerial victories added up to a lopsided advantage for the Sabres, the MiG pilots continued to hold the initiative.

Captain Jabara of the 4th Wing's 334th FIS got his first MiG on 3 April 1951. It was the beginning of a shooting spree. By 22 April 1951, Jabara had achieved the unprecedented by shooting down four MiGs. Jabara remained at Suwon after the 334th was routinely rotated back to Japan (one of the wing's squadrons customarily stayed in the rear area while two flew from Korean soil). He was thus flying with the 335th FIS rather than his own squadron when he finally got kill number five on 20 May 1951 (plus a sixth) while flying an F-86A-5 (49-1318). Jabara's achievement was all the greater because he got the kills

Capt. Bill Todd of the 335th FIS/4th FIW was flying this early F-86A (48-305) when a hit from a MiG damaged his horizontal stabilizer (shown) and canopy. The Sabre always had problems, not caused by any enemy, with its weak nosewheel, but most pilots credited the Sabre with some capacity to sustain battle damage. A pilot who flew with Todd, however, asserted that "the F-86 was not famous for durability," and felt it sheer luck that Todd made it home. Donald O. Griffith

This is what Sabre pilots called a max effort. With the troublesome pierced steel planking (PSP) of a taxiway dominating the foreground, 16 F-86A Sabres prepare to take off in formation and prowl the skies of MiG Alley. Speaking of wake turbulence from such a gaggle of Sabres, a pilot recalls, "If you were in the last flight, it got pretty bumpy." The black-and-white bands on these aircraft tell us that this is the 4th FIW within the first year after its arrival in the Korean War. Donald O. Griffith

At bases throughout Korea, in front of a variety of buildings, signposts proclaimed the aerial campaign being waged by the F-86 Sabre along the Yalu River. The 335th FIS, the Chiefs, was part of the 4th FIW, which fought most of the war from Kimpo. This tally of kills during the tenure of Lt. Col. Vermont Garrison comes late in the Korean conflict. Richard B. Keener

while flying off balance with a hung drop tank.

Crew Chief Talk

On the day America produced its first jet ace, Cpl. Albert N. (Norm) Kalow, a Sabre crew chief with the 335th FIS/4th FIW at Suwon, took notes on what an enlisted member's part of the F-86's war was all about. In Korea, crew chiefs often had no assistants, worked alone under grueling conditions of extreme cold and heat with minimal support facilities, and rarely got much credit. After breakfast at the chow hall, Kalow started his day:

"Time to preflight the Sabres for the morning mission to MiG Alley. I do my calisthenics for the day by removing the camouflage netting that covers the Sabre. We question its necessity, as the planes are parked on concrete. We think the contrast would make the planes more visible from the air to any would-be attacker.

"The pilots are coming to the flight line. Hope I don't get the 'Abort King.' This captain just flies to the bomb line to get credit for a mission, dreams up an imaginary problem with the Sabre, returns to base and we waste time finding out there is no problem. The C.O. has the engineering officer check out the plane every time he does this.

"Today, I'm in luck. Capt. Ralph (Hoot) Gibson flies my plane [F-86A-5 49-1311, the *Blazing Buckeye*]. We crew chiefs help each other with the APUs [auxiliary power units] used to start the J47 jet engines. They are clumsy but necessary. The jet engines require so much power to start that external help is needed. The APU is a big yellow box on wheels. In it is a light plane air-cooled engine coupled to a generator. Heavy black cables from the APU plug into the Sabre's fuselage.

Two key enlisted airmen had a direct role in keeping the Sabre up in MiG Alley. The crew chief usually receives more credit than the armorer, two of whom are shown here working on the Sabre's six .50cal M3 machine guns. Phyllis *is an F-86E-1-NA Sabre (50-0594) of the 51st FIW, which entered the fray shortly after the events described in this chapter.* Phillip A. Norton

"I check the oxygen, fuel tanks, oil level, and double check the Sabre in general. It looks good and there is time to see if the cooks have sent over any coffee and perhaps some leftover bakery for us. The P.A. system plays records today. The music reminds us of Japan. They play 'China Night,' 'Song of Arirang,' 'Tokyo Boogie Woo-

F-86A Sabres of the 335thFIS/4th FIW on the hardstand at Kimpo waiting for action. via Robert Esposito

gie.' New tunes from stateside are unfamiliar to us.

"'Herr' Schultz the armorer checks the .50 calibers on the Sabre. He is always bumming cigarettes. Says he left his on the piano. Schultz is a 'lifer'—was in bombers in WWII, shot down, and a POW, thus the title 'Herr' we bestowed on him.

"We're always warned about the dangers inherent in the Sabre's nose intake and treat it with respect. No problem with the jet exhaust—a person could be knocked down if he got too close but not burned or hurt seriously. The Koreans hired to sweep the taxiways never learn to steer clear of the jet exhausts and we get a kick of seeing a worker tumbling, butt over teakettle, white clothes flying.

"The Sabre's J47 engine requires more care in 'firing up' than, say, the F-80 Shooting Star. A 'hot start' will result in a large tongue of flame shooting out of the tailpipe and this causes a ruined ('Sayonara') engine. We crew chiefs have to be on the ball whenever we run up the engines but fortunately the learning curve is not excessively long.

"Hoot Gibson starts the engine and soon all the planes are taxying to the one and only runway. If they tangle with MiGs, we crew chiefs will have to hang drop tanks on them after their return. The C-119 is unloading more boxes of drop tanks for us so we'd better uncrate and build up several in case we need them. MiG Alley must be paved with them. We hear a set of drop tanks costs as much as a new Ford. If they fail to drop when the pilot wants to jettison, I lose a stripe. No longer a corporal."

For hours, crew chief Kalow waited. "The Sabres are returning. No drop tanks. The MiGs were up. They have light damage. The MiGs have cannons and can do serious damage if they are accurate. My plane is okay and Hoot apologizes for not getting a MiG. Great guy.

"But what's the excitement two planes over from mine? Crew chief Joe Menden is happy. His pilot, Capt. James Jabara, just made ace, shooting down MiGs number 5 and 6. The first jet ace in history. (If we had gotten to Korea sooner, I think Hoot Gibson would have had that honor). Pilots Roberts and Kemp hoist Jabara on their shoulders while *Life* photographers click away. Jabara lights up another cigar and beams happily...."

Jabara was a 27-year-old grocer's son from Wichita, Kansas, and had gotten three and one-half Luftwaffe kills flying the P-51 Mustang in World War II. In June 1951, he told *Newsweek*'s George C. Hamilton that the MiG could outrun and outclimb the F-86 above 30,000ft (9,144m). He said he wished he had four 20mm cannons instead of six .50cal machine guns. The American fighter's gunsight was better, but the MiG provided heavier armor protection for its pilot. "Lt. Col. Eagleston thought he hit one MiG 100 times but it didn't go down." The unwillingness of the MiG to fall from the sky, even when hit repeatedly, was to remain a major frustration. On balance, though, Jabara felt the F-86 was "the best jet in the world and the MiG is the second best."

Sabre pilots could shoot down MiGs. But they could not shoot down enough MiGs to alter the geography, politics, or progress of the war. And they could only contest the MiGs when the MiG pilots chose. One of Jabara's squadron mates, Capt. Michael P. Curphey, felt that the Sabre pilots were risking their lives for little gain. Curphey remembered one pilot who couldn't cut it. "This guy always had some reason why he couldn't get into the fight. We didn't have many like this, but he was a coward, plain and simple. As for the rest of us, we wanted to take on the bastards and whip their asses. Every time they hit one of our guys, we felt they were in charge of the situation and we seethed...."

To add to frustrations, the 4th Wing lost several F-86A Sabres in noncombat mishaps. Fighting along MiG Alley dropped to a low level in the spring of 1951, at the very time when a final spasm of terrain swapping came to an end and the Chinese spring offensive petered out. Now, battle lines on the ground really did begin to stabilize.

On 17 June 1951, an intruding Polikarpov Po-2LSh biplane dropped two bombs on Suwon. It was fashionable, even then, to dismiss the Po-2 as a nocturnal nuisance with no mission function except to annoy. Few, if any, Americans knew that Wehrmacht troops on the eastern front in World

War II feared the Po-2 and believed that it could look into each window to see if soldiers were inside a house. By blowing one F-86A Sabre (49-1334) to oblivion and seriously damaging eight more, this single incursion by Bedcheck Charlie, the Po-2 heckler, inflicted more harm to the Sabre force than the MiGs had, so far.

Along the Yalu, the MiGs became more aggressive in mid-June. In dogfights on 17–19 June 1951, two Sabres were lost and six MiGs were shot down. On 22 June 1951, Sabres mixed it up with MiGs while covering a raid by F-80s on the Sinuiju airfield south of the Yalu. One Sabre was lost, two MiGs shot down.

Lt. Col. Glenn Eagleston took three cannon hits during a 28 June 1951 engagement. A 37mm cannon shell exploded against the guns on the left nose and two 23mm shells ripped through steel farther back on the fuselage. Eagleston was thrown into a dive to 15,000ft (4,572m) and had to struggle home while Colonel Hinton covered him. The shell that gouged out major sections of the gun bay, had it struck a foot or two higher, would have hit Eagleston's head. Fortunately for Sabre pilots, the relatively slow rate of fire of the MiG cannons reduced the number of likely hits in any given instance and the Sabre itself was rugged and survivable.

Outnumbered

In June 1951, the Chinese possessed 445 MiG-15s while FEAF's 5th

Maintenance crews of the 336th FIS/4th FIW working on Sabres outside. The Sabre flown by Marine Corps exchange pilot Richard Rash is in the center. Weather in Korea swings from blistering, humid heat in summer to subzero snowstorms in winter, and maintenance people were sorely in need of better facilities. More important, they were desperate for improvement in the flow of supplies and parts. The Aircraft Out of Commission, Parts (AOCP) rate was so serious that the 4th FIW faced serious difficulty trying to maintain the initiative over MiG Alley. Richard Rash

Wing tanks. When a max effort was being mounted against the bandit trains and Sabres discarded their tanks, the falling metal was like a cascade of silver, raining from the sky. Unfortunately, there were not enough wing tanks, not when only NAA-built examples (shown) were available and not when Japanese-manufactured tanks entered the supply flow. Without wing tanks, there was no way the F-86 Sabre could journey to MiG Alley and prowl hostile skies. Yet commanders found themselves unable to obtain enough tanks to keep up the campaign against the MiG. Richard B. Keener

Air Force had 89 F-86 Sabres in theater inventory, of which 44 belonged to the 4th Wing's two squadrons then committed to Korea. While these numbers showed the Americans to be vastly outnumbered, the situation in fact was much worse than it looked: Col. Herman A. Schmid, who had replaced Col. George F. Smith as 4th Wing commander (in May 1951), was discovering that it took "maintenance miracles" to keep as many as half of his Sabres in the air. While it looked on paper as if Schmid was outnumbered 10:1, the truth was, his F-86 Sabre force had a 20:1 disadvantage vis-à-vis the Chinese. No amount of courage on the part of F-86 pilots could compensate for a losing situation that seemed to grow worse and worse.

The number two man in the 4th Wing, Col. David T. McKnight, was replaced by Col. Francis S. Gabreski, who was then—and still is— the top living American air ace, credited with 28 aerial victories in Europe. It's believed that Gabreski came to Kimpo expecting to take command of the 4th. As he took over the deputy commander's slot from McKnight, it's understood that McKnight uttered a gentle warning. "Our job is air superiority, Gabby. That means preventing the MiGs from getting through to shoot down our bombers and fighters. But the choice hasn't been in our hands so far. The MiGs don't usually get through, right now, because they don't usually try. The moment those bastards north of the Yalu start trying, we're going to be minced meat on the table."

In fact, Gabreski was destined to command a different unit entirely. Gabby was junior in rank to Col. Harrison R. (Harry) Thyng who was also on the roster for duty in Korea.

Although their numbers were to increase later in the year, Sabre pilots were to remain the most outnumbered band of fighter jocks in history—more than the Flying Tigers in China, more than the RAF in the Battle of Britain. Though many of the MiG pilots were no match for the Americans, a few who spearheaded the bandit trains coming across the Yalu were as good as they came. Some were Russian volunteers. 4th Wing pilot Capt. James A. Horowitz was to write a novel about a duel between the MiGs' aggressive fighter wing commander, Casey Jones, and a fictional American.

As the Korean War entered its second year, lines were joined on the ground, frustrating truce talks began, and the MiGs—while safe in their sanctuaries on the forbidden side of the Yalu—became more aggressive. In August 1951, the 5th Air Force settled on stationing its fighter wings at airfields in Korea, now deemed secure, which they would occupy for the remainder of hostilities. The only Sabre wing, the 4th FIW (334th, 336th FIS, with the 335th in reserve in Japan), was to remain at K-14 Kimpo AB. The 4th's maintenance and supply support was dispersed at several locations in Japan, but Sabre maintenance was soon consolidated at Tsuiki in western Japan. The 51st FIW (16th, 25th FIS)—still flying F-80s, but destined for a change sooner than anyone expected—was at K-13 Suwon AB south of Seoul. We shall hear more about the 51st Wing.

But what are we to make of reports that American pilots repeatedly sighted, and were attacked by, an F-86 Sabre flown by a communist pilot? Could somebody have landed an F-86 intact up there? The first such report surfaced at about the time Colonel Thyng came on the scene. In November 1951, an American Sabre pilot was fired upon—and missed—by a Sabre that bounced him from the north side of the Yalu. Though it gets ahead of our story, American pilots were to report a hostile F-86 again on 3 and 4 February 1952 and a South African pilot (Chapter 5) a few months later. In the research for this volume, it was determined that every American F-86 Sabre pilot from the Korean War has been accounted for, and that no American prisoners of war (POWs) landed their aircraft intact. But the mysterious communist F-86 had frightening symbolic importance. To some, it was more evidence that nothing was going well, nothing at all.

Intelligence officers determined that the Chinese were mounting a new campaign designed to establish air superiority over MiG Alley in late July 1951. Casey Jones and his wingmen began by experimenting with tactics. Taking advantage of their vast numbers and capability to fly higher, MiG pilots evaded Sabre patrols at the Yalu and continued southward at altitudes above 35,000ft (10,668m) as far as Pyongyang, the North Korean capital. It was arrogance for them to come as far as Pyongyang. It was a sign that the enemy's commander felt he was winning.

MiGs became more aggressive in challenging RF-80 reconnaissance aircraft and vulnerable F-80 and F-84 fighter-bombers. In mid-August, Sabres countered these MiG thrusts, overcame heavy numbers, and downed four MiGs.

At about this time, Navy LCdr. Paul Pugh took command of the 4th FIW's 334th FIS—the only naval aviator ever to command a USAF squadron in combat. He kept the post a mere four weeks before the USAF decided it couldn't have a tailhooker in charge of pilots in shade 84 blue.

Maj. Felix Asla, commander of the 336th FIS/4th FIW and holder of the Silver Star, was an experienced fighter pilot and an able leader. The long, grueling campaign over MiG Alley, with its frustrations and failures, was absolutely serious business, and Asla and his wingmen knew it, every minute. While the 4th FIW struggled to contain the MiG-15 without enough help and without adequate supplies, Asla was killed in combat along the Yalu River. Gordon Beem

Air Aces

Fighting grew heavier. On 2 September 1951, 22 Sabres battled 40 MiGs in a half-hour air duel that raged between Sinuiju and Pyongyang and shot down four MiGs. On 9 September 1951, a duel between 28 Sabres and 70 MiGs resulted in Capts. Richard S. Becker and Ralph D. (Hoot) Gibson each racking up their fifth MiG kills to become the second and third air aces of the conflict. In September, 14 MiGs and three Sabres went down in air-to-air fighting. But the ratio was deceiving. The Sabres were not doing well enough and it was becoming increasingly difficult to keep them aloft.

The USAF now faced a dilemma. F-86A Sabre day fighters were serving alongside F-86D interceptors in the Air Defense Command (ADC), guarding the North American continent against air attack by the Soviets. The top airman in the Far East, Gen. O. P. Weyland, warned the Pentagon that the Chinese "[may] be able to establish bases in Korea and threaten our air supremacy over the front lines," but in Washington chief of staff Gen. Hoyt S. Vandenberg was being told by advisors that no more F-86 Sabres could be despatched to Korea without impairing ADC. Vandenberg was also told that the means did not exist to support a second Sabre fighter wing in Korea. On 20 September 1951, almost certainly with pain in his heart, Vandenberg informed Weyland that the USAF could neither provide nor support additional Sabre squadrons in Korea.

When you didn't have enough to do the job, when you couldn't keep what you did have in the air, when you knew you were going to be outgunned every time you went north to fight, it was inevitable that some men were unable to hack it. The 334th FIS had one pilot who developed a fuel-flow problem or a mechanical glitch every time he got near MiG Alley. Another pilot found an excuse to drop out every time he was scheduled to go against the MiGs in a maximum effort. "We weeded these guys out," said one of the aces. "But it took time. In the meanwhile, we relied upon air discipline and teamwork. Every time a guy didn't hold up his part of the weight, it betrayed the rest of us."

When you were fighting 200mi (320km) behind enemy lines, in the high reaches of the stratosphere where so much seemed so impersonal, it was difficult to remember that this was war, that blood was spilled, that men died. "A guy would go down and you wouldn't see him any more, and that was it. You'd have an empty bunk. Once in awhile, when a guy bought it, you'd hear him over the R/T [radio], asking you to say so long to his parents, his wife, his kids, while his ship augered in." On rare occasion, a Sabre pilot actually got a glimpse of the face of his opponent in a MiG—often while in the process of killing him.

Even more rarely, grim reality got up close and personal: Capt. Robinson

It's doubtful that any commander of Americans in battle ever faced greater challenges than did Col. Harrison R. Thyng, who headed the 4th FIW when it stood alone against over 800 MiGs at four air bases on the Chinese side of the Yalu. Thyng (right, with the adjutant of Australia's No. 77 Squadron at Kimpo) was a World War II ace and became an ace again in Korea, but his greatest achievement was leadership. When supply problems threatened his ability to maintain air superiority, Thyng risked his career by going right to the top. Gordon Beem

Risner was hit by exploding MiG cannon shells that shattered his windshield and sprayed glass fragments into his face. Risner limped home, trailing smoke and debris, temporarily half-blinded, his face drenched in blood. Capt. Michael P. Curphey had his Sabre's fuselage ripped open by cannon hits. Leaking fuel and hydraulics, he flamed out 60mi (96km) north of Kimpo. He dead-sticked his way to runway's end, lost the always-troublesome nosewheel on landing, and came to a halt, tail-up. Curphey couldn't unstrap and climb out. There was blood everywhere and he was holding pieces of intestine in his hands.

Risner and Curphey lived to fight another day. Maj. Felix Asla, the much-respected commander of the 336th FIS and holder of the Silver Star, was lost in combat.

In October 1951, badly outnumbered and faced with numerous obstacles, the 4th FIW intensified its prowling of MiG Alley and fought some of the greatest air battles of history over northwestern Korea. Now the MiG force had increased to 525 aircraft (versus 44 Sabres) but Sabres destroyed two MiGs on 1 October, six on 2 October, one on 5 October, one on 12 October, and no fewer than nine (the biggest daily score yet) on 16 October 1951. But October 1951 also brought brutal MiG attacks on B-29 Superfortresses, a further increase in the size of the MiG force, and introduction of the MiG-15bis ("bis" stands for "improved") version with a more powerful engine. The Sabres were getting more kills, but the MiGs were perilously close to taking command of the air.

On 1 November 1951, Colonel Thyng replaced Schmid as commander of the 4th FIW, a job that many had expected Gabreski to occupy. (The official date is not precise: documents from the period show Schmid signing as commander on 4 November, Thyng on 17 November). Thyng was cautioned by an officer who greeted him that his pilots could not prevent bandit trains from breaking through the Sabres and shooting down B-29s, RF-80s, F-84s, and other UN warplanes.

Shortly after his arrival, Thyng had two pilots quit in one day. The two men told their flight leaders in plain English that they were afraid to, and couldn't continue to, strap themselves into five tons of wire and metal driven by a blowtorch, fly at the edge of the sound barrier into the pitch-black expanse of the stratosphere 200mi (320km) behind enemy lines, and come face-to-face with a numerically superior MiG force that held all the advantages.

World War II ace Capt. Philip E. (Casey) Colman, stuck in an F-80 outfit and eager to transfer to the air-to-air mission, visited Thyng and pleaded for an assignment to the 4th FIW. Though Casey Colman was exactly the kind of leader Thyng needed, the colonel found that it took mountains of paperwork to make it happen.

Frustrations

Colonel Thyng also spoke to a line chief who warned him that the numbers (which showed more MiGs being shot down than Sabres) were only part of the story. "Colonel," said S/Sgt. Fred Newman, "our pilots are being clobbered, sir. My crew chiefs are working 24hr but we don't have the parts we need, we don't have the wing tanks, and if we had to put up a maximum effort tomorrow morning, we wouldn't be able to."

Harry Thyng was a man to be taken seriously. His first fighter had been the Spitfire, and he'd shot down nine Luftwaffe aircraft in Europe. He'd also been on Okinawa as commander of a group of long-range P-47N Thunderbolts. Though he sometimes wore a .38 pistol hanging down from his hip, High Noon gunslinger style, Thyng was more a gentleman than a jock, a precise and thoughtful man with great presence who needed to say or do nothing to prove his courage. Harry Thyng was not a man who got upset, not ever, but they were asking him to wage an air war without enough of anything—not enough aircraft, not enough pilots, not enough wing tanks.

To understand the 4th FIW's dilemma, it must be remembered that maintenance and supply issues went hand in glove with combat performance. And it's necessary to use a little alphabet soup. As S/Sgt. Gordon Beem, chief clerk of the 4th FIW's message center remembers, the dilemma went like this:

"The 4th FIW was an Eastern Air Defense Force [EADF] outfit of the Air Defense Command [ADC] on temporary duty to Far East Air Forces [FEAF] and on detached service with 5th Air Force. Trying to get F-86 parts through normal supply channels was an administrative nightmare. When we tried OCAMA (Oklahoma City Air Material Area) they told us to go to FEAMCOM (Far Eastern Air Materiel Command) and FEAMCOM told us to go to OCAMA. In the meanwhile, whenever the 4th FIW was called upon to put up a maximum effort (which was frequently) less than half of the F-86s would be in commission. The AOCP [Aircraft Out of Commission, Parts] rate was at unacceptable levels.

"We had three squadrons, the 334th, 335th, and 336th. Each squadron was assigned 25 F-86s with a 10 percent augmentation 'for war.' Thus, the 4th FIW had some 80-odd F-86s to carry out its mission of 'maintaining air superiority in Northwest Korea.' From the classified message traffic that I handled, I believe that Colonel Thyng and the staff of the wing and its groups and squadrons did everything humanly possible to solve the problem of an unacceptably high AOCP rate. But the situation continued and when a maximum effort was laid on, the 4th FIW was hard-pressed to put more than 40 F-86s in the air over MiG Alley."

In those days, no one would ever have contemplated taking a step that Thyng now decided upon. Thyng would risk his command, his career, and certainly any chance he might have of ever wearing general's stars, by taking the problem not to 5th Air Force, not to FEAF, but directly to Washington, D.C., and to the USAF chief of staff, General Vandenberg.

As Beem remembers, "I had known Col. Harry Thyng to be an air warrior of high physical courage. He led the 4th FIW personally and with great valor. He made it clear when the wing received its first black fighter pilot, Lt. Dayton Ragland, that Ragland was to be treated for what he was, a highly skilled fighter pilot. When it was clear that the 4th FIW was not able to hold the line against the MiGs, he had the moral courage to do what was right even though there might be high personal cost involved. He believed that the men whose lives he was responsible for were at a disadvantage in MiG Alley due to the AOCP problem. After exhausting all other avenues, Harry took his career in his hands and sent a message that he knew was the right thing to do no matter what the cost to him personally or professionally."

Thyng was very much aware that no one might listen to what he had to say. He also knew that while some of his pilots were MiG happy and pressed an aggressive fight against the enemy—not always within the bounds of good judgment—others were demoralized by their inability to wrest the initiative from the MiGs. Speaking in part of the maintenance nightmare and in part of the MiGs' ability to fly higher, one pilot, after being asked several times, after being assured that he could answer truthfully, broke down and said, "Colonel, they are beating the shit out of us up there."

Beem reported for work one morning and was told by adjutant Maj. John Ross that Thyng had drafted an "Ops Immediate" message to send right away. Beem recalls: "Major Ross gave me a folder with a handwritten draft message in it that I took to my cubicle and read. It was a Top Secret, Operations Immediate message written in Colonel Thyng's handwriting. It was addressed to CSAF [the Chief of Staff of the USAF] with copies to CG [Commanding General] 5th Air Force, CG FEAF, CG ADC, and CG EADF. The message detailed the AOCP problem the 4th FIW had been, and was, experiencing, the situation with FEAMCOM and OCAMA; all the actions taken to resolve the matter and the lack of success achieved. Colonel Thyng detailed his deep concern in taking the available 4th FIW aircraft and their pilots into combat against the MiG-15s when the enemy had, and was capable of putting up, 8–10 times the number of F-86s we could muster...."

Neither Ross nor Beem believed that Thyng understood the message he was sending. He was laying his head on the chopping block. Says Beem, "I went into his office and he was in the final stages of dressing in his flight suit." Beem asked if he really wanted the message sent. Thyng replied, "Yes, there are too many lives at stake not to." With that, Thyng picked up his flight helmet and gear and went out his private door to his jeep, which would take him to his F-86 Sabre named *Pretty Mary and the 4 J's* for his wife and children. Colonel Thyng headed north to fight MiGs.

The key sentences of his message read, "PERSONAL TO VANDENBERG FROM THYNG. I CAN NO LONGER BE RESPONSIBLE FOR AIR SUPERIORITY IN NORTHWEST KOREA."

A year ago, China's entry into the war had overwhelmed the Americans. They'd fought hard to contain the onslaught and to stabilize the conflict. Now the USAF's supply problems, teething trouble with the F-86, and the lethality of the MiG-15 had combined to overwhelm them again. The air-to-air kill ratio—seven or eight MiGs falling out of the sky for every Sabre—was a salve for those who understood events only when looking at numbers, but the kill ratio was also a cruel hoax in a situation where, on any day, the enemy could do anything he wanted.

Pilots of the NAA F-86 Sabre were confronting terrible odds and fighting hard. But in the autumn of 1951, they were tasting something bitter and foul. To most of them, it was new. It was the taste of defeat.

312

CHAPTER THREE

North American FJ Fury Fighter

As World War II rushed toward its finish and the merit of the jet-powered warplane had been proven, the US Navy invested in four carrier-based fighters that, if hastily pressed into service, might have been available for the amphibious invasion of Japan, Operation Olympic-Coronet, scheduled for May 1946.

In December 1944 and early 1945, the US Navy awarded contracts for four jet fighters, the Vought XF6U-1, McDonnell XFD-1, McDonnell XF2D-1, and NAA FJ-1 (eventually named Pirate, Phantom, Banshee, and Fury). All had straight wings. All were single seaters. The FJ-1 had a low-mounted, very thin wing and a fuselage shape that today seems almost familiar. The shape of the FJ-1 fuselage is a bloated version of the F-86 Sabre it inspired.

The Navy went ahead with three prototypes of the XFJ-1 Fury, or company model NA-134 (bureau numbers [BuNos.] 39053/39055), powered by a 3,820lb (1,733kg) thrust General Electric TG-180 (later J35-GE-2) turbojet. This engine was initially built by Chevrolet. The USAAF decided against the straight wing and went back to the drawing board.

As it happened, the war ended in August 1945. After VJ Day, the frenetic pace of wartime aircraft development was sharply curtailed. With no enemy to combat, delays occurred in the development of the early jets.

The Navy's first XFJ-1 Fury (BuNo. 39053) took to the air on 11 September 1946 with Wallace Lien at the control. The ship was robust and portly. It looked like the pilot could just fling it around the sky.

The choice of wing planform imposed limited prospects on the FJ-1 in the newly unfolding jet age. In May 1945, the US Navy had ordered 100 (later cut back to 30) production FJ-1, or company model NA-141, aircraft (BuNos. 120342/120371). Though it looked like a performer, the FJ-1 Fury's principal characteristic was its mediocrity. In fairness, it was no more or less forgettable than the USAF's Republic XP-84 of the same period.

The FJ-1 Fury was credited with a top speed of 542mph (872km/h) at 16,000ft (4,876m). Armed with six .50cal (12.7mm) nose machine guns with 1,500 rounds but unable to handle ordnance loads beneath its thin wings, the FJ-1 Fury would have been an effective air-to-air combatant.

The FJ-1 Fury, held to subsonic speed by its aerodynamics and never meant to carry much of a payload, nevertheless reached one US Navy squadron, VF-5A Screaming Eagles at NAS North Island near San Diego, California. In fact, VF-5A received its first FJ-1 (BuNo. 120349) in December 1947 minus its 4,000lb (1,814kg) thrust Allison J35-A-4 powerplant. The absence of the engine prompted squadron skipper Cdr. Evan P. (Pete) Aurand to stage a gag in which pilots sat in a row in the plane's open, empty

A NAA FJ-2 Fury of the Marine Corps' VMF-122 Candystripers, commanded by Lt. Col. Johnnie M. Vance, takes a wave off from USS Coral Sea *(CVB-43) during operations in the Straits of Bonafacio on a Mediterranean cruise in June 1955. The FJ-2 was the first Fury version that drew from experience with the swept-wing F-86 Sabre. The Navy found this model not suitable for carrier work, so most were delivered to the Marines who usually operate from land bases—but within 14 months of accepting their first deliveries, the Marines were hanging out their tail hooks and going aboard ship.* Tad Riley

The first XFJ-1 Fury (BuNo. 39053) at the Naval Air Test Center, Patuxent River, Maryland, is sandwiched between two examples of a Navy fighter that achieved greater success than the straight-wing Fury. Number XF9F-1 model was built, so these two natural-metal Grumman XF9F-2 Panther prototypes (BuNos. 122475 and 122477), which began flight tests in November 1947, are the first of their breed, flown initially with no armament or ejection seat. By the time the Korean War came along in June 1950, the straight-wing Fury was past tense while the Panther was the Navy's primary fighter. via Larry Davis

Wearing the pre-1947 national insignia, with no red line inside the bar and as yet devoid of any meaningful Navy markings, the prototype XFJ-1 Fury (BuNo. 39053) poses over the High Sierra. This first Fury made its maiden flight on 11 September 1946 piloted by Wallace Lien. Here, the pilot is wearing an early, football-style helmet and back parachute, with no oxygen mask visible. He does not yet have an ejection seat and, if trouble were to arise, would have to climb out of the aircraft in order to parachute to safety. NAA

engine compartment and "rowed" the Fury with wooden oars. Once engines were available, an exhaustive familiarization program was carried out, including 200 field carrier landing practices (FCLPs), using an airfield marked-off to simulate a carrier deck. These mock carrier landings were done with the canopy to the rear and the landing signal officer (LSO) using paddles.

The honor of making the first operational landing of a Navy jet aboard a carrier went to Aurand when he brought an FJ-1 aboard USS *Boxer* (CV-21) on 16 March 1948, closely followed by his executive officer, LCdr. Bob Elder.

VF-5A did some pioneering with the first Pacific Fleet jet operations on *Boxer* and a squadron team won the Bendix Trophy by beating USAF F-80 Shooting Stars in a cross-country race. VF-5A also entered the Long Beach–Cleveland Bendix Trophy Race, won by Ens. Taylor Brown. Elder's contribution was limited to making a dead stick landing in an FJ-1 at Cleveland after running out of fuel at 43,000ft (13,106m) a full 80mi (128km) out. Aurand, Elder, Brown, and other VF-5A aviators were positive about the FJ-1 but noted that the straight-wing Fury had performance problems at maximum gross weight and was uncomfortable to fly due to lack of pressurization and temperature control.

Pilots flying the FJ-1 Fury operationally ran into problems with the wing-tip tanks. Apparently, the tanks were not compatible with the thin wing under certain conditions. The tanks were redesigned but the problem never entirely went away.

The squadron was redesignated VF-51 in August 1948, and operated the FJ-1 until July 1949 when the Grumman F9F Panther replaced it. FJ-1s then served with the Naval Air Reserve. With some aircraft prominently marked with a Weekend Warriors logo on the nose and an orange stripe around the rear fuselage, Reserve FJ-1s flew from Oakland, California, and served as transition trainers to give jet experience to pilots moving on to the McDonnell F2H-2 Banshee or the Panther. Reservists also flew the FJ-1 at Los Alamitos, Califor-

nia; Olathe, Kansas; and Dallas, Texas.

The aircraft was simple and straightforward: its axial-flow turbojet engine fed directly from the front and blew its exhaust straight out the back—allowing the Fury to have a simple, straight-through airflow. Still, the Fury incorporated some imaginative features. XFJ-1 prototypes had retractable, slatted speed brakes in the wing upper and lower surfaces, replaced in production by more conventional barn door style fuselage brakes. The top of the XFJ-1/FJ-1 fuselage behind the cockpit could be removed for maintenance access to the engine (this being the location of Aurand's oarsmen).

All Furys also had an ingenious tiny wheel mounted on the nosewheel strut that permitted the craft to "kneel" in supplicate fashion—nose down, tail up, for close-quarters shipboard parking. Most of these features were rarely used.

We know what happened after the USAAF halted construction of its version of the straight-wing FJ-1 Fury, took pause, and applied data from German reports. The result was a swept wing on a thinner fuselage—and the USAF's F-86 Sabre.

Swept-Wing Fury

The Navy was deliberate in moving towards swept-wing fighters because flying from carrier decks meant spending a significant part of each mission at low speeds, and reliable handling was of life-or-death importance after takeoff or on approach for

The portly FJ-1 Fury, which reached operational status with the fleet, was similar but not identical to the USAF's original straight-wing XP-86 pursuit ship. This FJ-1 Fury (BuNo. 120361), wearing the S tail code of Carrier Air Group Five (CVG-5) and assigned to VF-5A Screaming Eagles under Cdr. Evan P. (Pete) Aurand, is making an appearance at the Cleveland National Air Races in 1949. The straight-wing Fury went to sea aboard USS Boxer *(CV-21) and USS* Princeton *(CV-37) during its brief career in blue.* William Balogh

landing. As late as 1950, the Navy was still planning to use propeller-driven warplanes for a considerable time to come; the service was slow adopting jets, slower adopting swept wings.

The Navy's earliest swept-wing fighter, the Vought F7U Cutlass, combined swept wings with a radical, tailless shape. Production F7U-1 and F7U-3 Cutlasses ran afoul of developmental problems. Though design work began in August 1945, the Cutlass (sometimes called the Useless or Gutless Cutlass) did not enter service until 1955, by which time it had been leapfrogged by other types and was hopelessly outclassed.

Like the production Cutlass, the delta-wing Douglas F4D-1 Skyray and swept-wing McDonnell F3H-1N Demon suffered from the Navy's scandalous commitment to the Westinghouse J40 engine that failed utterly and almost paralyzed naval aviation in the early to mid-1950s (to the extent that early F3H-1N Demons had to be towed by road and shipped by barge to Memphis, for use as ground instructional trainers, never able to fly with a powerplant destined never to succeed). The Skyray (redesigned for the J57 engine) and the Demon were late evolving into operational, carrier-based fighters and had modest careers.

More successful was the Navy's effort to produce a swept-wing fighter by keeping the fuselage and powerplant of the F9F-5 Panther but sweeping the Panther's wings and tail. The resulting F9F-6 Cougar (and F9F-7 that followed) enjoyed some success. The mature F9F-8 Cougar had a more satisfying career with the Fleet.

In the crucible of war, pitted against the MiG-15—or, for that matter, the USAF's Korea-proven F-86 Sabre—Cutlass, Skyray, Demon, and Cougar were at best second-rate fighters. To be sure, as one pilot recalled later, "[You] probably shouldn't put the Cutlass and the Skyray in the same class; properly flown, the Skyray could be pretty good. And the Cougar, well flown, wasn't too far off the F-86 in performance." Whatever their flaws or strong points, all of these fighters arrived too late to fight in the 1950–1953 Korean unpleasantness.

Nearly a decade passed before the Navy made the leap from its 1945-vintage FJ-1 Fury to an advanced version of NAA's fighter. By then, straight-wing Navy fighters like the Banshee and F9F-5 Panther had drawn blood, and shed some, in Korea but had failed to mount any serious challenge to the MiG-15. The swept-wing F9F-6 Cougar was only beginning to enter service. Service versions of the Demon and Skyray still lay in the future.

Looking for air-to-air prowess for the US Navy and Marine Corps, the Navy's Bureau of Aeronautics (BuAer, from which BuNos. derive their name) made up for lost time by quickly ordering three XFJ-2 Fury prototypes and 300 production FJ-2 Furys (later reduced to 200), all based on the F-86E Sabre. Commander Aurand was appointed the Navy's project officer.

So quickly did BuAer move, indeed, that the production FJ-2 seems to have been finalized before exact details were ironed out in the configurations of the three test ships. This results in confusion: the airplane with the highest BuNo. of all 203 planes flew first, and all three prototypes had BuNos. (133754/133756) higher than the 200 production ships that followed. Documents from the period also prove that the later FJ-3 and FJ-4 variants had reached a well-advanced planning stage even when the FJ-2 was only beginning to take shape.

Why a Navy FJ-2, almost identical to the Sabre? A document classified confidential at the time and since made public tells us something about the US Navy's thinking:

"The FJ-2 Fury is the answer to the Navy's need for a day fighter to contest efforts of any enemy willing to build a fighter limited to daylight VFR [visual flight rules] conditions. The appearance of the MiG-15 in Korea has demonstrated the need for a high-performance day airplane, and the Navy has moved swiftly to put such a plane into operational service. Advent of the MiG-15 may have been a blessing in disguise, for prior to its arrival upon the combat scene, all fighters in the Navy's future procurement program were to be equipped with radars weighing from 500 to 1,000lb [227 to 454kg]. This gear, of course, would have limited the performance required for daylight operations because of [its] added weight."

Two published references tell us that the nickname Sea Sabre was shunned in favor of Fury for the FJ-2 because of "funding procedures." In fact, the idea of calling this airplane the Sea Sabre never entered anyone's mind. Fury had been the Navy's appellation fully three years before the USAF picked the name Sabre. Further, prefixing a Sea to a shipboard version of a landplane was a British, not American, naming practice. Though dollars flowed freely in the post-Korea years of Cold War confrontation, it may be true that fiscal constraints kept the Navy from treating the FJ-2 as a wholly new aircraft and, therefore, from calling it the F2J-1. However, there is equally strong logic in considering the swept-wing fighter a development of the FJ-1 Fury, as was done, and calling it the FJ-2.

One-off XFJ-2B

The first swept-wing Fury to fly, the sole XFJ-2B, actually wore the third BuNo. assigned to prototypes (BuNo. 133756) and was simply an F-86E-10 Sabre (the version that introduced an all-moving tail for improved maneuverability against the MiG-15) painted glossy sea blue and armed with four 20mm Colt Mark 12 cannons with 150 rounds per gun. The US Navy had always favored the cannon (which fires an explosive round) rather than the USAF's weapon of choice, the machine gun (which fires a bullet) and never hesitated in choosing cannon armament for its "Sea Sabre."

Next page

The third XFJ-1 Fury (BuNo. 39055) struggles to stay ahead of the only XFJ-2B Fury (BuNo. 133756). First flown on 27 December 1951 by Bob Hoover, the XFJ-2B was simply an F-86E-10 Sabre painted glossy sea blue and pressed into naval service, minus any equipment that would enable it to land on a carrier. The XFJ-2B was armed with four 20mm Colt Mark 12 cannons that became standard on the Fury series while two very similar XFJ-2 developmental airframes were equipped to land and take off from carrier decks but did not have the guns. Full arresting equipment and armament had to await the first production FJ-2 that followed.
NAA via Hal Andrews

756
NAVY
NAVY
39055

The second XFJ-2 Fury prototype (BuNo. 133755) gets a boost from a jeep generator on board USS Midway *(CVB-41) prior to a test flight on 13 August 1952. Robert Dose, Donald Engen, and other Navy pilots who did early developmental flying with the XFJ-2 found this naval version of the F-86E Sabre to be unsuitable for the rigors of day-to-day aircraft carrier operations, and urged the Navy to proceed directly from the FJ-2 to its own FJ-3 version. Production FJ-2 Furys ended up in the hands of the Marine Corps rather than Navy, but operated from carriers anyway.* USN via Hal Andrews

First flown 27 December 1951 in Los Angeles by Bob Hoover, the XFJ-2B or company model NA-185, went to Inyokern, California, for armament tests. The B suffix customarily meant a change of armament in a sub-series (as we'll see, for example, with the FJ-4B). In this case the XFJ-2B was armed with what the Navy had already chosen for production ships but the suffix helps us to distinguish the landbased XFJ-2B from a pair of carrier-capable XFJ-2 prototypes, which were unarmed.

Next to fly was the first XFJ-2, or company model NA-179 (BuNo. 133754), taken aloft on 14 February 1952 (or, according to one company document, on 19 February) by Bob Hoover. This aircraft had an earlier BuNo. and was completed to an earlier NAA specification than the XFJ-2B that had already flown, because the two XFJ-2s (BuNos. 133754/133755) had taken longer to prepare for flight. These first two XFJ-2 Furys were essentially F-86E-10s with no armament and navalized for carrier operation with V-frame arrester hook, and an extended nose gear leg to maintain a high angle of attack during takeoff and landing.

Based on initial success with the first three Furys, the FJ-2 went into production at NAA's newly activated, Navy-owned plant in Columbus, Ohio. This facility was transferred from Curtiss Wright's Airplane Division when it closed out the long history of Curtiss airplanes.

Production FJ-2

The first production FJ-2, alias company model NA-181 (BuNo. 131927), flew on 22 November 1952 at Columbus with James Pearce in the cockpit. The 200 production FJ-2 fighters introduced a modified canopy and folding wings, essential on tightly-cramped carrier decks. Production aircraft also lacked dihedral on the horizontal tail surfaces found on XFJ-2B and XFJ-2 test ships.

The FJ-2 apparently went into production before completion of successful development work with the X ships, which may explain why the FJ-2 had difficulties operating around carriers.

Production FJ-2s were powered by the General Electric J47-GE-2 engine of 6,000lb (2,722kg) thrust bringing the Navy fighter close to F-86F standard. Other changes for production included folding wings, an increased wheel track, greatly beefed-up landing gear, and—as we've noted—installation of four 20mm cannons. The FJ-2 had a Mark 16 Model 2 gunsight and AN/APG-30 radar. The FJ-2 also had a wheel track 8in (20.32cm) wider than the F-86.

The FJ-2 is credited with a maximum speed of 676mph (1,090km/h) at sea level, an initial rate of climb of 7,230ft (2,203m) per minute, and a

On 22 October 1954, the second production FJ-2 Fury (BuNo. 131928) looks pristine in its new Navy blue paint at NAA's Columbus factory. The production FJ-2, which ended up in Marine Corps livery, differed from the USAF's F-86E Sabre in having a slightly different canopy shape, V-frame arrester hook, catapults, and an extended nose gear leg to maintain a high angle of attack during takeoff and landing. This view shows to good advantage the leading-edge slats that enhanced low-speed performance around the carrier. NAA via Hal Andrews

An FJ-2 Fury (BuNo. 131977) of Marine Corps squadron VMF-235 Death Angels (also known as the Rednoses) under Lt. Col. Donald Sapp prepares for takeoff from Itazuke AB near Fukuoka, Japan, in the spring of 1955. At this time, tensions remained very high in nearby Korea, as evidenced by USAF F-86 Sabres racking up three MiG kills in 1955. VMF-235 was the second Marine Corps squadron to receive the FJ-2, and the first to operate the aircraft in the Far East. Bill Foy

combat range of 990mi (1,593km). One pilot recalls that, "You could reach Mach 1.0 without wing tanks in a low-G pull-through or push-over into a vertical dive from 40,000ft [12,192m]."

NAA delivered both XFJ-2 navalized test ships to the Naval Air Test Center, Patuxent River, Maryland, where they underwent carrier suitability trials on board USS *Midway* (CVB-41) and USS *Coral Sea* (CVB-43). Although properly equipped, the XFJ-2 produced less than satisfactory results in its shipboard tests. The new nose gear and arresting hook bumper proved too weak for carrier landings under realistic conditions. The Fury also received poor marks for its handling performance during approach and landing. It was decided to supply early production FJ-2s to an obvious, landbased user—the Marine Corps—while carrier problems were addressed.

Board of inspection and survey (BIS) report 21162, dated 14 October 1954 and classified confidential at the time, dealt with stability and control tests as part of the service acceptance trials of the FJ-2. The aircraft employed in these tests was a YFJ-2 (BuNo. 131932) with a nose boom installation containing pressure spires and a yaw vane to measure sideslip angle. This YFJ-2 was frequently grounded with various problems, including canopy failure, during the 1953–1954 trials; but 60 test flights were successfully made, some with a Douglas AD-3Q Skyraider as a pace aircraft.

The BIS report found the YFJ-2 Fury to be a stable and efficient gun platform during gunnery and strafing runs, but only in the hands of an experienced pilot. Ground handling and takeoff characteristics were deemed satisfactory. Several aspects of longitudinal stability and flight handling were found wanting. The report called for some restrictions and for a solution to rudder buzz, encountered in transonic flight. The BIS report's bottom line:

"It is recommended that the model FJ-2 airplane be accepted for service use as a carrier-based fighter airplane insofar as stability and control characteristics are concerned."

Because of the results with carrier suitability trials, and because the Grumman F9F-6 Cougar was considered more suitable for carrier operations, production FJ-2s went to Marine squadrons. A contract was also issued for wet 6-3 leading edge kits for the FJ-2s that eventually went to the Marines. (This 6-3 wing, so named because its leading edge was extended 6in [15.24cm)] at the root and 3in [7.62cm] at the wing tip with the slat removed, significantly improved combat performance in Sabres from the late F-86F onward).

It became clear, however, that the increased landing speed resulting from substituting the sharp leading edge for slats would preclude any possibility of safely operating from a carrier. But NACA-Ames had been experimenting with leading-edge camber and radius modifications on their F-86, so NAA-Columbus applied this research in developing a cambered version of the 6-3. Its wet configuration added 124gal of leading edge fuel, improved high Mach maneuvering comparable to the 6-3 on the F-86E/F, and finally, after considerable fence development by NAA's Pete Marshall and the Columbus team, resulted in a very suitable fighter. This cambered 6-3 wing came too late for the FJ-2 series but became standard on late-model FJ-3s.

Cherry Point, North Carolina-based VMF-122 Candystripers (later nicknamed Crusaders) took their first Fury deliveries in January 1954.

The FJ-3 Fury introduced a new engine and thus took the Navy somewhat away from the USAF's Sabre design. The second production FJ-3 (BuNo. 135788) is seen, replete with the new-style wing tanks adopted by the Navy, aboard Coral Sea *on 3 February 1955.* NAA via Hal Andrews

Though the Marines got the nod specifically to postpone Fury operations on shipboard, VMF-122 went aboard *Coral Sea* on a Mediterranean cruise that commenced on 28 March 1955. At a time when all Navy and Marine aircraft were painted blue overall, VMF-122's Furys flew in natural metal. One of the carrier-capable Marines in the silvery FJ-2 was future attorney F. Lee Bailey.

On the west coast, VMF-235 Death Angels (alias the Rednoses) under Lt. Col. Donald Sapp received FJ-2 Furys as replacements for the long-in-the-tooth Vought F4U-4 Corsair and used them to test some of the US Navy's first steam catapults, aboard USS *Hancock* (CVA-19). VMF-235 also fielded four FJ-2s retrofitted with strengthened tail hook bumpers and modified nose gear struts in an unsuccessful effort to solve the FJ-2 model's carrier problems. Serving with this squadron at MCAS El Toro, California, was VMF-451 Warlords, the Marines' other west coast operator.

FJ-3 Fury

With the FJ-3 Fury model (and the nearly identical FJ-3M), also known as the company model NA-194, the Navy finally tore itself free from the shackles of the landbased F-86 Sabre design with which it had been stuck, somewhat reluctantly. Now, the Navy could take the superb features of the swept-wing fighter and improve upon them for its very dangerous business of flying to, from, and around aircraft carriers.

The FJ-3 gave the Navy a more powerful engine in the 7,800lb

At the time the FJ-3 Fury was swinging into Navy squadron service, the Navy was preparing to dispense with its traditional blue paint. This FJ-3 Fury (BuNo. 135843) of VF-33 Tarsiers aboard USS Lake Champlain *(CV-39) belonging to Lt. F. W. Martin, illustrates the eye-catching markings that were made possible with no colors but blue and white.* via Larry Davis

(3,648kg) thrust Wright J65-W-2 (or W-4 on some airplanes), a version of Britain's Armstrong Siddeley axial-flow turbojet engine. Flight work with the engine began with the fifth production FJ-2, retrofitted with the new powerplant and referred to (possibly unofficially) as the YFJ-3. The FJ-3 also introduced a more cambered 6-3 wing, better fuel capacity, four 20mm cannons, and excellent maneuverability.

The pleasure of taking the first FJ-3 Fury (BuNo. 135774) aloft for its maiden voyage fell upon William Ingram. Columbus was the site of the 3 July 1953 first flight. By the end of 1954, composite squadron VC-3 at Moffett Field, near San Francisco, was flying six FJ-3s in addition to its mix of F7U-3 Cutlasses and F9F-6 Cougars, to indoctrinate new fleet aviators.

The FJ-3 joined the fleet at a historic juncture—a time of steam catapults, new-style carrier decks, new landing techniques, and even new markings. Together, the FJ-3 and the angled carrier deck joined the fleet (the angled deck was a British innovation that enabled aircraft to land without aiming themselves at other, parked aircraft).

At the same time, the US Navy developed a mirror system to partly replace the paddle-waving LSO in guiding a pilot's approach to a deck landing. On 22 August 1955, Cdr. Robert G. Dose made the first mirror landing in a blue FJ-3 Fury belonging to test and development squadron VX-3, aboard USS *Bennington* (CVA-20) in the Atlantic. The familiar Navy blue became a thing of the past, for on 16 February 1955 the Navy began painting its aircraft in a very different non-spectacular light gull gray (top) and gloss white (bottom) paint scheme that was destined to endure for 20 years. FJ-3 Furys were painted in these colors.

Yet another development occurred in 1955 when the Navy directed that all new fighters be equipped for in-flight refueling. Current aircraft, FJ-3 included, were retrofitted. Now, the Fury acquired a lengthy, offset, under-wing probe sticking out from its port wing. This installation had been tested with lukewarm results on a surviving FJ-2; it was subsequently adopted on the FJ-4 series. Interestingly, the earliest American use of air refueling in combat had been during the Korean War with the Republic F-84G Thunderjet and never, operationally, with the Fury's alter ego, the F-86 Sabre. Experience with the FJ-3 prompted the Navy to recommend that a refueling probe location for future fighters be determined "at the inception of [its] design."

Furys routinely refueled from twin-engine NAA AJ-2 Savages and buddy refueled from smaller tactical jets like the Douglas A4D-2 Skyhawk. In trials, the Navy's Martin P6M-2 Seamaster four-engine jet seaplane was fitted with an A-28D hose reel unit and was used to refuel an FJ-3 Fury. Cancellation of the Seamaster program, rather than any flaw in the Fury, ended this effort.

Navy pilots were happy to get the FJ-3, which offered dramatic improvements over fighters then in service. VF-154 Black Knights under Cdr. J. J. Boydston transitioned to the FJ-3 in August 1955, but compressor problems with the FJ-3's engine (of which, more below) prevented the squadron from joining USS *Wasp* (CVA-18) when it deployed in 1956. Despite the engine problems, Boydston spoke well of the FJ-3.

He was not alone. "It was light to the touch but was a tough airplane," recalls Capt. James R. (Dick) Powell. Powell served with VF-142 Fighting Falcons (later nicknamed Ghostriders) aboard USS *Hornet* (CV-12) when the squadron, commanded by Cdr. E. Ralph Hanks, converted to the FJ-3 from the Grumman F9F-6 Cougar in March 1956. Powell was impressed that the axial-flow engine offered far better performance and fewer mechanical hang-ups than the centrifugal-flow turbojet of the Cougar.

It was no small achievement to turn out an aircraft that measured up against a product of the Grumman "Iron Works," the Navy's prime supplier of carrier-based fighters. Compared to the Cougar, the dash three Fury "got off the ground a helluva lot faster" (according to Powell), offered its pilot

about the same degree of comfort, and "could out-fight any airplane in service in those days with the sole exception of the F-86H." LCdr. Russell N. McDowell, another FJ-3 pilot, insists that he consistently won fights with the very powerful F-86H, but is alone among those interviewed.

Most pilots who flew the FJ-3 were extremely fond of the ship, but even Powell, who is otherwise very positive, laments that its "APG-30 gun fire-control radar was the same shitty piece of equipment we had in the F9F-6."

Powell's own first flight in an FJ-3 was made on 27 March 1956 in BuNo. 139223, the first ship received by VF-142.

Like many naval aviators, he knew the missile age was coming and was pleased when the Navy improved the FJ-3 and brought into service the FJ-3M model, wired to handle the AAM-N-7 Sidewinder air-to-air missile. The FJ-3M was not a new-build airplane but was created by modifying FJ-3s soon after they were produced.

"I only ever got to fire one Sidewinder, but there was no doubt this was the way fighters were going to be armed in the future," Powell says. "You would get clicks in your earphones when the seeker head of the missile was latched onto a target." The infrared (IR) or heat-seeking missile was a relatively new concept in those days and one handicap was that Fury pilots had few chances to fire them. Powell's outfit spent more time firing cannons.

"We used the guns when we went out to El Centro [California]. We had damn few jams," says Powell. "The guns were farther apart than those on the F9F-6 but tighter, with a nicer pattern, converging at 1,000ft [310m]."

Cdr. Donald D. Engen, who flew FJ-3 Furys with VF-21 Freelancers aboard USS *Bennington* noted that "early versions of the FJ-3 had a vile operating-room green cockpit. I never understood why anyone would use such an unusual color."

Almost never seen in print are the bright colors worn by FJ-3 and FJ-3M Fury fighters that served with VF-53 Pukin' Dogs aboard USS Kearsarge (CVA-33) on Western Pacific cruises in the mid-1950s. This squadron's nickname was usurped in later years by a separate unit that did not exist in the Fury era, namely VF-143. The M suffix was appended to FJ-3 models that were modified to carry the Sidewinder air-to-air missile. Like many World War II carriers, Kearsarge had a re-covered wooden deck and was relatively unforgiving to errors in the Fury. Ralph Burr

Engine Woes

FJ-3 Fury fighters had engine problems that were not fully diagnosed until long after the dash three was in operation on carrier decks. Though the J65 also delayed the USAF's Republic F-84F Thunderstreak, some of which were parked on the line at Republic's Long Island factory awaiting engines, the powerplant had even more problems with the Fury and

The US Navy was years behind the USAF in putting the swept-wing Sabre design into action, but these seagoing NAA FJ-3 Furys (136049, foreground) of VF-191 Satan's Kittens on USS Yorktown (CV-10) enjoyed success with the fleet. This view shows to good advantage the 6-3 wing found on late F-86F Sabres and FJ-3 Furys that lacked leading-edge slats and introduced a vertical fence on the wing. NAA turned out 6,233 Sabres and 1,148 Furys. In four other countries, the Sabre total was boosted by Canadair with 1,815, Commonwealth (Australia) with 112, Fiat (Italy) with 215, and Mitsubishi (Japan) with 300. Thus, this 1956 view of FJ-3s on a carrier deck illustrates a pair of fighters out of a grand total of 9,823.
Richard E. White

the Fleet. Lt. (jg) Ralph Burr, who flew FJ-3s and FJ-3Ms with VF-53 Pukin' Dogs aboard USS *Kearsarge* (CVA-33) recalls that "we had less than complete confidence in the J65," in part because of lubrication problems that could cause an engine seizure during a catapult launch. Burr also remembers that "the turbine shaft central support bearing was gravity-lubricated and didn't work very well." The Navy placed some limitations on tactics or maneuvers in the FJ-3 and -3M; problems abounded.

It's unclear whether the Fury had more flameouts than other jets of its era. During a strafing mission in Nevada, Burr suffered not an engine seizure but a flameout. It took three attempts to air-start the J65, and the third attempt, had it failed, would have been Burr's last.

To make matters worse, experience with the rigors of shipboard flying demonstrated that the turbine blades of early J65s suffered fatigue, came loose, and, like shrapnel, blew out the side of the fuselage. This problem may have contributed to the loss of Cdr. Don Potter, operations officer of VF-62 Boomerangs, whose FJ-3 crashed in the landing pattern at NAS Cecil Field, Florida, in 1955.

Wright and Navy engineers devised a fix by replacing the bubble root (round) base of the turbine blade with a pine tree shaped section, and installed it on FJ-3s being flown at the Naval Air Test Center, NAS Patuxent River, Maryland. Ens. Don Primeau of VF-62 was one of four pilots detached to Patuxent for the sole purpose of putting flying hours on the engines with the new blades. Primeau remembers that "we flew our tails off for six weeks at Pax," solely to demonstrate that the engine was now trouble free.

Primeau's VF-62 then made a successful July 1956–January 1957 Mediterranean cruise in FJ-3s aboard USS *Randolph* (CV-15), one of the first US Navy carriers with the angled deck. Primeau remained with the squadron for a second FJ-3 cruise February–November 1958 aboard USS *Essex* (CV-9). This coincided with the Lebanon crisis in May of that year and included some shore operations from RAF Akotiri, Cyprus. Also in attendance during the Lebanon crisis was VF-21 aboard USS *Forrestal* (CVA-59). During this deployment, FJ-3 pilots flew night missions for the first time, although the aircraft remained essentially a day fighter.

An offshoot of this Fury variant was the FJ-3D, equipped as a drone director/chase aircraft for the Regulus missile and operated by the US Navy's Guided Missile Group Two, known in parlance as the Gum Group. The FJ-3D was periodically embarked with carrier air groups, including the first Randolph cruise, and performed its specialized mission effectively.

There was also a Guided Missile Group One, which flew FJ-3D Furys at Point Mugu, California. Legend holds that an AF F-86 Sabre pilot, in a late-night session at the O Club bar, conned this Gum Group into allowing him to try out an FJ-3D—and wrecked it.

During the Lebanon crisis in 1958, VF-62 Boomerangs operated from USS Essex (CV-9) and briefly from land at RAF Akotiri, Cyprus. In July 1958, FJ-3M Fury (BuNo. 139231), wearing new yellow-and-black markings introduced for this cruise, prowls a few miles from Beirut, ready for trouble. The nose seeker head of an AAM-N-2 Sidewinder missile is visible in this view, as is the Sidewinder pylon and the Fury's rather long air refueling probe. Note also the wing boundary layer fence that came with the wet 6-3 wing identical to that found on late USAF F-86F Sabres. Don G. Primeau

FJ-4 Fury

With the rapid production buildup of FJs, F-86s, and AJ-2 Savages (the Navy's first carrier-based nuclear bomber), the Columbus plant was approaching 7 million pounds of annual airframe output (it later exceeded 10 million). Although originally intended solely as a production facility, NAA recognized the need to maintain a tight feedback loop between fleet operations and engineering as well as with BuAer and its evolving new requirements. The manufacturer established a Confidential (Advanced) Design Group at Columbus headed by Frank Compton. Compton quickly became a key player in the Columbus engineering team, now headed by chief engineer George Gherkens.

It was the right time for NAA to have the right people on the job—a time of the severe fighter problem in the fleet. With the F3H-1N Demon abruptly out of the Navy's plans, a short delivery schedule was drawn up for a new Fury version that could meet or exceed the performance once expected of the Demon. The Navy's endurance requirement demanded doubling the internal fuel load of the FJ-3 while the Navy's high-speed (Mach 0.95) and combat-altitude (49,000ft/ 14,935m) requirements had never before been met without an afterburning engine. Gherkens' team produced the final version of the Fury and, arguably, the best performer in the entire F-86 Sabre/FJ Fury series—better even than the very powerful F-86H.

This was the FJ-4 Fury. In fact, design work on the FJ-4 had really begun almost as soon as the FJ-3 model was underway. The concept was to develop a 6 percent thickness ratio, cambered, integral fueled, and more highly tapered, 35deg swept wing of increased area to be used with the existing FJ-3 fuselage and other FJ-3 systems including the J65.

NAA engineers had to perform an intricate juggling act between wing area and planform, spar location and wing box size, and innovative new landing gear designs that, upon retraction, would leave enough space for an acceptable wing box. The resulting FJ-4 Fury was the most different looking aircraft in the series.

The first FJ-4 Fury, or company model NA-208 (BuNo. 139279) made its 59min maiden flight at Columbus on 28 October 1954 piloted by Richard

Its nickname painted over natural metal, the first FJ-4 Fury (BuNo. 139279) makes its 59min maiden flight at Columbus on 28 October 1954 piloted by Richard Wenzell. The FJ-4 version, and the very similar FJ-4B, introduced a new wing design to the Fury series. The two prototype FJ-4s had the same Wright J65-W-4 Sapphire turbojet engine as the FJ-3, while production FJ-4s, which began appearing in February 1955, had the 7,700lb (3,492kg) thrust J65-W-16A. To save weight, forward armor was removed in the FJ-4 and ammunition reduced from 600 to 576 rounds.
NAA via Hal Andrews

Wenzell and powered by a 7,800lb (3,538kg) thrust "dry" Wright J65-W-4. The aircraft is referred to in some documents as the YFJ-4, although the Navy normally used the Y or service-test prefix only during BIS trials. The two prototype FJ-4s had the same J65-W-4 engine as the FJ-3, while production airplanes, the company model NA-209, which began appearing in February 1955, had the 7,700lb (3,492kg) thrust J65-W-16A. To save weight, forward armor was removed in the FJ-4 and ammunition reduced from 600 to 576 rounds.

Remarkably, Wenzell's first flight came only 12 months after the go-ahead, with the first production airplane following just 5 1/2 months later. Navy BIS trials were completed just 30 months from contract start with a full squadron delivered for carrier operations. At a reunion of Patuxent River test pilots in the 1970s, Marine Corps Maj. Gen. Marion Carl, asked what was the greatest jet fight-

er he ever flew, responded, "Oh, the FJ-4, of course."

With its new "wet" wing, the FJ-4 had a 50 percent increase in internal fuel capacity. It was a tribute to Compton's engineering team that this was accomplished with virtually no sacrifice in performance.

The Marine Corps' VMF-451 Warlords became the first squadron to operate the FJ-4 in 1956. By March 1957, 152 aircraft in the FJ-4 series were delivered.

FJ-4B Fury

The FJ-4B Fury was an FJ-4 modified to carry an atomic bomb (not yet, in the 1950s, called a nuclear weapon) on an off-center pylon on its inboard left wing. The first FJ-4B (BuNo. 139531) made its first flight on 3 December 1956 piloted by Richard Wenzell. The first batch of these aircraft retained the company model NA-209 nomenclature while later aircraft were built to contracts NA-229 and NA-244. The FJ-4B was strengthened to use six underwing ordnance stations and, like the F-86H Sabre, had the Low Altitude Bombing System (LABS) to deliver an atomic weapon. The FJ-4B also had an additional pair of speed brakes beneath the tail, used to reduce speed during low-level attack.

The FJ-4B Fleet Indoctrination Program (FIP) began at Moffett Field, California, in 1957 with emphasis on loft-bombing with nuclear weapons. Eventually, 222 FJ-4Bs were built.

The doomsday mission of the FJ-4B highlighted the Navy's stubborn determination to keep up a nuclear mission so its aircraft-carrier fleet could compete with Strategic Air Command's bombers for defense dollars. So eagerly did the Navy promote the atomic mission that officers in the Pentagon drew up a map showing how carrier-based warplanes like the Fury could reach any target in the Soviet

This FJ-4B Fury (BuNo. 143494) wearing the XF tail code of squadron VX-4 Evaluators at Point Mugu, California, is carrying a most impressive load of six ASM-N-7 Bullpup air-to-surface missiles, though it's doubtful the Fury would have carried them very far without using its equally visible refueling probe. The FJ-4B was an FJ-4 modified to carry an atomic bomb on an off-center pylon (readily apparent here) on its inboard left wing. FJ-4B squadrons also rehearsed warfare with a wide variety of conventional ordnance loads. NAA via Larry Davis

Union. Critics saw that the map-placed carriers in the Black Sea, even the Caspian Sea, where the Fury would, indeed, be close enough to strike the Soviet heartland—but positioning a carrier in those waters would have been no less difficult than borrowing the Soviets' own airfields!

Nevertheless, some carrier air groups, which had Demons and Crusaders as their fighter force, had two squadrons of FJ-4Bs (12 aircraft each) with no other function than to "loft" an atomic bomb, a single-purpose role they shared in those days with the A4D-1 and -2 Skyhawk, which later took on other duties. The FJ-4B Fury "didn't have conventional weapons capability worth diddly squat," remembers RAdm. Rowland G. (Doc) Freeman III who, as a commander in 1960, flew the FJ-4B.

Freeman, a veteran of night-fighter action in World War II and Korea and one of the Navy's early experts on air-to-air missiles, was tapped in 1960 to command VA-144 Road Runners, one of two FJ-4B Fury squadrons aboard USS *Oriskany* (CVA-34). The other squadron on the ship was VA-146 Blue Diamonds, headed up by Roy Falk.

When first told he would fly an FJ-4B Fury, Doc Freeman had to ask, "What is it?" He was then told that his squadron was going to convert to A4D-2 Skyhawks anyway, and subsequently told that the FJ-4Bs would be retained. On 9 September 1960, Freeman organized a group of pilots who were assigned to VA-126 at NAS Miramar, California, to receive indoctrination in the FJ-4B. He made his first flight in an FJ-4B (BuNo. 143625) at Miramar on 14 November 1960.

Freeman has always liked the FJ-4B, which he calls an excellent carrier aircraft with good stability in the glide slope and a good craft to handle in the pattern around the carrier. In VA-144, "I inherited some well-maintained airplanes just back from a Westpac cruise," he remembers, referring to the Western Pacific. "I was able to develop tactics for night bombing in the airplane and it responded well to our needs."

Pilots often exaggerate, and Doc Freeman also remembered that the FJ-4B wasn't perfect. "It was a 'wet wing' airplane and it leaked like a sieve. It dripped everywhere. The original North American ejection seat was replaced by a Martin-Baker N5 seat and we had a lot of confidence in it, but it was uncomfortable and a pilot could easily suffer spinal compression.

"The FJ-4B was difficult to maintain. It was tired. The wet wing was a problem. We also had a problem with false fire warnings. We'd do a 4- to 6-G pullout after a dive and the engine fire warning light would come on. We also had drop-out [ram air turbine] generators that didn't work properly and at one point I simply disconnected them. The airplane could be unforgiving and if you got slow, it could roll on you."

The idea behind LABS was that a warplane would approach its target at treetop level, pop up abruptly, and "sling" its nuclear weapon at the target using the momentum of its own climb to carry the bomb some distance from the bomber. The aircraft would then complete its climb to a higher, safer altitude and get out quickly before the atomic blast. FJ-4B pilots refined this tactic so that they made a run-in at an altitude of 50 ft (15m), tossed the bomb, rolled the FJ-4B into inverted flight in order to come down out of the pop-up, and then continued in the same direction to exit the target area. Like many tactics developed during the atom-crazy 1950s, it was never tried in practice.

Doc Freeman was told to develop a conventional weapons capability. He found that the cannons on the FJ-4B were noticeably inaccurate and wouldn't stay boresighted. This was partly due to lack of use, since the guns were normally fired only during competitions. "When we practiced nuclear delivery, the cannons got jolted around and came loose in their mountings." Worse, the Navy's new family of conventional bombs, the Mark 81, Mark 82, and so on, had not been designed by anybody who'd ever looked at an FJ-4B. (In fact, design of the bombs slightly predates design of the FJ-4B). "The bomb fins dragged the ground," says Freeman. He redesigned a bomb rack for conventional ordnance, and it became standard on the FJ-4B only after Freeman got a nasty letter from the Navy's BuAer for his initiative in cheaply, effectively carrying out the sort of developmental work for which the US taxpayer had funded an empire of test plants and facilities.

It is widely understood that no version of the FJ Fury ever went into combat. But on the final cruise of the FJ-4B aboard USS *Lexington* (CV-16), covering the period 9 November 1961 through 15 May 1962, the Blue Ghost's two FJ-4B squadrons, VA-144 Road Runners and VA-146 Blue Diamonds are reported by one participant to have carried ordnance on sorties over Laos' Plain of Jars.

According to CPO John Gourley, a veteran of that *Lexington* cruise, a VA-146 Fury on a bombing mission—the date has been narrowed down to between 27 February and 20 March 1962—was hit by antiaircraft fire. The aircraft sustained damage over Laos, limped back to the carrier, and struck the round-down on impact. The damaged Fury's fuselage slid forward and caught fire. The pilot survived but the aircraft was struck. Gourley's reminiscences are not shared by another veteran of the same cruise, who remembers only "being on alert" for possible missions to Laos and no actual combat. ("They passed out kneeboard

Next page
The FJ-4 Fury was tested with a rocket booster motor in its tail in at least two different configurations. The first, seen here and unofficially known as the FJ-4(R), was BuNo. 139284. It was flown with a supplementary belly fuel tank. The rocket-boosted Furys demonstrated remarkable speed, climb, and altitude performance but no operational version was ever ordered or adopted. This portrait was taken early in the rocket test program, on 25 February 1956. NAA via Larry Davis

The second version of the rocket-boosted Fury, although still the same aircraft (BuNo. 139284) is this FJ-4F, which has the Rocketdyne rocket motor in the tail above the jet engine efflux outlet, and has now acquired a specially instrumented nose cone and pitot tube. These rocket-boosted Furys flew to phenomenal altitudes, possibly as high as 68,000ft (20,726m) and may have contributed to research for NAA's never-built XF-108 Rapier.
NAA via Larry Davis

4
139284
NAVY
DANGER
JET INTAKE

4
NAVY

Some of the most impressive markings on Fury fighters were worn by those aircraft assigned as drone controllers for missiles of the era, including the US Navy's Regulus, which was one of the first true cruise missiles. FJ-3D, FJ-3D2, and FJ-4 aircraft (shown) were used in this mission, though the last-named apparently was never designated FJ-4D as it should have been. This FJ-4 Fury with blue fuselage, black antiglare shield, and yellow wings and tail (BuNo. 139290) belongs to squadron VU-7 and is seen at Brown Field, California, on 30 April 1960. Clay Jansson

cards [with target information], briefed us as to who would drop bombs where, broke out the ordnance. But we never actually took off.") It's usually reported that the first US Navy warplanes lost in Southeast Asia were an A-1H Skyraider and an A-4C Skyhawk downed over North Vietnam on 5 August 1964. Though evidence is lacking, Gourley would make the first Vietnam-era casualty a Fury.

Rocket Fury

An experimental version of the FJ-4 Fury, with a 5,000lb (2,268kg) thrust NAA Rocketdyne AR-1 rocket in its tail set unofficial speed and altitude records of Mach 1.41 and 71,000ft (21,640m). Though the concept began earlier, the rocket-boosted Fury was pursued and refined, in part, because US officials overreacted to the 1956 Tushino air show where it became known that the Soviets possessed high-altitude Tupolev Tu-16 and Myasishchev Mya-4 jet bombers. The bombers were overrated by US intelligence, but it was true that no contemporary interceptors could effectively reach them.

Two aircraft (BuNos. 139282 and 139284) were modified with rocket power. The project began on 12 August 1955 and was referred to by company contract designations NA-234 and NA-248. At one point, one of the rocket-boosted Furys was referred to, perhaps unofficially, as the FJ-4(R). It preceded by at least three years a USAF rocket-boosted F-86F(R) Sabre of 1960. During prolonged tests at Patuxent and elsewhere, the two rocket-boosted Furys were designated FJ-4F. These were flown with and without a specially instrumented nose cone and a supplementary belly fuel tank. The FJ-4Fs demonstrated remarkable speed, climb, and altitude performance, but no operational version was ever ordered or adopted.

At the manufacturer's Columbus facility, NAA engineers proposed a final version of the Fury that would have been designated FJ-5. This aircraft took shape on drawing boards to compete with the Grumman F9F-9 Tiger (later redesignated F11F-1). Details have never been made public, but the aircraft is described as having a pointed nose and air intake above and behind the pilot, in the manner of NAA's F-107.

On 1 October 1962, the US Department of Defense (DOD) adopted a uniform system for the designations of aircraft of the US Army, USAF, Coast Guard, Navy, and Marine Corps. Under this system, variants of the Fury were redesignated as follows: F-1C (FJ-3), DF-1C (FJ-3D), MF-1C (FJ-3M), DF-1D (FJ-3D2), F-1E (FJ-4), and AF-1E (FJ-4B). F-1A and F-1B designations were not assigned. Most Fury variants were, by then, retired from service, although AF-1E Furys labored on in the Naval Air Reserve to the mid-1960s. As a footnote, if DOD's system were followed properly today, the McDonnell F/A-18 Hornet would be correctly designated AF-18.

The Fury's heyday falls almost precisely between the end of bloodshed in Korea and the beginning of more in Vietnam. Between November 1952 and May 1958, NAA's Columbus plant turned out 1,112 Furys for the US Navy and Marine Corps. At least a couple of thousand pilots flew them, thousands more helped get them into the air, and many Navy and Marine veterans remember the type with great fondness.

A civilian FJ-4B (BuNo. 143565, originally N400FS later N9255) was the last flying example of the Fury, operated by Flight Systems International in Mojave, California, on various military contract duties. Numerous Furys of various marks are on display in American museums.

As it turned out, the final version to serve with the US Navy was not an FJ Fury at all but an F-86 Sabre. Numerous F-86F and F-86H Sabres were operated by the Navy in the 1970s and 1980s as drones to serve, in effect, as flying targets. This aircraft, belonging to the Pacific Missile Test Center (PMTC) at Point Mugu, California, is an F-86F-40 Sabre (55-5057) that had formerly served with the Japan Air Self-Defense Force and is seen on 26 September 1987. Douglas E. Slowiak

Considered by many to be the most potent version of the terrible swift sword, this Commonwealth CA-27 Sabre Mark 32 (A94-983) is still flying as part of the Royal Australian Air Force's historical flight. A94-683 was delivered to the RAAF in November 1957, and transferred to the Malaysian Air Force in December 1971. Returned to the RAAF in 1978 and given civil registry VH-PCM, this down under Sabre is fully airworthy and is expected to be available for flying demonstrations well into the next century. Here, the Sabre is flying near RAAF Richmond. Denis Hersey

CHAPTER FOUR

Foreign Sabres

Even before fighting in Korea began, Canada was well advanced towards becoming the first non-US operator (and builder) of the Sabre. In the years that followed the war, several dozen countries operated Sabres.

Reports of small numbers of Sabres in some countries—for example, Ethiopia, Iran, and Iraq—cannot be confirmed by any reliable source. At least two countries, Israel and Uruguay, came so close to becoming F-86 users that intended aircraft had national markings painted on them. Israel's 1955 purchase of 24 spanking-new Canadair aircraft was halted, permanently, by the 1956 Suez conflict.

No full exposition of the countries that operated Sabres has previously been published. The following account has a few obvious gaps but is intended as a *tour d'horizon* of the Sabre overseas. Some of the details that follow, including s/n linkups, are published here for the first time.

Argentina

The Argentine Air Force, or Fuerza Aerea Argentina (FAA), operated 28 F-86F Sabres, the first of which was received on 26 September 1960. FAA s/ns C-101/C-128 were assigned. The corresponding USAF s/ns are not known.

The Sabres saw action during an April 1962 revolution inside Argentina when the Navy and some Army units attempted a coup against the established government. Four F-86F Sabres, together with some Gloster Meteor F.Mk.4s and Morane-Saulnier M.S.760s attacked the Navy base at Punta Indio and were credited with destroying a Navy C-54 on the ground. This attack squelched the uprising.

Argentina initially offered to sell F-86Fs to Venezuela in 1976, but the sale was embargoed by the United States. Then the aircraft were offered for sale to Uruguay, but the deal fell through even though the aircraft had been camouflaged for delivery and Uruguayan markings were about to be painted on.

These unsold Argentine Sabres were returned to operational service in the late 1970s and initially assigned to Escuadron CB-1 (from Grupo I de Caza-Bombardero) at Mendoza and later to Grupo 4 de Caza. In April 1982, trials were conducted at Mendoza to see if the Sabres could be safely operated from Port Stanley in the Falklands but this idea was abandoned as impractical. Sabres did not participate in the 1982 Falklands conflict although some F-86Fs were forward-deployed to Comodor Rivadavia (Argentina) in June 1982.

Sixteen aircraft were lost in operational mishaps in Argentine service. One known Argentine loss is C-102, which crashed on 25 August 1983.

Australia

The Commonwealth Aircraft Company (CAC) of Australia built the CA-27 Sabre. The mature Mark 32 version built down under was probably the most capable version of the F-86, with its 7,500lb (3,402kg) thrust Rolls-Royce RA.7 Avon Mark 26 turbojet, twin 30mm Aden cannons with 162 rounds each, and infrared GAR-8A (AIM-9B) Sidewinder heat-seeking missiles.

When the Royal Australian Air Force (RAAF) No. 77 Squadron began flying in combat in Korea in 1951 with Gloster Meteor 8s, Australia was caught up in the process of selecting a next-generation fighter aircraft. At least three aircraft were seriously con-

After giving thought to inducting the Grumman F9F Panther into its ranks, Australia settled on the F-86 design but took advantage of its own technology to create its CA-26 prototype, followed by the Avon-powered, cannon-armed CA-27 Sabre Mark 30, 31, and 32. A94-983 is painted in the colors of No. 75 Squadron's Black Diamonds aerobatic team. Superbly restored, A94-383 has become a familiar sight at air shows all over Australia. Denis Hersey

sidered by the RAAF, the Grumman F9F Panther, the Hawker P.1081, and the CAC-designed CA-23 tandem, two-seat, delta-wing fighter. The CA-23 was a remarkably advanced fighter that Australia abandoned in February 1950, mostly because of its cost.

Australia asked to purchase American-built F-86F Sabres to re-equip No. 77 Squadron and was told that none were available. The Meteor was outclassed by the MiG-15, and it was evident that a replacement was needed.

CAC director Lawrence Wackett proposed an Avon-powered Sabre, to be built under license in Australia. CAC eventually manufactured the Sabres and all but the first 22 of the engines.

The CA-26, as the prototype was designated, required considerable remodeling to accommodate the Rolls-Royce Avon engine and to ensure adequate airflow to it. The fuselage was deepened by 3.73in (9.47cm) at the intake, fairing into the original profile aft of the canopy. Because the new engine had to be moved aft (to maintain the center of gravity), the fuselage break point for engine removal was moved further aft, also. Thus, the tail section was shorter.

In all, 268 engineering changes were made from the F-86F model that served as a starting point. An Avpin isopropyl-nitrate starter was fitted, making it possible to make three engine starts independent of external power.

The RAAF ordered a prototype and 70 production aircraft in February 1951. The prototype CA-26 Sabre (A94-101) made its long-delayed 30min first flight on 3 August 1953. Although constructed at CAC's Fisherman's Bend facility, this first Australian Sabre flew from Avalon, with RAAF pilot Flt. Lt. W. Scott at the controls.

The first production Sabres were designated CA-27 Mark 30. The first of these (A94-901) flew on 13 July 1954 and was delivered to the RAAF on 18 August 1954. Twenty-two Sabre Mark 30s were built, followed by 20 Sabre Mark 31s, which differed mainly in the addition of a non-slatted 6-3 wing later retrofitted on many of the earlier aircraft. In addition, two Sabre Mark 31s (A94-938, A94-942) were fitted with extra internal wing fuel tanks, increasing capacity from 352 Imp gallons to 422. This became standard on future CAC Sabres.

The final production version was the Sabre Mark 32, of which 69 were built. The first 38 completed the initial order made in 1951. Further orders, placed in 1955 and 1957 for 20 and 21 aircraft respectively, completed Australia's production run. The Sabre Mark 32 had an uprated Avon engine and a dual-store wing. The final aircraft was delivered on 19 December 1961.

Numerous modifications were carried out on RAAF Sabres, the most important of which was the ability to carry the Sidewinder missile. The first aircraft (A94-946) was modified in 1959 for tests at the aircraft research and development unit. Two aircraft also tested the British Firestreak missile in 1956–1957, the first making its initial flight on 8 February 1956. The installation of this heavy and powerful missile involved a large amount of modification. It apparently proved impractical and the tests were curtailed.

The CAC Sabre served with five fighter squadrons and two operational training/conversion units of the RAAF. Squadron details:

No. 3 Squadron equipped with Sabres in March 1956 at Williamtown. The squadron moved to Malaya in November 1958 to join No. 78 Wing. It returned to Williamtown in July 1967 and continued to fly Sabres until converting to the Mirage III in February 1969.

No. 75 Squadron equipped with Sabres in April 1955 at Williamtown in April 1955. The squadron flew Sabres until converting to the Mirage III in August 1965.

No. 76 Squadron was reformed at Williamtown in 1960 with the Sabre under No. 81 Wing, and converted to the Mirage III in September 1966.

No. 77 Squadron, the Meteor veteran of the Korean War, equipped with the Sabre in November 1956 at Williamtown. The squadron went to Malaya in February 1959 to join No. 78 Wing at Butterworth. No. 77 Squadron returned to Williamtown in July 1969 and converted to the Mirage III soon after.

No. 79 Squadron reformed in May 1962 with Sabres at Singapore and moved soon after to Ubon, Thailand. Here, RAAF Sabres played a key role in the defense of Thailand in the early days of the Vietnam conflict, although they never flew in combat in Vietnam itself. The squadron transferred to Butterworth, Malaysia, in July 1968 and disbanded, transferring its aircraft to No. 77 Squadron.

No. 2 Operational Training Unit (OTU): The Sabre Trials Flight of this OTU received the Sabre in November 1954 at Williamtown. It was redesignated an Operational Conversion Unit (OCU) in 1958, and converted to the Mirage III in April 1970, transferring its aircraft to No. 5 OCU.

No. 5 OCU at Williamtown received the former No. 2 OCU Sabres in April 1970, and operated them until disbanding in July 1971.

Not surprisingly, improved versions of the already potent CAC Sabres were proposed, although never built. An intriguing 1955 study called for a 6,000lb (2,722kg) thrust Napier Double Scorpion rocket booster in a pod under the rear fuselage. Not dissimilar to the American F-86F(R) Sabre and FJ-4F Fury fighters that actually flew, this rocket-boosted Sabre would have had the fastest rate of climb of any aircraft of its era.

A separate project to test air-to-air capability led to an Australian Sabre being fitted with refueling probes on the front of its two 167 Imp gallon wing drop tanks.

After serving nobly and bulwarking Allied security interests in Southeast Asia—including their appearance in Thailand in support of the Vietnam War—the last RAAF Sabres were retired on 31 July 1971.

Throughout their career, RAAF Sabres were painted silver overall, with national markings in all of the usual places. Individual squadron markings were both colorful and individualistic. Thirty aircraft were lost in mishaps in RAAF service and 25 or so remain in Australia, including the prototype located at the Point Cook RAAF Museum. At least three have found their way to the United States for restoration to flying condition.

Sixteen CA-27 Sabres were turned over to Malaysia in October 1969. Eighteen were transferred to Indonesia in February 1973. Indonesia also acquired five more aircraft from Malaysia in July 1976.

Australian Sabre production:

CA-26 F-86 Sabre A94-101 (1)

CA-27 Sabre Mark 30/31 A94-901/A94-942 (42)

CA-27 Sabre Mark 32 A94-943/A94-990 (48)

A94-351/A94-371 (21)

Bangladesh

After the December 1971 conflict that transformed East Pakistan into an independent Bangladesh, the Bangladesh air arm found itself in possession of five Pakistani Air Force Canadair Sabre 6s (themselves former German aircraft). The Sabres and a few MiG-21MFs were formed into a mixed squadron at Tezgaon airfield near Dhaka, the capital. But spares shortages made it necessary to ground the Sabres, along with Bangladesh's sole T-33 trainer, in late 1973.

The five Sabre Mark 6s received by Bangladesh were Canadair constructor's numbers (c/ns) 1608, 1609, 1617, 1669, and 1723.

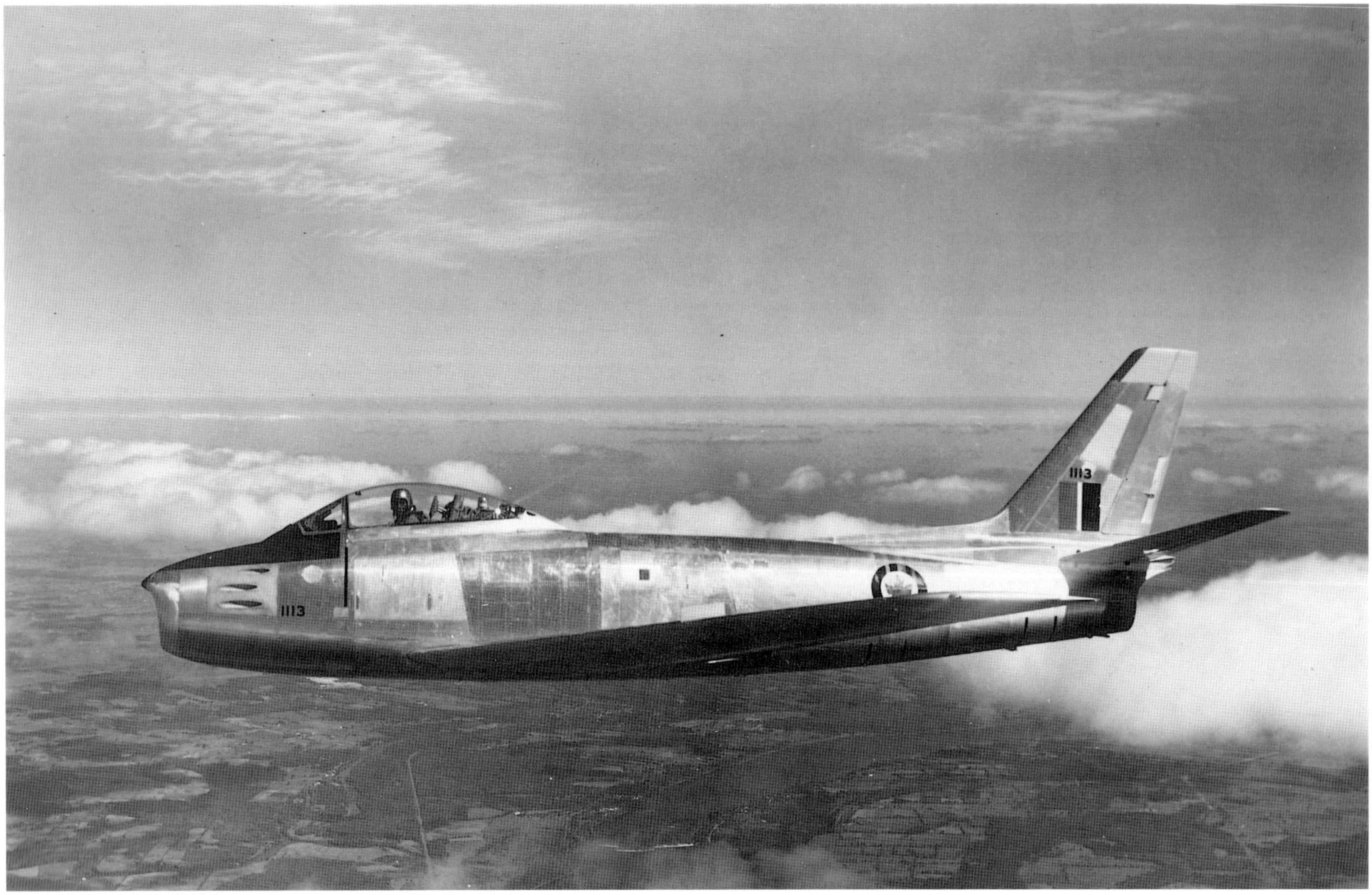

A vintage portrait from Canadair, added to the author's files in 1954. In natural metal, wearing its c/n 1113 rather than its RCAF s/n (23323), this Canadair CL-13A Sabre Mark 5, powered by the indigenous 6,355lb (2,883kg) thrust Orenda 10 engine is making its 26 August 1954 first flight. This version had the 6-3 wing and wing fences found on American aircraft beginning with the F-86F version. Canadair

Belgium

The Belgian Air Force, La Force Aerienne Belge, never had an operational squadron of Sabres. However, USAF delivery records show that F-86F Sabres were allocated to Belgium, namely 51-13202, 52-5305, -5362, -5367, and -5402. Possibly, these aircraft were evaluated by Belgian pilots, though they never entered service.

Bolivia

Bolivia's air arm, the Fuerza Aerea Boliviana , acquired about ten F-86F Sabres from the Venezuelan Air Force beginning in October 1973. The Sabres were assigned to Brigada Aerea 21, Grupo Aerea de Caza 32. Some sources give the total as nine, others as 11, although ten s/ns, 650/659, were assigned. Two of the Sabres were apparently written off when a civil Cessna crashed into their hangar at Santa Cruzon 11 July 1984. The remainder are not known to have been retired, so Bolivia may qualify as one of the very last F-86 active-duty operators.

Burma

Burma (which has since been renamed Myanmar) operated the Burmese Air Force, or Tamdaw Lay, which had 12 Canadair Sabre Mark 4s, obtained third-hand from Pakistan, beginning in the mid-1970s. Few details are available. Lack of spares and funds precluded a long service life and by the 1980s the Sabres were no longer flying.

Canada

The same Cold War tensions that produced an interceptor Sabre led to the 4 April 1949 creation of the North Atlantic Treaty Organization (NATO).

Sabres galore. Wearing the forest camouflage scheme that became standard for the RCAF, these Canadair CL-13B Sabre Mark 6s belong to the RCAF's No. 421 Squadron and are lined up at Prestwick in 1963. Canada's strong commitment to the defense of NATO prevented Ottawa from sending a Sabre squadron to fight in the Korean War, and is often overlooked as essential to the Cold War effort. Aircraft in foreground (23386) displays leading-edge slats to good advantage, although these aircraft eventually employed the 6-3 hard wing that NAA introduced with the F-86F series. via Jerry Geer

Canada was to make its contribution to guarding Western Europe against the Soviet menace by supplying squadrons of fighters for air defense. At Canadair Ltd. in Montreal, company leaders including program director Bob Raven knew almost immediately that the Sabre was the airplane they wanted. It took them a little longer to decide against the F-86D, mostly because of the latter's developmental hiccoughs, and to settle on an F-86E version.

Canadian pilots were eager to fight in the Korean War, and disappointed that their country was unable to put an RCAF fighter wing into the Korean peninsula, largely because the United States and other allies were relying on Canada to bulwark NATO defenses in Europe. Instead, in addition to building the F-86E-6s, Canada supplied some 22 pilots who served on temporary exchange postings with US units in Korea, logging 50 missions or six months, whichever came first.

The north of the border equivalent of the F-86E was produced under license by Canadair for use by both countries. Because Sabres were desperately needed in the second year of the Korean War, Canadair produced 60 F-86E-6s (52-2833/2892) for the USAF, most or all of which ended up in combat in Korea. Canadair also delivered 60 more F-86Es for Mutual Defense Assistance Pact (MDAP) delivery to allied countries and 230 similar CL-13 Sabre Mark 2s for the RCAF. The designation CL-13 Sabre Mark 3 went to a Canadair ship built to test the indigenous Orenda turbojet engine.

Canada's hands on experience with the Sabre begins with Canadair test pilot A. J. (Al) Lilly's first flight in a standard F-86A-5 (49-1170) at

The RCAF camouflaged its Sabres in Europe, as did the RAF and Luftwaffe. Here, a CL-13B Sabre Mark 6 (23749), coded as BH-749 with the RCAF's No. 421 Squadron, prowls the skies of Europe looking for trouble. In the 1960s, the old-style Canadian flag (partially visible on fin) was still in use and Canadian pilots used British-style ranks. The latter was changed in 1968 when a Canadian squadron leader became a major, and other ranks were switched, correspondingly, to the American system. via Jerry Geer

Wright-Patterson AFB, Ohio, on 3 August 1950. The first Sabre manufactured by Canadair was also the Montreal builder's only F-86A, or CL-13 Sabre Mark 1 (assigned RCAF s/n 19101). This ship was hand-assembled at Cartierville from F-86A-5 parts received from the United States. Lilly returned to Canada to make its first flight not at the company's Cartierville airfield, which was not yet ready for jet operations, but at nearby Dorval. Indistinguishable from the F-86A-5, 19101 was powered by a 5,200lb (2,360kg) thrust General Electric J47-GE-13 turbojet and armed with six .50cal machine guns. Lilly got airborne for this Canadian first flight on 9 August 1950.

Canadair moved onward to build 350 CL-13 Sabre Mark 2 fighters (19102/19199, 19201/19452), a figure that includes the 60 USAF F-86E-6s as well as 252 aircraft turned over to NATO countries. Wedged in among this production was the sole Sabre Mark 3 (19200).

In anticipation of Orenda production, a NAA-built F-86A Sabre (49-1069), known as the company model NA-167, was flown with the Canadian-designed Orenda engine on 5 October

1950. This aircraft was designated F-86J. This was not the same ship as the sole CL-13 Sabre Mark 3 (19200) test bed for the Orenda 3, which was first flown with a J47 on 14 June 1952 and subsequently converted to the Orenda 3 and flown with the latter engine on 25 September 1952.

This was followed by 438 CL-13 Sabre Mark 4 fighters (19453/19890), also referred to as F-86Es, retaining J47-GE-13 engines. Four hundred twenty-eight of these went to modernize the fighter squadrons of Britain's RAF. Identified for accounting purposes at the end of their RAF career as F-86E(M) models, these were later retrofitted with the 6-3 wing hard leading edges and passed on to Greece, Turkey, and Yugoslavia.

Canadian production now shifted to the CL-13A Sabre Mark 5 powered by the 6,355lb (2,883kg) thrust Orenda 10 engine. The first of these made its maiden flight on 30 July 1953. Of 370 built (23001/23370), 75 went to the newly formed West German Luftwaffe. The Sabre Mark 5 introduced a feature already in production by NAA that was the most fundamental change in the Sabre's history and, when applied to American aircraft, turned the tide in Korea. This was the 6-3 wing, so named because its leading edge was extended 6in (15.24cm) at the root and 3in (7.62cm) at the wing tip, with the slat removed. This change resulted in some degradation of low-speed handling but significantly improved performance in combat.

The CL-13B Sabre Mark 6 was the final Canadian production version, 292 of which (23371/23662) were built for the RCAF, six (2021/2026) for Colombia, and 34 (350/383) for South Africa. Subsequently, additional Mark 6 aircraft included 90 more (23663/23752) for the RCAF and 225 for the Luftwaffe.

There were numerous other Canadair Sabre designs that were never built or flown. The unbuilt Canadians included the CL-13C with afterburner, CL-13D boosted by Armstrong Siddeley Snarler rocket engine, CL-13G two-seat tandem version, CL-13H with all-weather radar and CL-13J, also with afterburner.

Canadair gave the designation CL-13E to the 21st Sabre Mark 5 (23021) when its fuselage was made "wasp-waisted" to test the area-rule configuration for improved performance in transonic speed ranges. There was no perceptible improvement in performance and this one of a kind Sabre eventually joined the civil register in the United States (as N1049D) where it crashed on 1 February 1980. It is not clear whether the designation CL-13F was used.

The RCAF initially left their aircraft in natural metal with red wing tips and stabilizers. In 1955, aircraft of No. 1 Air Division (Europe) were camouflaged with gloss dark green and dark sea gray upper surfaces and PRU blue undersurfaces. A matte-black anti-glare panel was forward of

This F-86D-30-NA Sabre (51-6123) coded F-123 with No. 726 Squadron, Royal Danish Air Force, is seen at Solingen AB, Germany, in April 1961. With its armament of 24 2.75in (6.98cm) FFARs, the radar-equipped F-86D was not at first approved for export, even to close NATO allies. As a result, most friendly air arms equipping for the interceptor mission used the F-86K version instead. Merle Olmsted

the windscreen on all aircraft. Squadron markings were applied and varied considerably over the years. Also the RAF-style fin flash was replaced by the Red Ensign in 1957, which was replaced by the current Maple Leaf Flag.

Preserved Sabres in Canada include CL-13A Sabre Mark 5 (23257) at Trention and CL-13B Sabre Mark 6s (23455, 23651) at Ottawa.

Chile

Chile was scheduled to receive 25 F-86F Sabres in 1966, but the aircraft were never delivered and Chile acquired 21 Hawker Hunters instead.

China (People's Republic of China)

A Chinese Nationalist F-86F Sabre (F86272) is preserved at a museum in Beijing.

China (Taiwan)

Taiwan, calling itself the Republic of China, operates the Chinese Nationalist Air Force (CNAF) which operated large numbers of F-86F Sabres.

The first four CNAF Sabres arrived on Taiwan (better known, then, as Formosa) on 29 November 1954. Reports differ as to whether the CNAF received a small number of F-86A models. By 1955, the CNAF had a full wing of F-86F Sabres in service. Eventually, three fighter wings operated the Sabre.

In the late 1950s, tensions with the mainland reached a peak, and sporadic fighting took place over the islands of Quemoy and Matsu. At least a half dozen air battles took place in the Taiwan Straits, between F-86F Sabres and the mainland's MiG-15s, MiG-17s, and MiG-19s. On 24 September 1958, amid a huge and furious air battle, Taiwan's F-86F Sabre pilots introduced the GAR-8 Sidewinder infrared homing missile. In this single battle, they shot down ten MiGs and claimed two further probable kills without loss. In all, between 14 August and 24 September 1958, the CNAF claimed 29 kills and eight probables, while losing only one F-84G Thunderjet and no Sabres.

One of Taiwan's Sabres was 51-2910, previously a Korean War veteran. It was the personal mount of ace Capt. Joseph McConnell and nicknamed *Beautious Butch II*. McConnell scored five of his 16 MiG kills in this aircraft, which was written off in CNAF service. Details on CNAF squadrons have not been published, but a nearly complete list of Taiwan's Sabres has belatedly come to light. CNAF aircraft included:

F-86F-1 51-2852, -2856, -2857, -2860, -2862, -2869, -2870/2874, -2877/2879, -2881, -2883, -2886/2887, -2891/2898, -2904/2905, -2910, -2912, -2914, -2918/2919, -2924.

F-86F-5 51-2927, -2930, -2932, -2934, -2937, -2940/2943

F-86F-10 51-12936/12937, -12939/12941, -12943/12946, -12949, -12951/12959, -12964/12965, -12967/12968.

F-86F-15 51-12974/12976

F-86F-20 51-13092/13093, -13096, -13110

F-86F-25 51-13170, -13172, -13174, -13176, -13190, -13196, -13198, -13205/13206, -13209, -13213, -13216, -13230, -13251, -13253, -13256, -13261, -13263/13264, -13271, -13273, -13275, -13282/13284, -13291, -13294, -13316, -13326/13327, -13329, -13332, -13334/13335, -13337/13338, -13343, -13346, -13353, -13359, -13363/13366, -13375, -13381/13382, -13386, -13392/13394, -13396/13397, -13405; 52-5337

F-86F-30 52-4344, -4373, -4384/4385, -4405, -4428, -4449, -4459, -4488, -4496, -4513, -4520, -4524, -4539, -4569, -4579, -4581, -4589, -4770, -4773, -4802, 4821, -4823, -4857/4858, -4900

Colombia

Colombia operated six Canadair CL-13B Sabre 6 fighters (identified by one source as Sabre 4s, and often referred to by the Colombians and American military assistance officers as F-86Es) delivered on 8 June 1956, plus two NAA F-86F Sabres that came from the Spanish Air Force as attrition replacements in January 1963.

The Sabres were operated by 10 Escuadron de Caza-Bombardero. Four of the Canadair aircraft were lost in mishaps. All Colombian Sabres were withdrawn from service in 1966. The Canadair ships were assigned s/ns 2021/2026, while the F-86Fs were assigned 2027/2028. One of the latter was 51-13226.

Denmark

The Royal Danish Air Force (RDAF), or Kongelige Danske Flyvevaben, operated 38 F-86D Sabres interceptors as part of the country's commitment to NATO's defense of western Europe. Because of their radar fire-control system and rocket projectiles, these aircraft were more sensitive, on security grounds, than the F-86K version. Their release to Denmark marked the first time the F-86D was exported.

Denmark's F-86Ds were modified to accept Martin-Baker ejection seats.

Assigned to Denmark's tactical air forces, the F-86D served with Nos. 726, 727, and 731 Squadrons. These Dog Sabres on alert in that tiny Nordic nation had to be taken into account by the Soviets when they pondered attacking NATO's vulnerable northern tier.

In recent years, surviving Danish F-86Ds were being used as decoys at Karup, Vandel, and Skydstrup. One Danish aircraft (F-453/51-8453) is preserved today near Copenhagen.

France

France's Armee de l'Air received the first of 60 F-86K Sabres, manufactured by Fiat in Italy, in September 1956. Deliveries continued until mid-1957 and some, or possibly all, of these late F-86Ks received Aero 3B Sidewinder launch rails.

In French service, the F-86K flew 36,382hr, of which over 6,500 were at night. Eight F-86Ks were lost in mishaps, with no loss of life. Twenty-two were eventually returned to Italy.

The following French squadrons operated the F-86K:

EC 1/13 Artois was formed in August 1956 at Lahr with the F-86K and moved to Colmar on 1 April 1957. The squadron initially used codes 13-GA to 13-GZ, and in April 1957 changed to codes 13-QA to 13-QZ. This squadron converted to the Mirage IIIC beginning in September 1962.

EC 2/13 Alpes was formed at Colmar on 1 May 1957 with the F-86K. For a few months after formation, codes were 13-HA to 13-HZ, soon changing to 13-PA through 13-PZ. The squadron also converted to the Mirage IIIC, beginning in April 1962.

EC 3/13 was formed at Colmar in April 1962 to fly the remaining F-86Ks

JB-234 is a Canadair CL-13B Sabre Mark 6 supplied to the West German Luftwaffe after the service first operated a batch of CL-13A Sabre Mark 5s, and is seen at Solingen AB in November 1964. In the hands of a rearmed Germany, the Sabre made a vital contribution during the Cold War as outnumbered allies stood up to the Soviet threat. Luftwaffe Sabre Mark 6s flew alongside RCAF Sabre Mark 6s, also stationed on German soil. via Jerry Geer

until the arriving of Mirages, and was disbanded in August 1962. Codes for this squadron were 13-SA to 13-SZ. Unlike most Armee de l'Air squadrons, EC 3/13 never received a name.

France had 62 F-86K Sabres. Aircraft s/ns were: 55-4814/4844, 55-4846/4865, 55-4867/4870, 55-4872/4874, 55-4876/4879.

Germany

The West German Luftwaffe picked the Canadair CL-13A Sabre 5 to serve as a lead-in trainer, to familiarize pilots with the Sabre in anticipation of 225 Canadair CL-13B Sabre 6s, which were ordered in December 1956. The Luftwaffe took delivery of 75 Sabre Mark 5s, all former RCAF, beginning in January 1957.

These Sabres were first flown to Renfrew/Abbotsinch, for overhaul by Scottish Aviation at Prestwick. The first ten Sabres arrived in Scotland on 15 January 1957 and the last three were delivered almost a year later on 1 January 1958.

Only 72 Sabre Mark 5s actually saw service with the Luftwaffe. The remaining three aircraft (BB+138, BB+148, and BB+157) were sent to Redifon, beginning in February 1958, for conversion to ground-based flight simulators.

It's hard to believe that pilot R. Y. Costain gets paid for having this much fun, especially after a military career in which he flew the F-89, F-94, F-100, A-1 Skyraider, and F-4 Phantom. Now, Costain is at the controls of Canadair Sabre Mark 6 c/n 1710, registered as N89FS, practicing for his job towing the TDU Dart gunnery target on contract with TAC. This Sabre, powered by a Canadair Orenda 14 engine, was manufactured for the West German Luftwaffe with the original s/n JB-240, later D-9541, and made its first flight on 18 April 1958. In later years, it went to Flight Systems (Costain's employer), first as N1039L, later as N89FS. Costain, incidently, ejected from an earlier failure but seems to have this ship well in hand at Peterson AFB near Colorado Springs on 11 August 1991. Robert Greby

The Luftwaffe began to receive its first aircraft on 10 May 1957, when RCAF pilots flew two ships to TSLw 3 (technical school) at Fassberg. Most of the aircraft, however, went to equip Waffenschule 10 (WaSLw 10) at Oldenburg, the first aircraft arriving on 9 September 1957. Oberstleutnant Herbert Wehnelt, commander of WaSLw 10, made his first flight on 29 November 1957, flying aircraft BB+123.

From a peak of about 65 airworthy Sabre Mark 5s in January 1959, the inventory was whittled down to around 25 aircraft by April 1960. This Sabre Mark 5 population remained constant until 9 March 1962 when the last ships were disposed of.

The Germans leaped ahead with the Canadair CL-13B Sabre Mark 6 version, the first of which arrived in 1959 and began to replace Sabre 5s in WaSLw 10. These aircraft eventually filled out three day-fighter wings, commencing with Jagdgeschwader 71 at Ahlhorn (code JA-) formed under Maj. Erich Hartmann on 6 June 1959. The other two wings were JG72 at Leck (JB) and JG73 at Oldenburg (JC). Plans for a fourth fighter wing (JD) were abandoned although a few aircraft were briefly painted with JD codes.

Luftwaffe Sabre Mark 6s participated in NATO's 4th aerial gunnery meet, at Leeuwarden, Holland, 26 June–7 July 1961. German Sabres routinely carried Sidewinder missiles. Though their primary role was always air to air, some were occasionally equipped with underwing, air-to-ground ordnance, including up to four launchers for four 2.75in (6.98cm) folding fin aircraft rockets (FFAR), four 5in (12.7cm) high-velocity aircraft rockets (HVAR), or two 750lb (340kg) napalm tanks.

Late in their careers, seven Sabre Mark 6s were modified for target-towing duties with DelMar towing equipment and served in this capacity with the Condor Flugdienst at Westerland. Although not strictly civilian aircraft, these carried civil-registry numbers typified by D-9522, which was written off on 9 January 1968 when power was lost on approach and the pilot ejected safely.

Eventually, five former Luftwaffe Sabre 6s reached the Pakistani, and subsequently, the Bangladesh Air Force.

German Sabres initially were flown unpainted, in natural metal finish. The color scheme adopted for Luftwaffe Sabre Mark 5s and 6s in 1960 consisted of dark green and dark sea gray upper surfaces with light blue undersurfaces. The national insignia, often called a Maltese cross although the term isn't strictly proper, were in the usual six positions (both sides of the fuselage; both sides of both wings), with a German flag serving as a fin flash on the vertical tail. Below the flag, in very small lettering, was placed the s/n in the format "Luftwaffe F86-xxx" with the last three numbers being the c/n assigned by the builder. The BB prefix, which signified WaSLw 10, was worn on the nose in 600mm-high figures over the machine gun ports (tactical numbers assigned to German Sabres changed on occasion, but not often). From autumn 1958, the two staffel of WaSLw 10 carried a colored band around the fin cap to identify their aircraft: white for 1/WaSLw 10 and red for 2/WaSLw 10. Codes also identified the two staffel as follows: BB+1xx for 1/WaSLw 10 and BB+2xx for 2/WaSLw 10.

Among surviving Luftwaffe Sabre Mark 5s are two at the Luftwaffe Museum, Uetersen.

The Luftwaffe also soared ahead on another front—investing in the NAA/Fiat F-86K Sabre for the all-weather intercept mission.

The 88 F-86Ks for the Luftwaffe were manufactured in the United States. They were not flown but shipped to Fiat in Turin, Italy. After test flights at Turin, the F-86Ks, without armament and with minimum instrumentation, were flown to Germany. They arrived at Oberpfaffenhofen in pairs, the first two on 22 July 1957, the final pair on 23 June 1958. At Oberpfaffenhofen, Dornier carried out acceptance checks. Still wearing USAF markings, the Sabres were then placed into storage awaiting formation of squadrons.

On 16 July 1959, Waffenschule 10 was formed to place the F-86K into German service. This unit received aircraft from 23 August 1959 to 24 August 1960 at their base at Oldenburg. Here, the Sabres were armed and readied for service. As it turned out, however, only 57 aircraft saw actual service. The remaining 31 remained in USAF colors until disposed of. The aircraft that saw service had been manufactured with extended wing tips, as also found on the F-86L.

The F-86K saw Luftwaffe service from October 1960 until their last flight on 5 January 1966. At first, these Sabre interceptors appeared in natural metal finish, with national insignia in the usual locations, and a squadron code followed by three numbers on the nose. Around the beginning of 1961, however, a camouflage scheme was adopted, comprising green and gray upper surfaces, with light gray undersides.

Only two Jagdgeschwader (JG), roughly equivalent to fighter groups, flew the F-86K, and after phaseout in 1966 most of the flying aircraft passed to Venezuela, as did many of the spare airframes.

Luftwaffe F-86K Sabre units were:

JG 75 (squadron code JE): formed at Oldenburg October 1960, moved to Leipheim 20 October 1960, disbanded 5 May 1961 and passed its aircraft to JG 74.

JG 74 (squadron code JD): formed at Neuburg in April 1961, received aircraft from JG 75 in May 1961, attached to NATO 5 October 1962; its first, second, and third squadrons of JG 74 operated the F-86K until May 1964 when the first Lockheed F-104G Starfighter arrived on the scene. All F-86Ks then passed to JG 74's third squadron until phaseout in January 1966. (Squadrons can be identified by the aircraft code, JD 100 is from JG 74 first squadron, JD 200 the second squadron, and so on.)

During their nearly seven years of service, only four Luftwaffe F-86K Sabres were lost to mishaps. Two of the aircraft (56-4133/JD 103 and 56-4119/JD 109) were lost in a tragic midair collision near Neuburg on 3 May 1962 in which both pilots were killed. Another (56-4130/JD 101) crashed on a road near Neuburg on 30 October 1963. The fourth (56-4157/JD 316) crashed near Schwabisch-Gmund on 24 November 1964. In these latter two crashes, the pilots survived.

Luftwaffe Sabre Mark 5s had the following Canadair c/ns: 792, 794, 798, 801, 807, 810, 815/820, 822, 833/835, 838, 840/841, 845/846, 849, 851/852, 854, 860, 866, 871, 877, 880/883, 895, 897, 901, 904, 913/917, 921/932, 934, 943, 948, 955, 960, 963/964, 967/969, 971/975, 977, 981/982, 984, 986, 989/990, 1095, 1111, 1117, 1138.

Luftwaffe Sabre 6s were assigned Canadair c/ns 1591/1815.

Luftwaffe F-86K Sabre interceptors on flying status were 55-4895/4898, -4907, -4911/4912, -4920, -4923, -4925, -4930, -4935, -4936; 56-4116/4144, 56-4146/4160. Non-flying spare F-86K Sabres belonging to West Germany were 55-4845, -4866, -4878, -4881/4882, -4888, -4899, -4901, -4904, -4908/4910, -4913/4919, -4921/4922, -4924, -4926/4929, -4931/4934; 56-4145.

Great Britain

Britain obtained three F-86E Sabres built by Canadair as CL-13 Sabre Mark 2s, all of which were loaned in preparation for delivery of 428 Sabre Mark 4s (out of 438 built). These were supplied to the RAF for use in Germany. The RAF kept Canadair's mark numbers but rendered them in British style as F.2 and F.4.

Subsequently, 59 of the Canadair Sabre Mark 4s were stationed on British soil for use by Fighter Command in the United Kingdom.

Deliveries of Sabres began with three Sabre F.2s and nine Sabre F.4s during December 1952. One Sabre F.4 (XB551) was procured separately to replace a Sabre F.2 (XB530) that was returned to Canada. One Sabre (XB534) crashed on delivery 3mi (4.8km) southeast of Prestwick on 19

An F-86E(M) Sabre, as it was temporarily designated for accounting purposes. This aircraft is British and not an American aircraft at all, even though it wears USAF ferry markings and a spurious USAF buzz number. Actually, this is a CL-13 Sabre Mark 4, or F.4, (19862) that has finished its service in Britain's RAF. The unusual markings are temporary during its transfer from the RAF to the Italian Air Force in 1958. Merle Olmsted

December 1952, another (XB925) at Kinloss on 28 September 1953. Deliveries of Sabres by air to Britain took place between 8 December 1952 and 19 December 1953 in Operation Bechers Brook.

RAF Sabre squadrons were No. 3 at Wildenrath (May 1953–January 1956), No. 4 at Jever (October 1953–July 1955), No. 20 at Oldenburg (October 1953–November 1955), No. 26 at Oldenburg (November 1953–June 1955), No. 66 at Linton-on-Ouse (December 1953–March 1956), No. 67 at Wildenrath (May 1953–March 1956), No. 71 at Wildenrath (October 1953–May 1956), No. 92 at Linton-on-Ouse (February 1954–April 1956), No. 93 at Oldenburg and Jever (April 1954–January 1956), No. 112 at Bruggen (January 1954–April 1956), No. 130 at Bruggen (August 1953–April 1956), No. 147 at Abingdon, Benson, and Lyneham (February 1953–February 1956), and No. 234 (November 1953–May 1956).

Between 1956 and 1958, 302 RAF Sabres were returned to the USAF (in camouflage, USAF markings and RCAF s/ns), at which time for record keeping purposes they were assigned the designation F-86E(M). In time, 121 of these were delivered to Yugoslavia and 179 to Italy. Of the remaining two aircraft, one crashed at Naples on delivery (XB733) and one (XB982) was transferred to a private owner.

British s/ns assigned to RAF Sabres were XB530/XB550 (21), XB551 (1), XB575/XB603 (29), XB606/XB646 (41), XB664/XB713 (50), XB726/XB769 (44), XB790/XB839 (50), XB856/XB905 (50), XB941/XB990 (50), XD102/XD138* (37), XD707/XD736 (30), XD753/XD781 (29)

*Later re-serialed as follows: XD102/XD105 became XB647/XB650; XD106/XD111 became XB770/XB775; XD112/XD116 became XB851/XB855; XD117/XD138 became XB978/XB999 (causing duplication of some in the XB941/XB990 batch). Separately XB901/XB905 became XB912/XB916 and XB941/XB990 became XB917/XB977, wiping out the duplication.

Greece

Greece's Royal Hellenic Air Force, as it was known when Greece was both a monarchy (from 1935) and a NATO member (from 1952), became a hand-me-down user of 82 Canadair CL-13 Sabre Mark 2 and Mark 4 fighters inherited from Britain's RAF and used in the day-interceptor role. Deliveries began in July 1954. These were part of the overall scheme of Allied cooperation in the defense of Western Europe, although Greece and Turkey also were known to point their aircraft at each other, and long-held hostilities occasionally flared.

In the late 1950s, Greece's former RAF Sabres filled out at least three of Greece's ten mira (squadrons) that together formed the country's only interceptor wing and would have transferred to NATO control in wartime as part of the 6th Allied Tactical Air Force.

Some sources credit the Greek Air Force with receiving 106 (or, according to one source, 110) Canadair CL-13 Sabre Mark 2s.

The first Sabre Mark 2s were delivered in mid-1954 and went to equip No. 341 Squadron (Mire) of No. 112 Wing (Pterighe). In 1955, a further two squadrons, Nos. 342 and 343, equipped at Elefsina, under No. 112 Wing. In 1956, the three squadrons transferred to Tanagra Under No. 114 Wing. Here, the Hellenic Flame aerobatic team was formed and flew displays in West Germany, France, Italy, and Turkey until disbanding in 1964. No. 343 Squadron disbanded in 1958, 341 in 1960, and 342 in 1962. The Sabres eventually went to Agchialos under No. 111 Wing, probably in No. 337 Squadron, until the end of their service.

In 1961, No. 343 Squadron was reequipped with F-86D Sabre all-weather interceptors. Details on Greek use of a small number of F-86Ds are sparse.

A nearly complete list of Greek Canadair Sabre Mark 2s, listed by their RCAF s/ns:

19102, 19104/19105, 19107/19111, 19121, 19125, 19127/19128, 19133, 19135/19136, 19140/19142, 19144, 19146, 19148, 19151, 19154, 19161, 19168/19172, 19174, 19182, 19186, 19188, 18191, 19196, 19199, 19202, 19209/19213, 19218, 19220, 19222, 19224, 19228, 19233, 19235, 19238/19239, 19243, 19250, 19254, 19267, 19269, 19271, 19273/19274, 19285, 19287, 19293/19294, 19305, 19307, 19320, 19323, 19344, 19347, 19349, 19355, 19363, 19374, 19377/19378, 19381/19383, 19390, 19392/19393, 19395, 19397/19398, 19403, 19407, 19409, 19416, 19418, 19423/19425, 19428/19430, 19432/19434, 19438, 19440, 19443/19444, 19447/19448, 19452.

Honduras

The Fuerza Aerea Hondurena (FAH) operated eight Canadair CL-13 Sabre Mark 2s or F-86E(M) (former Yugoslav), four F-86F, and five F-86K Sabres (former Venezuelan). The first of these began arriving in 1969 (F-86Ks) and others were on duty from July 1976 (F-86E(M)s) and July 1977 (F-86Fs). It is unclear what mission could have been effectively performed by such a small mix of aircraft: their only apparent action was harassment missions over El Salvador following the end of the 1969 "Soccer war." At least one aircraft was lost in a crash. The FAH museum at Tegucigalpa has a former German F-86K No. 1000, which was obtained from Venezuela in 1969. Serial numbers for 14 FAH Sabres are known: 1100/1103 (4) and 3001/3010 (10).

All surviving F-86Ks are now in the boneyard at Tegucigalpa while F-86Es and F-86Fs that survived will probably be put out to pasture at San Pedro Sula, their last operational base.

Indonesia

The Indonesian Air Force, or Tentara Nasional Indonesia–Angkatan Udara (TNI-AU) was supplied with 18 former Australian CA-27 Sabres in 1973. An advisory unit was operated by Australia from October 1972 to February 1975.

The first Sabres were delivered in February 1973. They equipped No. 14 Squadron at Madium in East Java.

To make up for attrition, a further five aircraft were supplied from Malaysia in 1976.

Aircraft supplied from Australia were: A94-352 (which crashed at Bali on delivery), -361, -366, -368, -945, -949, -952, -955, -957, -963, -968/969, -971/972, -975, -980, -988, -990. Of the five aircraft supplied by Malaysia, the identities of four are known: A94-353, -978/979, -987.

Italy

Fiat produced 121 F-86K Sabre all-weather interceptors at its Turin/Caselle plant from 1955 to 1958, and final-assembled up to 120 more F-86Ks built by NAA. Fiat, of course, had available for developmental work two NAA-built YF-86Ks (52-3630, 52-3804) both former F-86D-40 airplanes.

The export F-86K is almost identical to the American F-86D except that the latter's rocket projectile armament has been replaced with four 20mm cannons. Further, the F-86K is 8.5in (21cm) longer than the F-86D because of an extension of the tailpipe region.

Of the total Italian production run, 63 were supplied directly to the Aeronautica Militare Italiana (AMI). These were later joined by 22 Fiat-built former French F-86Ks in 1962, and eight more NAA-built F-86Ks transferred from the Netherlands Air Force in 1963, bringing the total AMI inventory to 93. The first Fiat F-86K (MM6185/53-8273) flew on 23 May 1955 at Caselle, with NAA representative Col. Arthur de Bolt at the controls.

The first unit to receive the F-86K was 6 Gruppo COT (Caccia Ogni Tempo, or All-Weather Fighter) of 1 Stormo at Istrana. The first two operational aircraft (MM6192/6193) were delivered from Turin on 2 November 1955. The final AMI F-86K was delivered by Fiat on 31 October 1957.

The F-86K continued in AMI service until 27 July 1973, when the last flight was flown from Rimini with Capt. Mario Pinna in aircraft 53-8291.

This cannon-armed F-86K Sabre (53-8316) was built by NAA but final-assembled by Fiat in Turin, and is seen here wearing its "plane in group" number as ship no. 21 in the 51st Aerobrigata, located at Istrana. Note the rifle-style sight on the forward fuselage just behind the radome. The natural metal, gruppo and brigata badges (fuselage and tail), and national insignia are typical of Aeronautica Militare Italiana (AMI) Sabres. Gerhard Lang

The following gruppi flew the F-86K:

6 Gruppo/1 Stormo received the F-86K in November 1955 at Istrana. 1 Stormo converted to the Nike missile on 1 May 1959 and its aircraft were taken over by 22 Gruppo.

17 Gruppo/1 Stormo received the F-86K in 1956 at Istrana. After 1 Stormo made the rather dramatic shift to the Nike, this unit's aircraft went to 21 Gruppo.

23 Gruppo/1 Stormo received the F-86K in December 1956 at Pisa. When 1 Stormo became a missile wing on 1 May 1959, these F-86K Sabres were transferred to 51 Aerobrigata. The F-86Ks moved to Rimini by the end of 1966, and transferred to 5 Stormo on 25 March 1973. 23 Gruppo converted to the F-104 Starfighter in July 1973.

21 Gruppo/51 Aerobrigata received F-86Ks from 17 Gruppo on 1 May 1959, at Istrana. When this unit converted to the F-104 in 1963, its Sabres passed to 12 Gruppo.

22 Gruppo/51 Aerobrigata received F-86Ks from 6 Gruppo on 1 May 1959, also at Istrana. When this unit converted to the F-104 in 1969, its Sabres went to 12 and 23 Gruppi.

12 Gruppo/4 Aerobrigata converted from the Sabre 4 (below) to the F-86K in 1963, operating from Gioia del Colle. This gruppo transferred to 36 Stormo on 1 August 1966, converted to the F-104 Starfighter in December 1971, and passed its Sabres on to 23 Gruppo.

Fiat-built F-86K aircraft delivered to the AMI from 1955-1957 were MM6185/6234 (53-8273/8322), MM6235/6237 (55-4811/4813), plus

In addition to its F-86K interceptors, Italy operated 180 CL-13 Sabre 4s transferred to the AMI from Britain's RAF. Wearing number 4-73, this camouflaged Sabre Mark 4 (19830), also known as an F-86M or F-86E(M) upon its transfer from England, is seen at an air base in Italy. The camouflage is as originally applied to the Canadair aircraft for service in the RAF. via Norman Taylor

the following which had no MM serials allocated: 55-4871, -4880, -4889/4893, -4903, -4905/4906.

Fiat-built F-86K Sabres transferred to the AMI from France in 1962 and not assigned MM serials were 55-4815, -4818/4821, -4824, -4829/4830, -4832/4833, -4837, -4843/4844, -4846, -4854, -4858/4860, -4863, -4865, -4868/4869.

NAA-built F-86K Sabres transferred to the AMI from Holland in 1963 were 54-1249, -1256, -1261, -1275, -1288, 1292, 1297, -1315.

In addition to F-86K interceptors, Italy belatedly operated 179 Canadair CL-13 Sabre Mark 4s, or F-86E(M)s, transferred to the AMI from Britain's RAF. Five of these aircraft were despatched to the Belgian Congo in

F-86F-40-NA Sabre 02-7985 (USAF s/n 57-6442) of No. 6 Hikotai (Squadron), 8th Wing, JASDF, poses on the hardstand at Tsuiki, the same Japanese air base that served as an overhaul center for American warplanes during the Korean War, on 20 August 1979. Both American- and Japanese-manufactured Sabres, totaling more than 400 airplanes, were operated by the JASDF well into the 1980s. Masumi Wada

1963 to support UN peace-keeping efforts there. A detachment of Philippine Air Force personnel operated these Italian Sabres from February to June 1963, reconnoitering roads and railroads and making force demonstrations over outlying villages.

Japan

The Japan Air Self-Defense Force (JASDF), or Nihon Koku Jietai, was one of the principal users of the F-86 Sabre.

The JASDF received 180 NAA F-86F Sabres during 1955–1957 and serialed them between 52-7401 and 72-7580, although the last 45 aircraft (72-7536/7580) were never used, partly because Japan lacked enough qualified pilots. These were returned to the United States in February 1959. All of these aircraft also had USAF s/ns.

Mitsubishi built an additional 300 F-86F Sabres under license between 1956 and 1961 (62-7701/12-7999 and 12-7000; it's not clear why the final aircraft wasn't assigned the s/n 12-8000, the next number in sequence). The F-86F equipped ten fighter hikotai (roughly, squadrons) numbered 1 through 10, as well as the well-known Blue Impulse aerobatic team, which re-equipped with the Mitsubishi T-2 during 1981–1982. The last combat unit to fly the F-86F was No. 6 Hikotai, which re-equipped with the Mitsubishi F-1 in 1980. Some F-86Fs were also operated by the Air Proving Group at Gifu and by the air defense headquarters squadron at Iruma. The last Japanese F-86F (62-7497) made its final flight on 15 March 1982.

Mitsubishi converted 18 F-86Fs to the RF-86F reconnaissance configuration in 1961–1962. These went to the 501st Hikotai, which used them until converting to the RF-4E Phantom on 1 October 1979.

All JASDF Sabres were initially unpainted; they were painted overall silver in the 1960s. Some retired F- and RF-86Fs were returned to the United States and converted to US Navy QF-86F target drones in the late 1970s and early 1980s. The QF-86Fs were operated by the Naval Weapons Center at NAS China Lake, California.

Once the F-86D Sabre all-weather interceptor became available for export, 122 F-86D Sabres (84-8101/04-8222) were supplied between 1958 and 1961. The JASDF organized four all-weather interceptor hikotai, numbered 101–103 and 105. A few F-86Ds were operated by the Air Proving Ground at Gifu. The last two F-86D hikotai were disbanded on 1 October 1968.

The linkups between JASDF and USAF s/ns for F-86F and F-86D Sabres are:

JASDF s/ns	**USAF** s/ns	**Model**
52-7401	52-4758	F-86F-30
52-7402	51-13474	F-86F-25
52-7403	52-4618	F-86F-30
52-7404	52-4684	F-86F-30
52-7405	52-4705	F-86F-30
52-7406	52-4845	F-86F-30
52-7407	52-4914	F-86F-30
52-7408	51-13376	F-86F-25
52-7409	51-13414	F-86F-25
52-7410	52-4679	F-86F-30
62-7411	52-4708	F-86F-30
62-7412	52-5327	F-86F-25
62-7413	52-4745	F-86F-30
62-7414	52-4905	F-86F-30
62-7415	52-4916	F-86F-30
62-7416	52-5439	F-86F-25
62-7417	51-13361	F-86F-25
62-7418/7419	51-13368/13369	F-86F-25
62-7420	51-13385	F-86F-25
62-7421	51-13390	F-86F-25
62-7422	52-4693	F-86F-30
62-7423	52-4699	F-86F-30
62-7424	52-4542	F-86F-30
62-7425	52-4836	F-86F-30
62-7426	52-4844	F-86F-30
62-7427	52-4909	F-86F-30
62-7428	52-4913	F-86F-30
62-7429	52-4923	F-86F-30
62-7430	52-4939	F-86F-30
62-7431	55-3822	F-86F-40
62-7432/7433	55-3818/3819	F-86F-40
62-7434	55-3820	F-86F-40
62-7435/7436	55-3823/3824	F-86F-40
62-7437/7438	55-3829/3830	F-86F-40
62-7439/7440	55-3833/3834	F-86F-40
62-7441	55-3855	F-86F-40
62-7442	55-3821	F-86F-40
62-7443	55-3825	F-86F-40
62-7444	55-3828	F-86F-40
62-7445	55-3838	F-86F-40
62-7446	55-3846	F-86F-40
62-7447	55-3853	F-86F-40
62-7448	55-3859	F-86F-40
62-7449	55-3864	F-86F-40
62-7450	55-3867	F-86F-40
62-7451	55-3869	F-86F-40
62-7452	55-3871	F-86F-40
62-7453/7455	55-3873/3875	F-86F-40
62-7456/7457	55-3877/3878	F-86F-40
62-7458/7459	55-3881/3882	F-86F-40
62-7460	55-3844	F-86F-40
62-7461	55-3889	F-86F-40
62-7462/7463	55-3893/3894	F-86F-40
62-7464	55-3896	F-86F-40
62-7465	55-3886	F-86F-40
62-7466	55-3863	F-86F-40
62-7467	55-3865	F-86F-40
62-7468	55-3868	F-86F-40
62-7469	55-3872	F-86F-40
62-7470	55-3892	F-86F-40
62-7471	55-3898	F-86F-40
62-7472	55-3904	F-86F-40
62-7473	55-3907	F-86F-40
62-7474	55-3879	F-86F-40
62-7475	55-3905	F-86F-40
62-7476	55-3907	F-86F-40
62-7477	55-3911	F-86F-40
62-7478	55-3914	F-86F-40
62-7479	55-3916	F-86F-40
62-7480	55-3917	F-86F-40
62-7481/7482	55-3908/3909	F-86F-40
62-7483	55-3817	F-86F-40
62-7484	55-3883	F-86F-40
62-7485/7486	55-3887/3888	F-86F-40
62-7487	55-3890	F-86F-40
62-7488	55-3897	F-86F-40
62-7489	55-3910	F-86F-40
62-7490/7491	55-3912/3913	F-86F-40
62-7492/7493	55-3918/3919	F-86F-40
62-7494	55-3921	F-86F-40
62-7495	55-3924	F-86F-40
62-7496	55-3926	F-86F-40
62-7497	55-3937	F-86F-40
62-7498	55-3880	F-86F-40
62-7499/7502	55-900/3903	F-86F-40
62-7503	55-3923	F-86F-40
62-7504	55-3885	F-86F-40
62-7505	55-3899	F-86F-40
62-7506	55-3915	F-86F-40
62-7507	55-3922	F-86F-40
62-7508	55-3925	F-86F-40
62-7509/7510	55-3927/3928	F-86F-40
62-7511	55-3930	F-86F-40
62-7512/7514	55-3932/3934	F-86F-40
62-7515	55-3940	F-86F-40
62-7516	55-3891	F-86F-40
62-7517	55-3931	F-86F-40
62-7518	55-3939	F-86F-40
62-7519/7520	55-3942/3943	F-86F-40
62-7521	55-3948	F-86F-40
62-7522	55-3951	F-86F-40
62-7523	55-3954	F-86F-40
62-7524	55-3816	F-86F-40
62-7525	55-3895	F-86F-40
62-7526	55-3920	F-86F-40
62-7527	55-3929	F-86F-40
62-7528/7529	55-3935/3936	F-86F-40

Mitsubishi F-86F Sabre 82-7847 (USAF s/n 56-2849) belonging to No. 1 Hikotai, taxies at Hamamatsu AB, Japan, on 5 June 1978. The yellow-and-black checkerboard on this Sabre's tail is a squadron marking and is typical of individualized colors placed on Japanese Sabres. Masumi Wada

JASDF	USAF	Model
62-7530	55-3938	F-86F-40
62-7531/7534	55-3944/3947	F-86F-40
62-7535	55-3949	F-86F-40
62-7701/7705	55-5048/5052	F-86F-40
72-7706/7770	55-5053/5117	F-86F-40
72-7771/7773	56-2773/2775	F-86F-40
82-7774/7868	56-2776/2870	F-86F-40
92-7869/7880	56-2871/2882	F-86F-40
92-7881/7940	57-6338/6397	F-86F-40
02-7941/7991	57-6398/6448	F-86F-40
12-7992/7000	57-6449/6457	F-86F-40
84-8101	51-8368	F-86D-36
84-8102	51-8344	F-86D-36
84-8103	51-8375	F-86D-36
84-8104	52-4042	F-86D-45
84-8105	51-5858	F-86D-26
84-8106	51-5957	F-86D-31
84-8107	51-5955	F-86D-31
84-8108	51-5996	F-86D-31
84-8109	51-6002	F-86D-31
84-8110	51-6019	F-86D-31
84-8111	51-6030	F-86D-31
84-8112	51-6033	F-86D-31
84-8113	51-6042	F-86D-31
84-8114	51-6080	F-86D-31
84-8115	51-6086	F-86D-31
84-8116	51-6095	F-86D-31
84-8117	51-6098	F-86D-31
84-8118	51-6129	F-86D-31
84-8119	51-6132	F-86D-31
84-8120	51-5898	F-86D-26
84-8121	51-5941	F-86D-26
84-8122	51-6094	F-86D-31
84-8123	51-5922	F-86D-31
84-8124	51-5974	F-86D-31
94-8125	51-5992	F-86D-31
84-8126	51-6013	F-86D-31
84-8127	51-5967	F-86D-31
84-8128	51-5989	F-86D-31
84-8129	51-6008	F-86D-31
84-8130	51-6032	F-86D-31
84-8131	51-6040	F-86D-31
84-8132	56-6066	F-86D-31
94-8133	51-5982	F-86D-31
84-8134	51-5986	F-86D-31

Two Mitsubishi-modified RF-86F Sabre reconnaissance aircraft of the 501st Hikotai (62-6425 and -6428) take off from Iruma AB, Japan, on 9 December 1974. The United States, Japan, and South Korea operated various photo-reconnaissance versions of the Sabre, beginning with Project Ashtray RF-86As flown by Americans in the Korean War, Project Haymaker RF-86Fs also developed for US forces, and the Japanese RF-86Fs shown here.
Shinichi Ohtaki

JASDF	USAF	Model
84-8135	51-6039	F-86D-31
94-8136	51-6077	F-86D-31
94-8137	51-5894	F-86D-31
94-8138	51-5973	F-86D-31
94-8139	51-6104	F-86D-31
84-8140	51-6135	F-86D-31
84-8141	51-5879	F-86D-26
84-8142	51-5901	F-86D-26
84-8143	51-5964	F-86D-31
94-8144	51-5970	F-86D-31
94-8145	51-5912	F-86D-26
94-8146	51-6023	F-86D-31
84-8147	51-6050	F-86D-31
84-8148	51-6121	F-86D-31
84-8149	51-5980	F-86D-31
84-8150	51-6003	F-86D-31
84-8151	51-6049	F-86D-31
84-8152	51-5889	F-86D-26
94-8153	51-5988	F-86D-31
84-8154	51-6005	F-86D-31
84-8155	51-5857	F-86D-26
84-8156	51-5949	F-86D-31
84-8157	51-5991	F-86D-31
84-8158	51-6015	F-86D-31
84-8159	51-5892	F-86D-26
94-8160	51-8278	F-86D-36
04-8161	51-6155	F-86D-36
04-8162	51-6166	F-86D-36
04-8163	51-6198	F-86D-36
04-8164	51-6200	F-86D-36
04-8165	51-6202	F-86D-36
04-8166	51-6214	F-86D-36
04-8167	51-6244	F-86D-36
04-8168	51-6246	F-86D-36
04-8169	51-6250	F-86D-36
04-8170	51-6258	F-86D-36
04-8171	51-8275	F-86D-36
04-8172	51-8289	F-86D-36
04-8173	51-8302	F-86D-36
04-8174	51-8333	F-86D-36
04-8175	52-3920	F-86D-45
04-8176	52-3898	F-86D-45
04-8177	52-3969	F-86D-45
04-8178	52-3949	F-86D-45
04-8179	52-3953	F-86D-45
04-8180	52-3970	F-86D-45
04-8181	52-3972	F-86D-45
04-8182	52-3975	F-86D-45
04-8183	52-3979	F-86D-45
04-8184/8185	52-3984/3985	F-86D-45
04-8186	52-4009	F-86D-45
04-8187	52-4013	F-86D-45
04-8188	52-4068	F-86D-45
04-8189	52-4299	F-86D-50
04-8190	52-10001	F-86D-50
04-8191	52-10014	F-86D-50
04-8192	52-10093	F-86D-50
04-8193	52-3989	F-86D-45
04-8194	52-10119	F-86D-50
04-8195	52-9998	F-86D-50
04-8196	52-10003	F-86D-50
04-8197	52-4071	F-86D-45
04-8198	52-4247	F-86D-50
04-8199	52-4105	F-86D-45
04-8200	52-4024	F-86D-45
04-8201	52-4038	F-86D-45
04-8202	52-4045	F-86D-45
04-8203	52-4301	F-86D-45
04-8204	52-9987	F-86D-50
04-8205	52-9989	F-86D-50
04-8206	52-10147	F-86D-50
04-8207	52-3992	F-86D-45
04-8208	52-4240	F-86D-50
04-8209	52-10000	F-86D-50
04-8210	52-3965	F-86D-45
04-8211	52-10020	F-86D-50
04-8212	52-3967	F-86D-45
04-8213	52-4005	F-86D-45
04-8214	52-10153	F-86D-50
04-8215	52-4280	F-86D-50
04-8216	52-10005	F-86D-50
14-8217	52-3966	F-86D-45
14-8218	52-4297	F-86D-50
14-8219	52-10126	F-86D-50
14-8220	52-10145	F-86D-50
14-8221	52-10021	F-86D-50
14-8222	52-10103	F-86D-50

Malaysia

The Royal Malaysian Air Force (RMAF), or Tentara Udara Diraja Malaysia, announced in April 1969 that it would receive ten CA-27 Sabres amounting to $10 million in grant aid from Australia. The deal included a simulator, spares, and 90 Australian personnel to train RMAF pilots and technicians.

The first Sabres arrived in October 1969. Two nonflying aircraft were also supplied as training aids. In November 1971, six more Sabres were delivered to the RMAF, bringing the total to 18.

The Sabre was phased out of RMAF service in April 1976, and five were then sent to the Indonesian Air Force in July and August of that year. Of the remainder, one aircraft (A94-983) was flown back to Australia, in 1978, inside a C-130, for restoration to flying condition for the RAAF Historic Flight.

Malaysian squadrons:

No. 11 Squadron, formed in 1969, operated the Sabre from Butterworth.

The squadron replaced its Sabres with Northrop F-5A and F-5B Freedom Fighters in 1975–1976.

No. 12 Kilau (Lightning) Squadron, formed 31 May 1975 at Butterworth and operated Sabres briefly until receiving the F-5A and F-5B in April 1976.

RMAF Sabres were supplied in overall silver color scheme but soon received olive drab upper surface camouflage, with light gray undersides. National insignia were applied above and below the wings.

Malaysian Sabres: A94-353/354, -359, -362, -363, -364, -365, -367, -369, -371, plus nonflying A94-356/357. Aircraft delivered in November 1971 were A94-946, 948, 978/979, 983 and 987.

Netherlands

Holland's Koninklijke Luchtmacht (KLu) purchased 57 NAA-built and six Fiat-built F-86K Sabres. The NAA aircraft were delivered by sea between October 1955 and April 1956, while the Fiat-built Sabres followed a year later. The first batch of 15 were shipped aboard USS *Tripoli* on 1 October 1955. These 63 aircraft equipped three squadrons, the last serving until June 1964. Sixteen F-86Ks were written off in KLu service, and eight were returned to Italy in 1963. The remaining Sabres were scrapped in 1963–1964.

All KLu Sabres flew in natural metal, and initially displayed a two-figure squadron code followed by a number. This system lasted until 1 September 1959, when Q followed by the last three digits of the USAF s/n was painted on the nose. Dutch pilots reportedly referred to the F-86K, which played such a vital role in defending NATO air space during the Cold War, as the Kaasjager, Dutch for Cheese Fighter. Another explanation often quoted is that the F-86K is nicknamed after Mr. Kaasjager who was prominent in Holland in the 1950s and proposed that the canals of Amsterdam be filled in to create car parks.

The following Dutch squadrons flew the Sabre:

No. 700 Squadron (code 6A) was formed in January 1956 at Soesterburg and moved to Twenthe in 1959. This squadron flew Meteor T.7s as conversation trainers alongside the Sabres until August 1956.

F-86K Sabre interceptor of the Royal Netherlands Air Force (RNAF) on display in the RNAF Museum, Soesterburg, Holland, on 6 April 1984. Roger Wasley

No. 701 Squadron (code Y7) was formed in June 1956 at Twenthe, and also flew Meteor T.7s for a time. The squadron was disbanded in 1963.

No. 702 Squadron (code ZX) was formed as the operational conversion unit for the Sabre, also at Twenthe, in January 1957.

F-86Ks that served in Holland and were scrapped in 1963–1964: 54-1237/1238, -1244, -1246, -1253/1257, -1259, -1273, -1277/1278, -1280, -1291, -1296, -1299, -1301, -1305, -1307, -1310, -1317, -1323, -1327, -1329/1330, -1333, -1336/1337. -1339, -1343/1346, -1350; 55-4875, -4877, -4887, -4900, -4902.

This F-86K Sabre (54-1312) all-weather interceptor belonging to the RNAF's No. 332 Squadron is seen on a visit to Baden-Baden, Germany, in May 1961. In addition to the standard armament of four 20mm cannons, Norwegian F-86Ks carried inboard launch rails for two GAR-8A Sidewinder infrared homing missiles (redesignated AIM-9B in 1962). These interceptors plugged what would have been a major gap in the air defense of NATO's lightly-armed northern tier. Merle Olmsted

Pakistani Sabres fought in the 1965 and 1971 Indo-Pakistani conflicts and were retired in 1980 after brief exposure to further fighting along the Afghan border. This F-86F-40-NA Sabre (55-5005) is now on display at Peshawar with the checkerboard markings and distinctive badge of No. 15 Squadron. This Sabre racked up the Pakistani Air Force's first jet-versus-jet aerial victory on 15 September 1965 when Flight Lieutenant Choudry fired an AIM-9B Sidewinder missile blind at night to shoot down an Indian Canberra PR.57 reconnaissance aircraft (IP988). A day earlier, a PAF F-104 Starfighter failed in a similar attempt to destroy a nocturnal Canberra intruder. Peter R. Foster

F-86K Sabres that served in Holland and were written off in mishaps: 54-1239, -1250, -1252, -1255, -1263/1264, -1269, -1286, -1293, -1308, -1311, -1321/1322, -1325, -1340, -1349; 55-4885.

F-86K Sabres that served in Holland and were returned to the Italian Air Force, February–June 1963: 54-1249, -1256, -1261, -1275, -1288, -1292, -1297, -1315.

One F-86 Sabre that served in Holland has been preserved: 54-1283 (Q-283) is a gate guardian at Twenthe AB. A second Sabre preserved in Holland is an impostor in that it never served in the Dutch air arm: 53-8305 (Q-305), now at the Militair Luchtvaart Museum, Soesterburg, was flown to Deelen, Holland, on 10 June 1973 from Rimini, a gift from the Italian Air Force. Finally, the cockpit (only) of 54-1244 (Q-244) is preserved at the same museum.

Norway

The Norwegian Air Force flew the F-86K and, beginning soon after, the F-86F.

Norway operated 60 NAA-built F-86K Sabre interceptors, beginning in June 1955, as part of its commitment to NATO's northern tier. Fifty-nine were delivered between September 1955 and October 1956. The remaining aircraft was lost during acceptance trials in the United States and was not replaced until January 1960.

A hangar fire destroyed four aircraft on 10 March 1956, and four Fiat-built F-86Ks were delivered in June 1956 as replacements. Norway then suffered its first ejection on 20 January 1962 when 1st Lt. Bjornar Vollstad of No. 339 Squadron ejected through his canopy at about 12,000ft (3,657m) while in inverted flight on a mission from Bodo. A few other mishaps followed in the early 1960s.

The F-86K force stood down in 1966–1967, and since the aircraft were not needed elsewhere, most were scrapped in Norway.

F-86F Sabres were assigned to Norway through the US military aid program as replacements for the F-84G Thunderjet. Delivery of 90 F-86Fs began in March 1957 and was completed in May 1958. As attrition replacements, Norway received two subsequent batches of F-86Fs, consisting of six and 19 aircraft.

Norwegian squadrons:

No. 331 Squadron at Bodo converted to F-86F from F-84G in April 1958. The squadron flew Sabres until they were replaced by the F-104G Starfighter in April–May 1963.

No. 332 Squadron at Rygge was the first Norwegian squadron to convert to F-86F from F-84G in April 1957. The squadron moved to Bodo in 1962, converted to the F-86K interceptor, and was merged with No. 337 Squadron, and continued operating as No. 332 until being disbanded in the fall of 1964.

No. 334 Squadron at Bodo converted to F-86F in August 1958 and to F-86K in August 1960. This squadron merged with No. 339 Squadron on 1 September 1963. The last F-86K was surrendered on 15 July 1967.

No. 337 Squadron was formed with F-86K interceptors at Gardermoen on 1 September 1955 and was disbanded in the autumn of 1963 with its aircraft and crews transferring to No. 332 Squadron.

No. 338 Squadron at Orland had a brief interlude with the F-86F Sabre in the summer of 1958, resumed F-84G Thunderjet operations for a time, and finally converted to the F-86F in April 1960. The squadron operated its F-86Fs until they were replaced in the summer of 1966 by Northrop F-5A and F-5B Freedom Fighters.

No. 339 Squadron formed with the F-86K at Gardermoen on 13 July 1956, moved to Bodo on 1 September 1960, and disbanded on 1 September 1963, transferring its crews and aircraft to No. 334 Squadron.

Two F-86F-30-NA Sabres belonging to the Philippine Air Force taxi at Clark Field in 1955. This is shortly after transfer of these fighters to the Philippines. The aircraft at right (52-4890) has not yet acquired Philippine national insignia and, like its partner at left (52-4852) wears a USAF-style buzz number at the rear of the fuselage. Pat Tomelden

Norwegian F-86F aircraft: 51-13453, 52-4671, -4734, -4888, -5021, -5026, -5031, -5056, -5058, -5069, 52-5105, -5107, -5109, -5124, -5132, -5136, -5145, -5160, -5164/5167, -5172/5174, -5177, -5186/5187, -5190/5192, -5195/5196, -5200, -5202/5203, -5211/5216, -5218/5219, -5223/5225, -5227, -5229, -5232/5234, -5236, -5238, -5245, -5250, -5255/5257, -5264, -5266, -5269, -5301, -5306, -5319, -5338, -5377, -5382, -5452, 53-1078/1079, 53-1082, -1086, -1089, -1093, -1096, -1098, -1104/1105, -1112/1113, -1117/1118, -1120, -1123, -1126, -1128/1129, -1137/1139, -1141, -1143, -1146, -1148, -1150/1151, -1153, -1161/1162, -1166, -1168/1169, -1175, -1178, -1191, -1195, -1200, -1206, -1210/1211, -1218/1220, -1226/1227.

Norwegian NAA F-86K aircraft: 54-1231/1234, -1236, -1240/1243, -1245, -1247/1248, -1251, -1254, -1258, -1260, -1262, -1265/1268, -1270/1272, -1274, -1276, -1279, -1281, -1284/1285, -1287, -1289/1290, -1294/1295, -1298, -1300, -1302/1304, -1306, -1309, -1312/1313, -1316, -1318/1320, -1324, -1326, -1328, -1331/1332, -1334/1335, -1338, -1341/1342, -1347/1349.

Norwegian Fiat F-86K aircraft: 55-4874, -4884, -4886, -4890.

Pakistan

Introduction of the Sabre to the Pakistani air arm began in 1954, and Sabres remained in service until 1980 when the last fighters were withdrawn following a spate of fatigue-related accidents. One hundred two F-86F-35-NA and F-86F-40-NA Sabres came straight from the factory and were delivered under the Mutual Defense Assistance Pact (MDAP), the very last airplanes off the American production line. Following the 1965 Indo-Pakistani war, these were augmented by 90 former Luftwaffe Canadair CL-13B Sabre Mark 6s with Orenda 14 engines known in Pakistan, inaccurately, as F-86Es.

Sabres were operated by the Pakistan Air Force's (PAF) Nos. 14, 15, 16, 17, 18, 19, and 26 Squadrons. Both

NAA and Canadair Sabres saw action in the 1971 Indo-Pakistan war. Numerous Sabres remain on display in Pakistan. Among them, at PAF Base Peshawar, is an F-84F-40 (55-5005) that scored the country's first jet kill when it shot down Indian Air Force Canberra P.R.57 IP988 on 15 September 1965.

Sabres fought in Pakistan's short-lived 1965 conflict with India. The Sidewinder was a trump card for the Pakistani side. Less than 25 percent of the Sabre force—in fact, only 22 aircraft—was equipped to carry the AIM-9B, but the Indian side had to assume that these potent infrared missiles equipped any Sabre they encountered. Sabres performed well against Indian Hawker Hunters and less well against the Folland Gnat fighters. Only seven Sabres were lost in air combat in the 1965 fray.

When Pakistan and India fought again in December 1971, the Sabre played a critical role, accounting for a large portion of the PAF's 141 aerial victories. Kills of Indian warplanes included Folland Gnats, MiG-21s, and Su-7s.

Pakistan's Canadair CL-13B Sabre Mark 6s, as identified by their Canadair c/ns, were: 1592, 1594/1595, 1606/1608, 1614, 1616/1618, 1621/1624, 1626/1627, 1629, 1632, 1634, 1636, 1639, 1650, 1652/1653, 1655/1658, 1661, 1663, 1665, 1669/1670, 1674, 1683, 1689, 1692/1693, 1695, 1701/1703, 1705, 1709, 1718/1720, 1722, 1728, 1733, 1735, 1738/1739, 1742, 1747, 1749, 1751, 1754, 1756, 1763/1766, 1771/1772, 1777/1778, 1781, 1783, 1786/1790, 1792, 1794, 1797/1798, 1800, 1802/1804, 1808/1809/1812, 1815.

Peru

TheFuerza Aerea del Peru (FAP) operated 26 Sabres, most or all of which were NAA F-86Fs. These arrived on 1 July 1955. At least two squadrons, and possibly more, operated the Sabres. Attrition was heavy. At least nine Sabres were lost in mishaps by December 1963. Wing spar cracks became a serious problem, as FAP pilots tended to fly the aircraft aggressively in mock combat against rival Hawker Hunter-equipped units. Interestingly, the USAF mission in Lima rated the FAP pilots "very highly qualified," though the Sabres never saw any action before being retired in 1971.

Known serial numbers for Peru's aircraft are 51-13227, -13249, -13255, -13491, -13494/13495, -13499/13503, -13505; 52-5286, -5289, -5295.

Philippines

The Philippine Air Force, or Hukbong Himpapawid ng Pilipinas (HHP) received its first modern aircraft in 1957 with the arrival of its first batch of F-86F Sabres. At about the same time, the service received F-86Ds

The F-86Fs equipped the 6th and 7th Tactical-Fighter Squadrons of the 5th Fighter Wing and the 8th and 9th Tactical-Fighter Squadrons of the 6th Fighter Wing. The 9th squadron was the last to use the Sabre, ending up with the final half dozen aircraft. All of these units at one time or another were located at Basa airfield in northern Luzon that was viewed as the Philippines' principal air defense base. In all, the Philippines received 36–40 F-86Fs (in F-86F-25-NA, F-86F-25-NH, F-86F-30-NA, and F-86F-35-NA versions) and 20 F-86D-35-NA Sabres as part of a US military assistance package.

The F-86D was withdrawn from service in 1969, the F-86F in 1979.

Portugal

A full NATO partner, Portugal obtained 50 F-86F Sabres under the MDAP in 1958 and assigned them s/ns 5301/5350. Some of these had formerly been operated by the USAF's 531st Fighter-Bomber Squadron (FBS) at Chambley. Subsequently, 15 more operable Sabres (s/ns 5351/5365) were obtained from a batch of about 50 former West German Canadair CL-13B Sabre Mark 6s, the remainder being broken up for spares. A small number of former Norwegian Air Force F-86F Sabres were also purchased for spares in 1968–1969. Two Portuguese squadrons (Esc. 51 and 52) flew Sabres although Esc. 52's role was short lived. The Portuguese Sabres were based at BA 5 (Base Aerea 5), Monte Real.

The Sabre wore Portuguese colors at the very time Portugal was losing its grip as a colonial power in Africa. In August 1961, eight F-86Fs from BA 5 were deployed to Bissau Airport, Portuguese Guinea, in a mission code-named Atlas and intended to show the

F-86F-35-NA Sabre (Portuguese s/n 5357, USAF s/n 53-1164) on the flight line at Ota in 1958. Forca Aerea Portuguesa (FAP) pilots were enthusiastic about the Sabre, which was employed in a flag-waving show of force, and subsequently in combat, in the West African colony of Guinea-Bissau. via Norman Taylor

flag. What was originally scheduled as an eight-day deployment ended up keeping the Sabres outside Portugal until October 1964!

The detachment was led by Maj. Ramiro de Almeida Santos, and the ferry flight began on 9 August 1961, the aircraft arriving on the 15 August. The 2,300mi (3,680km) trip was the longest flight made by Forca Aerea Portuguesa (FAP) aircraft at the time.

Portuguese forces were fighting guerrillas in what was to become Guinea-Bissau (as well as in another colony, Mozambique). The Sabres went into action at Port Guinea as ground-attack and close-support aircraft. Over time, they flew 577 combat missions. Though every one of the Sabres was hit by ground fire at one time or another, none was lost. The last Sabre mission of the Guinea-Bissau conflict was flown by Maj. Barbeitos de Sousa on 20 October 1964.

At one time, the Portuguese had plans to obtain Canadair CL-13B Sabre 6s from West Germany and to deploy them to Mozambique, another segment of Africa where they were losing in the struggle for colonialism. The FAP's Col. Gomes do Amaral test-flew the Sabre 6. However, the United States and Canada applied pressure on the West German government not to transfer the Sabre 6s. A compromise was reached under which West Germany supplied 40 Fiat G.91R4 aircraft instead.

Initially, FAP F-86F Sabres were flown in natural metal with the national insignia on the vertical fin and the Cruz de Cristo (national insignia)

Canadair CL-13B Sabre Mark 6, aircraft 361 (23680) was one of the first Sabres to be withdrawn from SAAF service, and never received the camouflage scheme seen on SAAF Sabres in the 1970s. At Lanseria airport near Johannesburg, 361 wears the natural metal and the blue fuselage band associated with No. 1 Squadron (the other South African Sabre unit, No. 2 Cheetah Squadron, had a red band on its Canadair aircraft). This Sabre is to be preserved for the SAAF Museum. L. J. Vosloo

In 1974, South Africa began painting its surviving Sabres, piecemeal, in a camouflage color scheme consisting of deep buff and olive drab upper surfaces and light Admiralty gray undersurfaces. By this time, most surviving Sabres were being transferred to No. 85 Advanced Flying School at AFB Pietersbury, Northern Transvaal. The school's badge appears on the tail of the Sabre. L. J. Vosloo

on both sides of the fuselage and both wings. Squadron identification was in the form of painted vertical tail, wing tips, and intake ring. On early paint schemes, the intake ring was not painted on its internal surface. Colors were dark blue for Esc. 51 and red for Esc. 52. In later service, FAP Sabres were painted pale gray overall, with similar national markings. At all times the last three numbers of the s/n were applied to the nose, below the cockpit, in 1.6ft (0.5m) numbers.

Portuguese squadron details:

Esc. 51 was formed as Esc. 50 at BA 2, Ota, in October 1958 and was renamed Esc. 51 that same month. The squadron moved to BA 5, Monte Real, on 4 October 1959. To further confuse its brief history, the squadron was renamed Esc. 201 but was disbanded when Sabres were removed from FAP service. The squadron was known throughout its career as the Falcoes (Falcons).

Esc. 52 was formed at BA 2, Ota, in October 1958 and moved to BA 5, Monte Real, in October 1959. Named Aguias (Eagles) and later Galos (Cockerels), the squadron was disbanded in 1961.

The 65 F-86Fs assigned to Portugal, in the order of their FAP numbers (5301/5365) were: 52-5168/5169, -5171, -5176, -5178/5180, -5183, -5189, -5194, -5206/5208, -5210, -5240, -5242/5243, -5254, -5262, -5268; 53-1090, -1097, -1154, -1209, -1213; 52-5170, -5181/5182, -5201, -5205; 53-1144, -1225; 52-5184/5185, -5197/5199, -5204, -5220/5221, -5252, -5263, -5265, -5267, -5271; 53-1073, -1083, -1092, -1100, -1110, -1115/1116, -1134, -1136, -1152, -1156, -1164, -1170, -1188, -1190, 1204, -1223/1224; 52-5083/5084.

Saudi Arabia

The Royal Saudi Air Force received 16 F-86F Sabres in 1958, all from the United States, and may have received three more F-86Fs from Norway in 1966. Not all of these entered service because of a spares shortages but those that did served with No. 7 Squadron at Dhahran. Withdrawal of the Sabres from service began in 1966 but was not completed until the early 1970s when they were replaced by Northrop F-5 Freedom Fighters.

Known serial numbers for the Saudi F-86Fs are 52-4497, -5021, -5056, -5136, -5278; 53-1072, -1089, -1098, -1114, -1122, -1133, -1185.

South Africa

The SAAF's No. 2 Squadron Flying Cheetahs fought in the Korean War in F-51 Mustangs, which they surrendered on 31 December 1952. The squadron then moved to K-55 Osan AB, Korea, and received the first of 22 F-86F-30 Sabres on loan from the USAF. After intensive training, operational flying was resumed on 16 March 1953. In addition to ground-attack work, the squadron then undertook fighter sweeps along the Yalu and Chonjong rivers, and routine patrols, and by the time the armistice was signed on 27 July 1953, SAAF Sabres had flown 2,032 sorties with the loss of four aircraft (plus one postwar loss). The squadron returned to South Africa in October 1953, returning its Sabres to the USAF.

In 1955, South Africa selected the Canadair CL-13B Sabre Mark 6, and 34 were ordered from Canada (SAAF s/ns 350/383, RCAF s/ns 23669/23702). Delivery began in April 1956. No. 2 Squadron, home from Korea at Waterkloof, flew the Sabres until converting to Mirage III fighters in the mid-1960s. No. 1 Squadron, also at Waterkloof, then operated CL-13B Sabre Mark 6s until 1976 when it became the first unit to receive Mirage F.1AZ ground-attack fighters.

F-86F-30-NA Sabres operated by the SAAF in Korea:

SAAF	USAF	Disposition	Nickname
601/A	52-4352	Returned to USAF, to CNAF	*Shernador II / Renlins*
602/J*	52-4361	Returned to USAF, to CNAF	*Imp VIII*
603/B	52-4315	Returned to USAF, to CNAF	*Ruth 1*
604/K	52-4311	Returned to USAF, to CNAF	*Black Dick*
605/C	52-4313	Returned to USAF, to CNAF	*Sharonne*
606/L	52-4316	Returned to USAF, to CNAF	*Little Phylis / Tomtitt*
607/D	52-4320	Returned to USAF, to CNAF	*Just Joan*
608/M	52-4348	Written off 28 February 1953	
609/E	52-4321	Returned to USAF, to CNAF	*Malobola*
610/N	52-4333	Returned to USAF, to CNAF	*Glow Worm*
611/F	52-4310	Returned to USAF, to CNAF	
612/O	52-4326	Returned to USAF, to CNAF	*Stardust*
613/G	52-4327	Written off 21 April 1953	*Bevkeneve*
614/P	52-4355	Written off 28 August 1953	
615/H	52-4331	Written off 19 April 1953	*Kevric*
616/Q	52-4368	Written off 21 July 1953	
617/I	52-4346	Returned to USAF, to CNAF	
618/?	52-4359	Returned to USAF, to CNAF	
619/M	52-4344	Written off 19 May 1953	
620/?	52-4386	Returned to USAF, to CNAF	
621/G	52-4412	Returned to USAF, to CNAF	
622/R	52-4572	Returned to USAF, to CNAF	

RF-86F Sabre reconnaissance aircraft (52-4874) of the 10th Fighter Wing, ROKAF, taxying at Kimpo AB in May 1968. This aircraft was converted to its reconnaissance role in Project Haymaker and has different camera systems than the RF-86A of the Korean War. Note the red / maroon canopy rail with the pilot's name inscribed in hangul, the Korean phonetic alphabet. The USAF buzz number has been reduced to the last three digits of the s / n, minus the FU prefix found on American Sabres.
Stephen H. Miller

South Korea

The Republic of Korea Air Force (ROKAF), or Taehan Minguk Kong-gun, operated F-86D, F-86F, and RF-86F Sabres. The first batch of five F-86Fs were delivered on 20 June 1955. Little information about ROKAF structure has ever been released, but it's understood that all Sabres served in squadrons under the ROKAF's 10th Wing.

The ROKAF ended up being one of the last users of the Sabre. Of 122 F-86Fs and RF-86Fs and 40 F-86Ds supplied to the Koreans from 1955 to 1958, as many as 50 were retired from service only in the late 1980s. In fact, as late as 1988 plans existed to convert surviving F-86Fs into unmanned surface-to-surface cruise missiles, similar to the Martin TM-61A Matador of the 1950s.

Only a partial list of ROKAF s/ns has surfaced. These are F-86F-25-NA and F-86F-30-NA Sabres turned over to the Koreans between June 1955 and June 1956:

51-13175, -13187, -13191/13192, -13199, -13201, -13203, -13207, -13215, -13217, -13229, -13243, -13246, -13248, -13260, -13270, -13272, -13279, -13289, -13317, -13324, -13336, -13345, -13389, -13413, -13422; 52-4305, -4308, -4388, -4565, -4631, -4647, -4651, -4753, -4755, -4761, -4764, -4789, -4791/4792, -4837, -4854, -4907, -4912, -4917, -4919, -4921/4923, -4925/4926, -4940, -4946, -5459, -5454, -5468, -5402, -5417, -5424, -5428/5429, -5441, -5445, -5455, -5499, -5517.

Spain

Though it refrained from joining the NATO alliance at the height of the Cold War, Spain has always had close ties with the United States and has

R.O.K. AIR FORCE
RESCUE

enjoyed a military relationship based on the Spanish-American Defense Treaty of 26 September 1953. In the 1950s, the air defense of Spain rested in the hands of a three-wing day interceptor force of the country's air force, or Ejercito del Aire, which operated 270 F-86F Sabres, beginning in 1955. Each of the three wings comprised three squadrons of 25 aircraft each.

The creation of the Sabre force was preceded by arrival in Spain in 1954 of US training personnel and equipment. A jet school, or escuela de reaccion, was established at Talavera la Real, Badajoz, where six USAF-staffed mobile training units familiarized pilots with jet operating techniques. The first 25 Sabres arrived in September 1955.

The F-86F Sabre was given the Spanish designation C.5. In keeping with the Spanish air arm's custom, all Ejercito del Aire Sabres were given new s/ns C.5-1 to C.5-270, although at least one was apparently mistakenly numbered C.5-259.

Ala de Caza 1 (Fighter Wing 1) was based at Manises beginning in 1955 with Escuadrone 11 (Fighter Squadron 11), which was assigned the squadron color red. The squadron was redesignated Esc. 101, and its parent unit was redesignated AdC 11 in 1965. This interceptor wing was also host to Esc. 12 at Manises from 1955, color blue. This fighter wing formed an aerobatic team, the Ascuas, named after the call sign of one of the pilots who was known as Ascua (Arrowhead). The flight demonstration team used at least four Sabres, painted in a wild yellow-and-red paint scheme, from the early 1950s until being disbanded in 1963.

AdC. 2 was based at Zaragoza from 1955, with Esc. 21, color black.

Sidewinder-equipped F-86D-50-NA Sabre all-weather interceptor (52-9985) of the ROKAF's 10th Wing at Suwon AB on 8 May 1968. In more recent years, an F-86D has been preserved as a gate guardian at the entrance to Suwon, the base from which American Sabres operated during the Korean War. Unfortunately, details about squadrons and s/ns are difficult to obtain from ROKAF headquarters in Yongdongpo. Stephen H. Miller

AdC. 4 made its home at Son San Juan from 1955 until disbanding in (apparently) 1964 and was responsible for Esc. 41, green.

AdC. 5 was based at Moron from 1955, with Esc. 51, having an orange squadron color.

AdC. 6 at Getafe was parent unit for Esc.61, which was formed on 1 April 1958 with 25 Sabres and six T-33A Shooting Stars. In May 1959, this squadron moved to Torrejon, the best-known Spanish air base near Madrid, and continued operating Sabres until re-equipping with the Lockheed F-104G Starfighter in March 1965. This squadron's color was white. This squadron and wing were redesignated Esc. 102/Adc. 16 in about 1965, possibly before giving up its last Sabres.

Other Spanish squadrons, on which details are sparse, include Esc. 103, 151, 201, and 732. The last user of the Sabre was Esc. 732, which phased out its last aircraft (C.5-199, coded 732-9) at the end of 1974.

The last Sabre was delivered in 1958. All of these were F-86F-20, 25, and 30 block airplanes and most were modified to F-86F-40 standard by CASA.

Today, a dozen or so Sabres are preserved in Spain and one example is in Ascuas colors at the Museo del Aire, Cuatro Vientos. One Sabre is on display at Torrejon, namely C.5-82 (former USAF 55-3966) while another is mounted on exhibit at Moron (C.5-231, alias former USAF 52-5307). Two Spanish F-86Fs were delivered to Colombia in January 1963.

Aircraft that served in Spain include: 51-13079, -13086, -13088, -13089, -13116, -13118, -13121, -13125, -13126, -13130, -13137, -13145, -13152, -13164, -13180, -13182, -13186, -13189, -13192, -13194, -13218, -13220, -13226, -13228, -13232, -13234, -13236, -13237, -13239, -13245, -13254, -13267, -13312, -13315, -13328, -13333, -13339, -13340 (all of the preceding being F-86F-20); and 51-13094, -13098, -13099, -13179, -13200, -13211, -13258, -13277, -13287, -13308, -13313, -13325, -13341, -13351, -13354, -13358, -13370, -13378, -13388, -13398, -13402, -13404, -13408, -13412, -13417, -13418, -13421, -13427; 52-5292, -5376 (all F-86F-25); and 52-4502, -4566, -4570, -4571, -4585, -4599, -4602, -4606, -4612, -4644, -4668, -46789, -4680, -4712.

A linkup between USAF s/ns and the numbers assigned by Spain has not previously been published. They are:

Spanish s/ns	**USAF** s/ns	**Model**
C.5-1	51-13194	F-86F-25
C.5-2	51-13239	F-86F-25
C.5-3	52-5376	F-86F-25
C.5-4	51-13086	F-86F-20
C.5-5	51-13125	F-86F-20
C.5-6	51-13137	F-86F-20
C.5-7	51-13152	F-86F-20
C.5-8	51-13079	F-86F-20
C.5-9	51-13089	F-86F-20
C.5-10	51-13121	F-86F-20
C.5-11	52-4612	F-86F-30
C.5-12	52-4668	F-86F-30
C.5-13	51-13118	F-86F-20
C.5-14	51-13130	F-86F-20
C.5-15	51-13164	F-86F-20
C.5-16	51-13218	F-86F-25
C.5-17	51-13339	F-86F-25
C.5-18	51-13274	F-86F-25
C.5-19	51-13145	F-86F-20
C.5-20	51-13180	F-86F-25
C.5-21	51-13126	F-86F-20
C.5-22	51-13234	F-86F-25
C.5-23	52-5292	F-86F-25
C.5-24	51-13301	F-86F-25
C.5-25	51-13189	F-86F-25
C.5-26	51-13269	F-86F-25
C.5-27	51-13116	F-86F-20
C.5-28	51-13233	F-86F-25
C.5-29	51-13193	F-86F-25
C.5-30	51-13303	F-86F-25
C.5-31	51-13236	F-86F-25
C.5-32	51-13267	F-86F-25
C.5-33	51-13288	F-86F-20
C.5-34	51-13307	F-86F-25
C.5-35	51-13312	F-86F-25
C.5-36	51-13328	F-86F-25
C.5-37	51-13182	F-86F-25
C.5-38	51-13088	F-86F-20
C.5-39	51-13237	F-86F-25
C.5-40	51-13254	F-86F-25
C.5-41	51-13228	F-86F-25
C.5-42	51-13293	F-86F-25
C.5-43	51-13333	F-86F-25
C.5-44	51-13186	F-86F-25
C.5-45	51-13226	F-86F-25
C.5-46	51-13232	F-86F-25
C.5-47	52-4500	F-86F-30
C.5-48	51-13220	F-86F-25
C.5-49	51-13245	F-86F-25
C.5-50	52-4712	F-86F-30
C.5-51	52-4678	F-86F-30
C.5-52	52-4566	F-86F-30
C.5-53	52-4644	F-86F-30
C.5-54	51-13315	F-86F-25
C.5-55	51-13340	F-86F-25
C.5-56	52-4570	F-86F-30
C.5-57	52-4585	F-86F-30
C.5-58	52-4594	F-86F-30
C.5-59	52-4606	F-86F-30
C.5-60	52-4502	F-86F-30
C.5-61	52-4602	F-86F-30
C.5-62	52-4680	F-86F-30
C.5-63	52-4571	F-86F-30
C.5-64	52-4655	F-86F-30
C.5-65	52-5369	F-86F-25
C.5-66	52-4600	F-86F-30
C.5-67	52-4722	F-86F-30
C.5-68	52-4642	F-86F-30
C.5-69	52-4677	F-86F-30
C.5-70	52-4683	F-86F-30
C.5-71	52-4718	F-86F-30
C.5-72	52-4685	F-86F-30
C.5-73	55-3950	F-86F-40
C.5-74	55-3952	F-86F-40
C.5-75	55-3953	F-86F-40
C.5-76	55-3957	F-86F-40
C.5-77	55-3958	F-86F-40
C.5-78	55-3959	F-86F-40
C.5-79	55-3960	F-86F-40
C.5-80	55-3963	F-86F-40
C.5-81	55-3965	F-86F-40
C.5-82	55-3966	F-86F-40
C.5-83	55-3970	F-86F-40
C.5-84	55-3980	F-86F-40
C.5-85	52-4653	F-86F-30
C.5-86	52-4672	F-86F-30
C.5-87	52-4561	F-86F-30
C.5-88	52-4670	F-86F-30
C.5-89	55-3941	F-86F-40
C.5-90	55-3955	F-86F-40
C.5-91	55-3964	F-86F-40
C.5-92	55-3968	F-86F-40
C.5-93	55-3962	F-86F-40
C.5-94	55-3973	F-86F-40
C.5-95	55-3974	F-86F-40
C.5-96	55-3975	F-86F-40
C.5-97	55-3979	F-86F-40
C.5-98	55-3982	F-86F-40
C.5-99	55-3983	F-86F-40
C.5-100	55-3984	F-86F-40
C.5-101	55-4000	F-86F-40
C.5-102	55-3993	F-86F-40
C.5-103	55-3995	F-86F-40
C.5-104	55-3990	F-86F-40
C.5-105	55-3961	F-86F-40
C.5-106	55-4002	F-86F-40
C.5-107	55-3981	F-86F-40
C.5-108	55-3994	F-86F-40
C.5-109	55-3976	F-86F-40
C.5-110	55-3956	F-86F-40
C.5-111	51-13094	F-86F-20
C.5-112	51-13142	F-86F-20
C.5-113	55-3967	F-86F-40
C.5-114	55-3969	F-86F-40
C.5-115	55-3972	F-86F-40
C.5-116	55-3977	F-86F-40
C.5-117	55-3978	F-86F-40
C.5-118	55-3986	F-86F-40
C.5-119	55-3987	F-86F-40
C.5-120	55-3988	F-86F-40
C.5-121	55-3996	F-86F-40
C.5-122	55-3997	F-86F-40
C.5-123	55-3999	F-86F-40
C.5-124	55-4003	F-86F-40
C.5-125	55-4007	F-86F-40
C.5-126	55-4009	F-86F-40
C.5-127	55-3989	F-86F-40
C.5-128	55-3992	F-86F-40
C.5-129	55-4001	F-86F-40
C.5-130	55-4004	F-86F-40
C.5-131	55-4005	F-86F-40
C.5-132	55-4006	F-86F-40
C.5-133	55-4008	F-86F-40
C.5-134	55-4012	F-86F-40
C.5-135	55-4014	F-86F-40
C.5-136	55-4016	F-86F-40
C.5-137	55-4017	F-86F-40
C.5-138	55-3991	F-86F-40
C.5-139	52-4503	F-86F-30
C.5-140	52-4661	F-86F-30
C.5-141	51-13098	F-86F-20
C.5-142	51-13200	F-86F-25
C.5-143	55-3971	F-86F-40
C.5-144	55-3985	F-86F-40
C.5-145	55-3998	F-86F-40
C.5-146	51-13211	F-86F-25
C.5-147	52-4593	F-86F-30
C.5-148	52-4601	F-86F-30
C.5-149	52-4713	F-86F-30
C.5-150	51-13277	F-86F-25
C.5-151	51-13287	F-86F-25
C.5-152	51-13325	F-86F-25
C.5-153	53-13439	F-86F-25
C.5-154	51-13468	F-86F-25
C.5-155	51-13481	F-86F-25
C.5-156	55-4015	F-86F-40
C.5-157	52-5276	F-86F-25
C.5-158	52-5347	F-86F-25
C.5-159	51-13308	F-86F-25
C.5-160	51-13428	F-86F-25
C.5-161	51-13507	F-86F-25
C.5-162	52-5277	F-86F-25
C.5-163	52-5372	F-86F-25
C.5-164	52-5354	F-86F-25
C.5-165	51-13487	F-86F-25
C.5-166	51-13415	F-86F-25
C.5-167	52-5371	F-86F-25
C.5-168	51-13408	F-86F-26
C.5-169	51-13432	F-86F-25

Spanish	USAF	Model
C.5-170	51-13444	F-86F-25
C.5-171	51-13469	F-86F-25
C.5-172	55-4011	F-86F-40
C.5-173	51-13430	F-86F-25
C.5-174	51-13451	F-86F-25
C.5-1755	1-13466	F-86F-25
C.5-176	51-13354	F-86F-25
C.5-177	51-13402	F-86F-25
C.5-178	51-13427	F-86F-25
C.5-179	51-13370	F-86F-25
C.5-180	51-13378	F-86F-25
C.5-181	51-13391	F-86F-25
C.5-182	51-13431	F-86F-25
C.5-183	51-13470	F-86F-25
C.5-184	51-13388	F-86F-25
C.5-185	51-13482	F-86F-25
C.5-186	52-5405	F-86F-25
C.5-187	51-13400	F-86F-25
C.5-188	51-13457	F-86F-25
C.5-189	51-13409	F-86F-25
C.5-190	51-13437	F-86F-25
C.5-191	51-13455	F-86F-25
C.5-192	51-13099	F-86F-25
C.5-193	51-13418	F-86F-25
C.5-194	52-5329	F-86F-25
C.5-195	51-13351	F-86F-25
C.5-196	51-13485	F-86F-25
C.5-197	52-5423	F-86F-25
C.5-198	52-5310	F-86F-25
C.5-199	52-5330	F-86F-25
C.5-200	51-13421	F-86F-25
C.5-201	51-13441	F-86F-25
C.5-202	52-5274	F-86F-25
C.5-203	52-5272	F-86F-25
C.5-204	52-5311	F-86F-25
C.5-205	52-5336	F-86F-25
C.5-206	52-5328	F-86F-25
C.5-207	51-13412	F-86F-25
C.5-208	51-13464	F-86F-25
C.5-209	52-5304	F-86F-25
C.5-210	52-5324	F-86F-25
C.5-211	52-5317	F-86F-25
C.5-212	52-5333	F-86F-25
C.5-213	52-5275	F-86F-25
C.5-214	52-5312	F-86F-25
C.5-215	52-5341	F-86F-25
C.5-216	52-5343	F-86F-25
C.5-217	52-5360	F-86F-25
C.5-218	52-5287	F-86F-25
C.5-219	52-5296	F-86F-25
C.5-220	52-5318	F-86F-25
C.5-221	52-5285	F-86F-25
C.5-222	51-13443	F-86F-25
C.5-223	51-13450	F-86F-25
C.5-224	52-5409	F-86F-25
C.5-225	51-13458	F-86F-25
C.5-226	51-13500	F-86F-25
C.5-227	52-5315	F-86F-25
C.5-228	51-13424	F-86F-25
C.5-229	52-5273	F-86F-25
C.5-230	52-5293	F-86F-25
C.5-231	52-5307	F-86F-25
C.5-232	52-5392	F-86F-25
C.5-233	52-5314	F-86F-25
C.5-234	52-5375	F-86F-25
C.5-235	51-13417	F-86F-25
C.5-236	51-13463	F-86F-25
C.5-237	51-13221	F-86F-25
C.5-238	51-13446	F-86F-25
C.5-239	51-13454	F-86F-25
C.5-240	51-13459	F-86F-25
C.5-241	51-13462	F-86F-25
C.5-242	51-13498	F-86F-25
C.5-243	52-5291	F-86F-25
C.5-244	52-5416	F-86F-25
C.5-245	51-13434	F-86F-25
C.5-246	51-13478	F-86F-25
C.5-247	52-5355	F-86F-25
C.5-248	52-5398	F-86F-25
C.5-249	52-5350	F-86F-25
C.5-250	52-5379	F-86F-25
C.5-251	51-13399	F-86F-25
C.5-252	51-13489	F-86F-25
C.5-253	51-13358	F-86F-25
C.5-254	52-5400	F-86F-25
C.5-255	52-5241	F-86F-25
C.5-256	51-13483	F-86F-25
C.5-257	51-13497	F-86F-25
C.5-258	52-5281	F-86F-25
C.5-259	51-13404	F-86F-25
C.5-260	51-13416	F-86F-25
C.5-261	51-13398	F-86F-25
C.5-262	52-5284	F-86F-25
C.5-263	52-5418	F-86F-25
C.5-264	52-5290	F-86F-25
C.5-265	52-5308	F-86F-25
C.5-266	52-5334	F-86F-25
C.5-267	52-5435	F-86F-25
C.5-268	52-5359	F-86F-25
C.5-269	51-13493	F-86F-25
C.5-270	52-5302	F-86F-25

Thailand

The Royal Thai Air Force (RTAF) operated 40 F-86F Sabres, the last of which was delivered in March 1962, until they were replaced in 1966 by Northrop F-5 Freedom Fighters. Thailand was also the only export customer for the F-86L Sabre.

The F-86F Sabres served with Nos. 12, 13, and 43 Squadrons. The F-86Ls served with No. 12 Squadron.

Tunisia

Information about Sabre operations by Tunisia's modest air force has eluded many researchers in the United States and Europe. It appears that 15 F-86F Sabres (12, according to some sources) were delivered to Tunisia in 1969, all of them being former USAF inventory aircraft. Tunisia replaced these with the Macchi MB-326K in 1978.

Turkey

The Turkish Air Force, or Turk Hava Kuvvetleri (THK) operated a variety of Sabres beginning in July 1954 when 102 Canadair CL-13 Sabre Mark 2s, also known as F-86E(M), were delivered from Canada. These aircraft formed the core of Nos. 141, 142, and 143 Squadrons at Merzifon and Eskisehir, providing fighter cover over Turkey. Turkish forces are part of NATO and would come under NATO command in wartime, but they also maintain Ankara's long standing animosity with its Greek neighbor.

Turkey also received 12 NAA F-86F Sabres in 1958, by which time the THK was suffering major spares deficits despite direct support from Canadair. Soon thereafter, 50 NAA F-86D Sabres were delivered and took over part of the air-defense mission from the F-86E(M) and F-86F fighters. Subsequently, Turkey also acquired 40 F-86Ks.

The F-86E(M)/F squadrons served until 1966. The F-86D and F-86K aircraft remained in service until 1969.

A nearly complete list of Turkish Canadair CL-13 Sabre Mark 2s, listed by their RCAF s/ns:

19103, 19120, 19124, 19126, 19129/19130, 19134, 19138/19139, 19147, 19150, 19153, 19157, 19160, 19162, 19164/19166, 19173, 19175/19176, 19179/19180, 19183/19184, 19190, 19192, 19194/19195, 19197/19198, 19203, 19207, 19214/19217, 19223, 19226/19227, 19230/19232, 19236, 19241/19242, 19247/19249, 19268, 19270, 19275, 19286, 19289, 19301, 19314, 19317/19318, 19325, 19335, 19337/19338, 19342, 19353/19354, 19359, 19364, 19371, 19373, 19375/19376, 19379/19380, 19385/19387, 19389, 19391, 19394, 19396, 19399, 19401, 19405/19406, 19408, 19410, 19412/19415, 19419/19421, 19427, 19431, 19435, 19437, 19439, 19441, 19445/19446, 19449/19451.

Venezuela

The Venezuelan air arm, or Fuerzas Aereas Venezolanas (FAV)

A F-86F Sabre, one of 30 operated by the Venezuelan air arm, or Fuerzas Aereas Venezolanas (FAV), possibly seen in Miami while en route for delivery in October 1955. Very little information about Venezuela's use of the Sabre has been disclosed. Harold G. Martin

operated 30 NAA F-86F Sabres and 74 NAA/Fiat F-86K Sabres.

The F-86Fs were delivered in October 1955 (6 aircraft), February 1957 (5), and December 1960 (19). Only the s/ns of the first six have been confirmed, these being 52-4614, -4660, -4682, -4689/4690, -4736. F-86F units included Grupo Aerea de Caza No. 12, Escuadron de Caza 36 Jaguares, and possibly Escuadron de Cazas 37 and 38

Included in its own F-86K total, Venezuela received many of West Germany's 51 NAA F-86K Sabre all-weather interceptors from the Luftwaffe's total of 67 flyable and 31 non-flyable airframes. F-86Ks were flown by Escuadron de Cazas 34 and 35, and may have equipped 36 (with F-86Fs) for a time.

Four F-86Fs joined in an attempted revolt on 1 January 1958, making a number of low-level flights over Caracas. They strafed the heavily-defended presidential palace at Miraflores, the ministry of defense, and the national security headquarters. At least one was hit by antiaircraft fire.

At least six F-86Fs were lost to accidents and at least nine were sold to Bolivia. The F-86Ks proved a maintenance nightmare, with at least 27 mishaps attributed to various causes. Most, if not all, were grounded July 1969 with over-age hydraulic hoses. Of the total, at least 15 still wore their original USAF colors and s/ns as of October 1990 in a storage area and FAV s/ns for these, while assigned, were obviously not worn.

The Venezuelan s/ns applied to Sabres are a prototype for the Byzantine art of number-crunching. F-86Fs were initially serialed as, for example, 1 B 36, 2 C 36, etc., in "plane in group" fashion with the first number the individual aircraft within escuadron, the letter (A,B, or C) indicating the esquadrilha within the escuadron. Later, a completely random serialing system was adopted and at least 14 F-86Fs received random numbers (0310, 0674, 9478, 0900, 9518, 0493, 5936, and so on).

F-86Ks received random s/ns from the outset, including 0002, 0005, 0011, 0926, 0960, 1130, and others. It appears that of the total of 74 F-86Ks received, about 27 were cannibalized for parts from the outset while five others were sold to Honduras in 1969.

F-86K Sabres transferred to Venezuela from West Germany were: 55-4866, -4895/4896, -4898, -4901, -4907, -4910/4913, -4923, -4925, -4930; 56-4116/4118, 56-4121/4126, -4128/4129, -4131/4132, -4134/4144, -4146/4156, -4158/4160. An additional 24 F-86Ks may have been transferred solely for use as spares.

Yugoslavia

The Yugoslav Air Force, or Jugoslovensko Ratno Vazdhoplovstvo (JRV) began to receive 121 modified Canadair CL-13 Sabre Mark 2s and Mark 4s, also known as F-86E(M)s, in 1956. These were former RAF Sabres that temporarily belonged to the USAF during the transfer. Yugoslavia also purchased F-86D Sabres.

During a border incident in the late 1950s, a JRV Sabre Mark 4 shot down a Hungarian MiG-15.

Early JRV Sabre Mark 4s were delivered in the RAF camouflage for that period—upper surfaces in dark green and dark sea gray, and lower surfaces in PRU blue. Later aircraft arrived in natural metal finish.

Pilots from the 335th FIS (left to right): Capt. James Horowitz got one MiG and later wrote the novel The Hunters. *2nd Lt. James F. (Dad) Low became the 17th ace of the war six months out of flight school. Lieutenants Al Smiley and Coy Austin both seem impressed by the cigar belonging to Capt. Philip (Casey) Colman, one of several Korean War pilots who got four MiG kills. Red stars for aerial victories are painted on the barracks wall behind Horowitz's head, while Colman is holding a "Mach Riders of the Sky" patch.*
Martin Bambrick

CHAPTER FIVE

Pilot Talk

Capt. Karl Dittmer, 335th FIS/4th FIW, K-14, 1952, F-86F

Our biggest problem was locating MiGs. If someone spotted MiGs and had time, they'd usually give a call to let other flights know their location and general heading—like, "BLUE Flight here, we've got MiGs crossing the river near Antung, headed south." If you had just departed Kimpo, you'd have to make a guess as to how far the darn MiGs would get while you were traveling toward them. Some flight leaders would head for the place the MiGs were first spotted, then wonder why they never seemed to find MiGs.

Near the end of my tour they assigned a captain to my flight who had been teaching fighter tactics at Nellis. He was quite aggressive, and would be given my flight as soon as I rotated. For his first few missions I had him on my wing. My element leader was also aggressive, and would quite often spot other aircraft that he believed to be MiGs. I'd check them out and almost always decided they were friendly. Since it is quite difficult to maintain flight integrity in a fight, I'd always humor him and tell him to go check them out, that I would see him back at Kimpo. In addition, whenever another flight called out MiGs I'd head for their expected position.

My new man got quite cool toward me, and I'm sure he had decided that I was trying to avoid a fight. That changed when he learned I wasn't. The two of us found about 50 MiGs in one large loose gaggle. We jumped into the middle of them. This may sound stupid, but we had one very good advantage. I knew where my wingman was and he knew where I was, and we could shoot at everything else! We both had a grand time. I have no idea how many MiGs I hit, but got strikes on several. Finally I noticed a MiG cross below and in front of me. I made a turn that aligned me for an attack, used the excess altitude to get into excellent shooting position, then squeezed the trigger.

Nothing happened. I was out of ammunition. I was also very, very angry. If it had been possible, I would have yanked out the control stick and beat him on the head with it.

"Two, I'm out of ammo. Let's go home."

"Roger!"

He didn't mind flying with me after that.

One of the chores assigned to flight leaders was having to monitor our pilots during departure and arrival. The term for it was mobile control. We had to perform this function in what can best be called an auxiliary control tower that was towed to a spot about 50ft [15m] to the right and near the approach end of the runway.

Our function was to check for fluid leaks and proper configuration on birds pulling out onto the runway for takeoff, giving advice to pilots coming back with a problem, and warning pilots who appeared to be making unsafe approaches. I have a hunch the Wheels instigated this precaution after that guy messed up coming in after an earlier flyby.

One bright afternoon found me in the mobile-control unit on the north end of our airstrip. From the chatter on our radio, it was obvious the troops had found the MiGs. Shortly, flights were coming in with their noses blackened from firing their six .50cal guns.

Traffic had pretty well quit. When I heard a pilot call, "Kimpo, I'm about 30mi [48km] out at 15,000 [4,644m], flamed out."

"Roger, we're landing toward the south."

Capt. Karl Dittmer poses beside his F-86E Sabre, Betty Boots *of the 335th FIS/4th FIW at K-14 Kimpo AB. One of the few pilots who flew F-86F Sabres with rocket-assist bottles, Dittmer was both a MiG killer and a talented artist whose paint brush was very much in demand by other Sabre pilots.* Karl Dittmer

Three Marine Corsairs were taxying toward the runway. I pressed my mike button. "Kimpo Tower, hold those Corsairs short. We have an '86 coming in flamed out."

The Corsairs continued on. I repeated my call. No luck. They went onto the runway, with the leader and Three on the left, Two on the right. I screamed at the tower, "Get those damn Corsairs off the runway!"

The leader added throttle, took his time checking both magnetos, then slowly added power and accelerated down the runway. I continued to holler at the Corsairs to get the hell off.

Once the leader was well down the runway, Two went through his mag check, released brakes, and headed down the runway. I was still fuming over the mike. Three was just finishing his mag check when the flamed-out F-86 swooshed by him and touched down. Three, as if nothing had happened, released his brakes and passed the F-86 on his takeoff roll!

An acquaintance of mine was standing mobile duty on a day when traffic was toward the north and the MiGs were up. As the late arrivals were coming in two pilots reported coming in flamed out. One reported on a high base leg for landing toward the north. The other called, "I can't make it. I have to land toward the south." My acquaintance pressed his mike button. "Both of you keep to the right side of the runway!" Then, according to him, he closed his eyes. They got away with it.

When Dittmer wasn't hosing MiGs, he was decorating Sabres of the 335th FIS/4th FIW. Dittmer painted this F-86E-10-NA Sabre (51-2794) as the Newark Fireball for Capt. Henry A. (Hank) Crescibene (shown), who racked up a couple of MiG kills. Aircraft in the F-86E-10-NA series were actually F-86F Sabres in every respect except for the engine; they were redesignated F-86F-2-NA when retrofitted with the F model's more powerful version of the J47 turbojet engine. Karl Dittmer

The '86 pilots as a whole were doing their best to get into a fight with the MiGs. We usually put up one spare on most missions, to fill in should one bird in the group have mechanical problems. The 51st generally put up a spare, too. Both groups had the spare orbit over Cho Do Island until it was apparent they were not needed. Often, they wouldn't be needed and it was not unusual for the two pilots to join formation, hunt for a common radio channel using hand signals—and when they found a common frequency, to go north as a team. Some of these teams managed to get MiG kills.

On one nice day when I was not scheduled on the mission, a light colonel who commanded the Air Base Group flew *Betty Boots*, my bird [F-86E]. His wingman was flying one of the few F-86A models in our squadron. The A model had a conventional flight-control system, while all later birds had hydraulic-operated flight controls. The colonel spotted a MiG quite low, so he and his wingman made a very steep dive to attack. The colonel pulled out a bit too hard and blacked out briefly. Ain't no wonder, for the gauge that records Gs that have been applied to the aircraft leaves a needle at the highest reading and it indicated 11G. The bird is supposed to break at more than nine, but is stronger than engineered. Anyway, the colonel loused up his attack due to blacking out. His wingman's bird wouldn't come out of the dive as he intended and he ended

ROSIE

Dittmer's fellow pilot Marty Bambrick was standing next to an USAF photographer when Bambrick clicked off this shot, which is almost identical to an official picture. In the foreground is Bambrick's F-86A Sabre (49-1272), alias Wham Bam. *In the background, wearing two MiG kills at the time, is the F-86E Sabre (51-2769) nicknamed* Bernie's Bo, *belonging to Capt. Robert J. Love, the war's 11th jet ace.* Martin Bambrick

Previous page
Wearing a flying suit left over from World War II stocks, Capt. Troy G. Cope poses beside his F-86E Sabre, Rosie. *Cope was killed in combat in an engagement when rocket-boosted F-86F Sabres sought to engage MiGs at high altitude.* Karl Dittmer

up well below the MiG, so he didn't do any good either.

The overstress left some small wrinkles on the fuselage, just above the trailing edge of the wing. My bird was a bit faster after that.

After I had painted *Betty Boots*, Sabre pilot Henry Crescibene said he'd give me a case of beer to paint *Newark Fireball* on his bird. Next, I painted *Beep* for Nolli and *Gopher Patrol*, with a Disney-type gopher peering over the name for Major Thomas. I did *Chuck and Randy* for Manning and *Rosie* for Troy G. Cope. My final paint jobs were *Wham Bam* with a couple of Bugs Bunny-type rabbits for Marty Bambrick's bird, and *Jolley Roger*, with a skull and crossbones pirate flag on a splash of blood on the front of Clifford Jolley's hard hat. Both Bugs Bunny and Cliff's new helmet were on their first flights, after being painted, on the same mission.

The MiGs were up. Bambrick jumped a MiG only to have the MiG snap into a spin. MiG pilots sometimes had trouble recovering from spins, so Bambrick spiraled around his expected victim hoping the guy would punch out. He didn't. Instead, he recovered and hosed off a burst at Bambrick. One 23mm shell hit Bambrick's left wing close to the fuselage—right under the bird's new name. Bambrick limped his badly damaged bird home.

[Interviewed separately, Bambrick remembers that this hit was a 37mm. Separately, a 23mm went through the cockpit.].

Meanwhile, Cliff Jolley got into a fight and with fuel way low, broke out and headed for home. However, he didn't get away unscathed. A MiG

1st Lt. Martin G. Bambrick ought to be smiling, as he peers down at the harm inflicted to the main structure of his F-86A Sabre's wing by a 37mm cannon shell from a MiG-15. Bambrick was hit twice while flying with Jolley, Dittmer, Cope, and others in the 335th FIS. Martin Bambrick

hosed his bird with one cannon shell knocking off the left earpiece of his helmet. Jolley didn't have enough fuel to make it back, and had to eject over the Yellow Sea. He dropped the ruined helmet when approaching the water in order to see how close he was to it. Fortunately, the rescue helicopter picked him up OK. However, for some reason I got no more requests for paint jobs.

About the middle of September 1952, our squadron, the 335th FIS, was given six secret weapons. These were early F-86Fs that had been modified with three internal JATO [jet-assisted takeoff] bottles. These could be fired simultaneously or in train. The switch was to the left and a little aft of the throttle on the cockpit sidewall. Three of these birds had wing slats like our As and Es, while the other three had hard leading edges on the wings. We took two of each up on a local flight and played around with them. There was enough difference between the two that Cliff decided we would use them in pairs with the same wing configuration rather than mixing them in a flight. Our tests also indicated that the JATO was most effective when all were fired at once.

I flew three missions in the F in September and had mixed feelings about it. At altitude the bird would not hold altitude, but would insist on gaining height for several seconds, then losing it. No matter how hard I tried, I could not stop the damned thing from doing this. We only flew them as a two-ship element, with a floating lead, and they always seemed to be out of phase with each other. In a hard turn, they reacted worse than a Mustang with a full aft-fuselage tank. I mean they tried to swap ends and it took considerable forward stick to break the inevitable stall.

On the plus side, it sure was nice to have that extra 3,000lb (1,360kg) of thrust when you needed to close the gap between you and a MiG. And once the units were fired, the bird flew normally. I was flying one with Jolley shortly after he had his dunk in the Yellow Sea. Someone had reported MiGs well up river from Antung. We got into the area, but didn't see anything until we both hit bingo fuel. Just as we turned toward Kimpo, I spotted a lone MiG going toward Antung, on our side of the river. I called Jolley, and headed for him. Jolley mentioned our marginal fuel state. I elected to attack anyway, and closed to about 2,000ft (609m), barely in range for our .50s. I caught him with numerous bursts, but was hurrying my attack, and ran out of ammo before I realized I was closing to really effective range. I doubt that he made it to Antung, but we couldn't wait around to see.

I ran into MiGs on almost all of my last ten missions. I had discovered the significance of 32,000ft, which put me just below 10,000m. Apparently the MiG pilots liked to have the hands of their altimeters pointing at a nice round number!

Coming back from one mission, I spotted a MiG going south just below Ping Pong. He was about 300–400ft (91.5–122m) above me and I ended up about 200–300ft (61–91.5km) behind him on my intercept. I had my bird almost on a stall, trying to get more space and altitude. He knew I was trying for him. He S'ed a couple of times trying to get behind me. I was just starting to yank the nose up and fire a burst in front of him, in the hope that I could nail him before falling out of the damn sky, when he broke hard right. I broke right, but found him well out of range after my turn. Nuts.

Troy G. Cope and I had a couple of the secret weapons early in October. We were headed toward Antung about 50 or so miles out [80km] when Cope got behind a MiG and opened fire. After he fired his JATO and hosed off a few bursts, I saw a couple of MiGs coming up behind Cope. They were almost within range, so I called, "Cope, you have a couple coming up behind. Call the break when you get tired of shooting at that guy."

"DITT, BREAK LEFT!"

Hell, I was to Cope's left...I made a hard break to the left and saw a MiG go past my right wing, close enough to reach out and touch. I turned back to hose him.

"NO! NO!"

I whipped back to the left as another MiG went by less than 100ft (30.5m) to my right. By then my bird was in a complete stall. I pushed forward hard on the stick, trying to break the stall, then glanced back at both MiGs as they tried to get into shooting position and found myself still stalling and falling. They gave up after about 270deg of my stalled turn. I climbed back up to altitude and the two of us headed more or less parallel to the river, toward the coast. Shortly, I saw a pair of MiGs followed by another pair crossing in front of us. I made a turn to attack, approaching at about a 30deg angle to them. As we approached, I noticed that I was on a collision course with a third pair of MiGs! The leader was at my left and slightly high. If Cope was watching me he might not notice this pair. I called, "Cope, watch out for that other pair!"

By then I was at a critical spot, and whipped my bird up and to the right in a half roll that put me directly

Marty Bambrick and Hank Crescibene strike up typical fighter pilot poses beside Wham Bam, *alias F-86A Sabre (49-1272), the aircraft in which Bambrick shot down a MiG-15 in September 1952. Not seen in this photo is a Bugs Bunny likeness on the other side of the Sabre, painted by pilot and artist Karl Dittmer.* Martin Bambrick

Dittmer poses with Bambrick's Wham Bam *at Kimpo AB.* Karl Dittmer

over the lead MiG. That put him in a bad spot. I watched as he started to turn left, then right, then into a hard left turn. I rolled left and down. He crossed about 200ft (61m) in front of me and I considered hosing off a burst. I should have, because I could have ripped him to shreds. As it was, he headed up and swung back toward the north. I knocked a few holes in his tail, then fired my JATO in an attempt to catch him. While the JATO was on I called, "Cope, I've fired my weapon. Do you have me in sight?"

No response.

"Oh, hell," I thought. "He's hit that other MiG." As I approached the area I noticed numerous MiGs at different altitudes. All were milling around a pair of smoke columns coming up from the forest below.

I started to make a high-speed pass to see if I could identify the types of the crashed birds, but decided against it. I wish I had taken the chance, though it wouldn't have changed anything.

Ivan A. Holshausen, No. 2 Squadron, SAAF, 18th FBW, K-55, 1952, F-86F

Pilots in No. 2 Cheetah Squadron initially were World War II vets who stayed on in the SAAF as career officers. As time went on, most of this pool of pilots had done their tour in Korea, so young pilots who qualified during their national-service training were asked to volunteer for service in Korea.

At the time, there were three courses a year getting their wings with plus/minus 20 pilots per course getting their wings. A lot of these young guys, myself included, accepted three-year short service commissions.

The technical side followed much the same pattern. When I went on my operational training course, the SAAF knew the change from F-51s to F-86s was going to happen in the near future. So to cover all eventualities, my course did a full OTC [operational training course] on Spitfires, as all previous courses had done, and then we repeated the whole lot on Vampires. This was done at AFB Langebaanweg, which is 100mi [161km] north of Cape Town. There was only one more OTC [after mine] and only about six of them came out to Korea as replacements, mainly to fill the gaps left by guys returning home sick.

During the period we operated F-86s, we only had one aircraft shot down and one disappear, with a num-

Ivan Holshausen's aircraft was this F-86F-30-NA Sabre (52-4315), coded 603/B with No. 2 Cheetah Squadron and seen during a visit to Tsuiki AB, Japan, from its home airfield at Osan. While the 18th FBW had only one South African squadron, its two American squadrons also wore the South African colors seen on the vertical fin of Ruth II. *This F-86F has leading-edge slats, which Holshausen preferred. The 6-3 hard wing came with later F-86F models.* Richard Keener

ber suffering various degrees of damage. We were extremely lucky with the '86s, as the two USAF squadrons with us in the 18th FBW really had some bad times.

As an example, on the last napalm mission the '86s flew—policy was then changed so that '86s did no more napalming—20 aircraft took part. The date was 15 June 1953 and the target was a troop concentration at a village known, in the terminology we used then, as YD2477.

The first 16 Sabres to strike the target were USAF aircraft. The last four were SAAF, myself being number four, the last aircraft on the target. We dropped the bombs at about 50ft [15m] at around 350 knots [700km/h]. We were unable to drop at higher speeds because the fuses were not igniting the mix. The napalm tanks were fused at both front and back.

On that mission, five USAF aircraft suffered damage but no SAAF aircraft were hit. That's the luck of the draw. F-86s did not fly a lot of napalm missions and only our F-86F models were equipped to carry napalm.

When the decision was made for the 18th FBW to change to '86s, we then flew the F-51s back to Japan at the end of December 1952. We also moved to a new base that was still under construction, K-55 [Osan]. A technical training team came from either Japan or the USA and we did a ground school.

Whilst all this was going on, the brand-new F-86Fs started arriving and then the flying started. What a wonderful experience, flying the brand-new, fastest fighter in Korea! All our initial aircraft were the slotted leading-edge type, followed much later on by the solid leading-edge type. I much preferred the slots—a very docile aircraft that handled extremely well under all conditions.

We used to do a very tight circuit after the formation break with a very steep final and a very low quick flare, no problem. Not, however, with the solid leading edge as it would quite viciously drop a wing. On takeoff, with the solid leading-edge aircraft, one had to be careful to pull up the nose wheel before 90 knots, otherwise the nose wheel would not unstick. The upper air characteristics of the solid leading-edge aircraft I'm afraid I cannot recall, probably because it didn't frighten me so much away from the ground.

The F-86 was a real gentleman's aircraft. It was strong. It handled beautifully. It had a good ceiling. Not as good as the MiGs, though. It had good armament. It was a good gun platform. It carried a useful bomb load of either two 500-pounders or two 1,000-pounders, plus drop tanks.

When operating in the high altitudes in battle formation, one was sitting on the edge of maximum performance, so the widespread turns had to be handled very gently and they required a lot of experience to execute properly. If number two, three, or four in the formation fell behind in a turn, you were to put your nose down in a gentle dive to increase speed, get underneath the rest of the formation, and then gently over a period of time climb back into your position.

Most of our missions were ground attack, though we were called on from time to time to do air-to-air patrols along the Yalu and the Chongchon. My oddest air-to-air mission was when a single, unpainted '86 passed about 10,000ft [3,048m] below us, heading north. Radar told us to investigate. I was flying wingman to the leader, so the pair of us peeled off in an effort to overtake, but he was too far ahead and when he started losing height in the area of Mukden [across the Yalu] we were recalled.

In the last few weeks of the war, the Gooks started moving MiGs onto airfields just south of the Yalu. We were tasked to bomb these airfields. They were max range missions that we had never had occasion to do before.

We carried 500-pounders and, I think, 120gal drop tanks. The missions were worked out very carefully with the performance graphs, so the steep climb was performed very accurately. After each aircraft completed its attack, you turned and headed south, on your own, as there were insufficient fuel reserves to allow the formations to re-form.

A typical mission:

The wing would be tasked. It would then task the squadron or squadrons involved. In No. 2 Squadron, we had an A and B Flight. Our flight commanders would put up the pilots' names on the notice boards in our bungalows.

For briefing, we went to the main briefing room where the various specialist officers gave us the details. For example, the type of mission, where it was going, targets, defenses, latest call signs for Rescap, weather and intelligence. We marked our maps. Each squadron then went to its own operations room and kitted up— thermal suits in winter, in case one went for a swim—and then you were taken by truck to your aircraft. You did a thorough preflight check, strapped in, and waited for the start-up time.

The '86 is a very easy aircraft to start. After start-up—instruments and control checks, followed by radio check-in—the aircraft all taxied out in correct order to the runway, lining up in pairs. Each flight spooled up their engines, then took off in pairs, each pair being quite close to the pair ahead. Each four joined up on the climb out. The flight leaders checked with ground stations—one call sign, I remember, was KODAK.

On the climb out, each four checked in with its leader. You switched on the gunsight and gave a quick burst to check that guns were operating and that the tracer went through the pipper on the gunsight. We only used a few tracer at the beginning of the belts for this check, the theory being that tracer distracted your aiming if you used them all through the belt.

The four, or fours, were to all be in battle formation on the climb out and at operating height. On a ground attack mission, the leader would identify the target and, at the appropriate time, roll into the dive. Generally, we spaced ourselves out and did not follow the aircraft ahead, for obvious reasons.

On the climb out, we all climbed on a determined heading and joined up again and headed back to base. After landing, there was the usual debrief with a quick drink of whiskey, which was good for you, and a cigarette. One more to write up in your logbook. There were about 30 South African pilots who flew the F-86 in Korea. I managed to finish 75 missions, which was the highest total for a SAAF pilot.

During our training, naturally everybody tried to break the barrier at the first opportunity. On my first try, I climbed up to 35,000ft [10,668m], built up speed straight and level, then eased the nose forward into a steep dive. This was obviously the wrong technique. Even though the Mach meter was nudging 0.98 and then 0.99, the aircraft was vibrating terribly. Then the headrest came lose and fell onto the panel. I eased out of that dive, replaced the headrest, and analyzed the situation. I came to the conclusion that by putting it into a dive I was forcing it too much and was getting too much drag from the tailplane. So I again built up speed straight and level, rolled onto my back, and let the nose drop. At an angle of about 45deg, I got slight wing roll, and then I was through the barrier, showing, if I remember correctly, 1.07 Mach. It was as easy as that, and inverted as well.

Another time, an interceptor-wing F-86E came into our area and pulled in close to me, probably looking at my strange markings. It was an F-86E with the wide yellow band on the fuselage and fin, possibly from the 51st FIW. There we were, flying alongside each other. He then opened his throttle and raised his nose. I did the same. The F outclimbed the E and also left him behind. That extra bit of power certainly made a difference.

On photographs of 18th FBW aircraft, you will note the orange, white, and blue stripes on the fin. These are obviously the South African flag colors. The 18th FBW colors initially were a wide dark blue band with small white stars. This marking gave the impression of a high tailplane, similar to the MiG-15, so it was decided to change to the SAAF markings and all squadrons in the 18th, not just ours, used this tail marking.

Capt. Leonard W. (Bill) Lilley, 335th FIS/4th FIW, K-14, 1952, F-86E

As a 12-year-old, I made my first flight with Roscoe Turner. Turner's signature was a lion cub for a copilot. At an old pasture in Nebraska, after paying five dollars for the ride, I strapped into the airplane.

Roscoe Turner came out with a lot of fanfare, with the lion cub. He put the lion cub in the copilot's seat, closed everything up, and took off. Fumes from the engine quickly filled the cockpit, quickly filled the passenger cabin, and became mixed with the fumes of the lion cub. That was it, I decided. I swore at that point that I was never going to get off the ground again.

In 1942, I went to the US Military Academy with every intention of becoming an infantry officer like my dad. Then I found out what the infantry was all about. I changed my mind.

I was fortunate enough to qualify for pilot training. I went through that. I graduated at West Point and put my wings on in 1945. We had the accelerated course [at West Point], the three-year course. I flew P-40s, P-47s, and went to the Pacific with P-51 Mustangs. Eventually—by the time the Korean War came around—I had spent a lot of time in fighters and it was all post-World War II. I had listened to all the great stories, in the bars but had not flown in combat.

By the time Korea came along, I had 1,000hr in Mustangs but arrived in Korea with 40hr of F-86 time. I was a little bit uneasy about the airplane because I didn't feel completely comfortable with all its systems at the time.

I arrived in June 1952. The war had been going on for two years and was very stabilized. Though one of the more experienced fighter pilots in the USAF, I was far behind others who'd had 18 months to rack up MiG kills.

We had 150 F-86s in Korea at the time. The enemy was 19mi [30.5km] away [on the ground]. It was a very active war.

The MiGs were 200 nautical miles away, up behind the Yalu River. There were 1,500 MiGs at the various bases in Manchuria, Antung, Tatangkou, and Fen Chen. We could fly along that river and with binoculars we could count the airplanes on those airfields. Usually two of us went up and made a count—not of all 1,500 because Fen Chen was a little bit further. Technically we were not allowed to go up into Manchuria, although hot pursuit was authorized at times and that was very liberally interpreted.

My squadron had 25 airplanes. We had a mix of F-86A and F-86E Sabres, and the newer F-86F was just beginning to arrive. I flew the F-86E. Yellow [recognition] bands on the aircraft were very necessary because at more than 3,000ft [914m] angle-off, at certain angles-off, it was very difficult to tell the difference between a MiG and an F-86. Both had swept wings. The MiG had a big barn-door tail. Ours was rather narrow. The yellow stripe really helped us to tell the good guys from the bad guys.

Our average mission was 1hr 20min. The MiGs liked to come up and

Capt. Leonard W. (Bill) Lilley was an experienced fighter pilot when he became the 22nd American air ace of the Korean War during his 82nd mission on 18 November 1952, while flying a Canadair F-86E-6 Sabre (52-2834). Lilley racked up seven kills in all, while flying various Sabres. The others: 30 August 1952 (52-2855), 4 September 1952 (51-2764), 14 September 1952 (51-2764), 16 September 1952 (52-2833), 16 December 1952 (51-2815), and 14 January 1953 (50-0625). Lilley stressed the importance of teamwork and air discipline during his missions to MiG Alley.
USAF via R. A. Stevens

F-86 Sabres of the 4th FIW on the line at Kimpo. In the foreground is a well-traveled F-86E-1-NA Sabre (50-0625), in which Capt. Bill Lilley shot down his seventh MiG-15 during his 98th combat mission on 14 January 1953. Some of the aircraft in Lilley's 335th FIS were Canadair F-86E-6-CAN models. Karl Dittmer

have us drop those external tanks early because that then limited our time in the sensitive area. Every time we dropped those tanks it plucked at my heartstrings. One of the things I wanted at that time was a Chevrolet convertible. A Chevrolet convertible cost $2,000 and every time we punched those tanks off, it was $2,000. People in North Korea loved these tanks because they made them into water reservoirs and you see all kinds of pictures of very ingenious utilization of those tanks. When they had a big flight airborne and we got to punch off those tanks it looked like some of the chaff dropped in World War II, particularly when the sun was in the right position: it was really beautiful.

On my 34th mission, 30 August 1952, I was credited with a MiG kill. I felt that one of the Sabre's principal advantages was its all-flying tail, introduced in the F-86E model, which enabled the Sabre to make tight turns even in transonic ranges around Mach 1.0. With its six .50cal M3 machine guns with 267 rounds per gun, the Sabre had 17sec of fire compared with the MiG's 7sec. I noted, though, that when I scored hits, the Sabre's air intake was like a vacuum cleaner, sucking pieces of MiG. In most respects, in fact, the two fighters were about equal, but the MiG-15 could fly higher while the Sabre was being flown by more experienced pilots.

That all-flying tail was probably the secret of one of the great successes of the F-86 against the MiG. That tail was a hydraulically-activated tail. Just touching the control stick with your thumb when you're on the Mach turned you beautifully at that speed.

The MiGs didn't have that. And so therefore we were able in many cases to turn inside the MiG at those speeds if we could get them at those speeds—which was not often the case.

At K-14 Kimpo AB near Seoul, we always had four airplanes on alert. When we sat on alert, auxiliary power units [APUs] were all hooked up. Many times when the situation was a little [tense] we were in the cockpit, so all we had to do when we got the bell was start the airplane. Some of the troops were so eager that they pulled out the APU prematurely. We didn't have a lot of good luck on alerts at different times because people were so eager to get airborne. We'd get hot starts. We'd get a frenzy of activity where people would taxi into one another. There was no question at all of the overall desire and keenness of the American pilot to get at the MiGs.

Life at Kimpo was tense for those who worked on the Sabres. The crew chiefs would be all excited when our guns were fired—when you came back with the nose all smoked-up from firing. They knew that something had happened and they were very keen to get the story firsthand, to be the first to know what had happened.

My wingman was Canadian Sq. Ldr. Eric Smith. He flew night intrud-

Sq. Ldr. Eric G. Smith, on an exchange posting from the RCAF flew as wingman for Capt. Bill Lilley in the 335th FIS/4th FIW. When a friend held his camera for this portrait, however, Smith was climbing not into his own Sabre but into 1st Lt. Earl Brown's. The contribution of fully two dozen Canadian F-86 pilots in the 1950–1953 conflict is frequently overlooked. Canada had wanted to deploy its own fighter wing to Korea, but instead provided people and aircraft. Eric G. Smith

On 18 November 1952, Capt. Bill Lilley taxies in at Kimpo after shooting down his fifth MiG-15 to become the war's 22nd jet ace. Lilley achieved this feat while flying Col. Charles W. King's Canadair F-86E-6-CAN (52-2834). Confronting MiG bandit trains along the Yalu River, Lilley and his wingmen were almost always outnumbered and not all of their opponents, as advertised, were Chinese. Lilley came eyeball-to-eyeball with a MiG-15 pilot who was East German or Russian. Eric G. Smith

ers and Mosquitos in World War II, out of France. He was a Canadian exchange officer. A lot of people don't know that the Canadians rotated fighter pilots into our two groups to give them a taste of combat—as did the British and the South Africans.

We kept our airplanes in revetments and lived in crude buildings. We used to get visited by Bedcheck Charlie, which was a little, open-cockpit North Korean [Po-2] airplane. Bedcheck Charlie would come over and just harass us and drop hand grenades and mortar shells and the like. We had quad .50 antiaircraft guns and they hadn't been fired in so long that they wouldn't stop firing. I remember standing by one quad .50 and the sergeant kept telling the troops to stop firing. They wouldn't. Pretty soon you could see the barrels become red hot, and white hot, and then move on down the barrel and then the bullets just started wobbling out. They wobbled down into the revetments. We had something like six or eight [of our] aircraft damaged on one raid by our own guns.

The fighting along the Yalu River was often intense. In more recent times we tend to forget, but in Korea it was not uncommon for 300 jet fighters to be tangling with each other across hundreds of square miles of sky. After I had been credited with four MiGs, my big moment came on 18 November 1952 when I taxied in at Kimpo in a Canadair F-86E-6 (with the name Col.

Charles W. King on the canopy rails) after getting my fifth kill.

What was a typical mission like? One quick look at a mission. We flew with four aircraft. The aircraft took off in twos. As soon as you were airborne, the leader throttled back, very quickly, so three and four could catch up. Then the leader advanced the throttle until somebody started dropping back. Then he'd reduce the throttle, and lock the throttle. We'd climb at 400 knots to altitude. We cruised into the area. And we would normally set up a patrol along the Yalu River.

Those guys [the enemy] who had us on radar would wait until we had patrols on—unless we had fighter-bombers who were bombing the airfields, around Pyongyang. Then they would come over and try to intercept our fighter-bombers. At which point things got pretty active.

We always tried to stay together. At least two [of us]. [We sought] flight integrity with four aircraft—two down, two high. We worked very hard on tactics. We had excellent air discipline. That's probably the third reason that we did as well as we did: the people who were shot down, who came out of prison camp later, were people who invariably had been separated from their wingman and were locked on a MiG. In this game, at this time, you could not clear yourself. You could not work on your gunnery problem [alone]. It was totally impossible. You had to have that wingman clearing you all the time. Never take your eyes off the target. A guy I knew came out of prison camp and I said, "What happened?" They invariably said, "Well, I didn't watch my wingman but I was locked on to this guy, I had him cold, and...." He wasn't clearing himself and became a target.

A close-up of Sq. Ldr. Eric G. Smith's F-86E-6-CAN (52-2875). From this angle, details include the Sabre's speed brakes, all-flying horizontal tail, and yellow recognition bands. Eric G. Smith

A mission was 1hr 20min. If we became engaged, we had to drop our tanks. That limited our time in the area. We tried to leave [MiG Alley] with a thousand pounds of fuel. Many times, we didn't have that much fuel.

2nd Lt. James F. Low became the 17th and most junior American ace on 15 June 1952. Low was not the youngest ace, as often reported. He'd been an enlisted sailor in the Navy during World War II and, at 24, was a year older than the 51st Wing's Lt. Henry Buttelmann. Low's first-person account on these pages marks the first time he has described his controversial MiG killing spree, which brought his fifth kill a mere six months out of flying school. USAF via R. A. Stevens

We could get back [as far as Pyongyang] at 35,000ft [10,668m], we'd shut the engine down. Fortunately, we had tail winds from the northwest, coming out of Manchuria. If you shut down at 35,000ft over [Pyongyang] at 250 knots, you could arrive over [Kimpo] at 10,000ft [3,048m]. Then we would start up. That would give you enough fuel to make a power landing. Sometimes it wouldn't restart and you could usually make a dead-stick landing if there weren't too many other pilots making dead-stick landings.

The only time I ever saw the face of the enemy was when I was behind a MiG and fired at him. I was getting very good hits and pieces were coming off. I was very conscious of being close. At one point, I was getting ready to fire when his jet stream sort of punched me up and as I fired my tracers went right along the top of his fuselage as he ejected, and I saw strikes on his seat. The seat appeared to malfunction and rocked like this for a millisecond.

It was one of these moments in life that I'm sure all of you have had, where it was just an impression that you'll never forget as long as you live. I can see that just as clearly as I can see your face right now. His face went over my canopy. In fact, it missed my canopy by a foot. But it was such a flash, and there was this big shock of blond hair and a terribly distorted face, like the pictures you've seen of someone in a wind tunnel or in a centrifuge. And that's exactly what it was.

I went back to my CO [commanding officer], Col. Harrison Thyng later and he said, "How did it go?" I tried to explain because I was a little emotional and he was not very sympathetic with my emotions because [killing an enemy pilot] just represented one less person who would be up there tomorrow trying to make things difficult for us. That's what war's all about, I guess. We were pretty sure we were seeing Czechs and Russians and East Germans, Poles, all the satellite air forces.

Plus the Moscow Air Defense Force, we just loved them. Those guys were the hotshots. When they came up, we had very great battles with them. They were very good pilots. But we scored well against them because, again, I don't think they had the knowledge of air tactics that we did. I don't know if there really was an enemy pilot like Casey Jones, the character [in a novel]: we never saw the same guy twice. The only other time that I saw a fellow bail out, I made the mistake of flying by his parachute. Everything was black—his helmet, his suit, his gloves.

They were always fighting over their own territory. They never came south of the bomb line. So they could be very fierce. Some of the more experienced pilots felt that the safest thing to do when a Sabre was behind you was to hunker down behind the armor plate until the [MiG] was on fire and then eject, get out.

I never heard any stories about anybody being strafed in a parachute. In our squadron, we shot down 38 airplanes in the fall of 1952. We lost one man. He came out of prison camp after the war. We spent a lot of time playing ping-pong and working on aircraft recognition—there weren't that many aircraft to worry about—not like World War II.

I was hit one time with a 37 and a 23 and it had a tremendous impact, like the airplane just stopped. This fellow that I was scissoring with, I had overtaken him trying to get behind him. I didn't realize that he was shooting. I was pulling so hard trying to get behind him. And all of a sudden my airplane stopped: it felt like it stopped.

He hit me. Now, he should not have been shooting. He was 90deg angle-off and the first thing any fighter pilot is ever taught, you don't shoot at 90deg angle-off. You try to get down in the 30-degree cone. But he was shooting 90deg angle-off. The 37 went through the left wing and the 23s went through the right wing but missed all of the main spars and the airplane [survived].

Which guns were best, the Sabre's or the MiG's? I liked the idea of having 17sec to fire, because I did a lot of missing. It was nice to have something in reserve. They did a lot of missing, too. They didn't have anything in reserve.

[If I had been an enemy officer talking to his pilots] I would have emphasized the advantages that they had. The MiG flew higher than we did. Our service ceiling was around 40,000ft [12,192m]. We could get to 45,000 [13,716m], but if you got up there, you just were hanging in the air. You couldn't do any violent maneuvering. The reason we went to 45,000 in October the troposphere comes down and you could get above the contrail level. So we would climb above the contrail level, sort of hiding up there, waiting for them to come across the river, hoping they came by lower than we were.

They could do very well at 50,000ft [15,240m]. We never got up to fight them at 50,000. But they could fly comfortably, in formation, at 50,000ft. I've been at 45,000ft [13,716m] and had four MiGs, line abreast, come down out of an azure sky. Four planes, line abreast, all shooting at you. That was a fighter-versus-bomber technique they used to shoot down a lot of B-29s. Finally, they took the 29s out of combat over there. Their altitude advantage could be translated into an airspeed advantage.

An F-86F-30-NA Sabre (52-4519) of the 334th FIS/4th FIW on a combat mission in Korea in 1952 or 1953. The F-86F was late in reaching the combat zone and the hard-wing F-86F (shown) arrived even later. Until then not everyone was prepared to rate the Sabre as superior to the MiG-15. Traditional fighter-pilot skills, among them good eyesight and quick responses, remained important to American Sabre pilots. Gene Sommerich

2nd Lt. James F. Low, 335th FIS/4th FIW, K-14 , 1952, F-86F

I went to Perrin AFB, Texas, in November 1950 for primary flight training. I had some measure of success. I was the only one in the class who flew a perfect stage—that's six takeoffs and landings, landing on a spot. After that, I went to F-51s. I did great in the '51. From there, I was sent to Williams AFB, Arizona, for jet upgrade and to Nellis AFB, Nevada, for gunnery. An instructor named Andrew Ritchie wanted to put me into F-80s to penalize me for the failings of several other trainees, but I was given a checkout in the F-86 and a chance to be assigned to the F-86.

The first flight I had on the gunnery pattern, I shot 40 percent, which meant I out-shot my gunnery instructor. I was lucky, but I knew I could fly and that was the name of the game.

I graduated in F-86s and went overseas, first to Tachikawa [Japan], then onward. Kind of like in *The Hunters*. I was Pell in that book. Dick Powell made a movie of it and he did a pretty good job. Robert Wagner played my part.

I got to Tachikawa in April 1952. Again, I was fortunate. I was assigned

An F-86E-15-NA Sabre (51-12976) after suffering battle damage and taking refuge on the offshore island of Paenyongdo, also known as K-53. Richard I. Sudhoff

to the 4th FIW instead of the 51st. We paraded in there, we second lieutenants, my classmates. Again, I was lucky. I was assigned to the 335th FIS and, not only that, I was chosen by D Flight. Casey Colman was the flight commander. He had shot down several airplanes in China. Then he came to the 4th and he made ace there. [Capt. Philip E. (Casey) Colman was credited with five kills in World War II and four in Korea]. Horowitz was in there, a.k.a. James Salter. He didn't particularly like me, obviously.

After I was assigned to Dog Flight, they checked me out and gave me some good information. The 335th was getting more MiGs than any of the other squadrons. The reason was, they were spending more time in the combat area. The other squadrons would race up there, fly around, and come right back at Mach 0.92 and log a mission. That's all they were interested in. Well, Dog Flight was interested in getting MiGs.

My first mission was what they called a bomb-line mission. We took off and went just north of Seoul, on the bomb line, just to look around. The next time I went up, I was flying with Jim Kasler and we were hosing around Pyongyang. I was just flying his wing and, all of a sudden, four MiGs jumped us. They'd never been that far south before.

Kasler says, "Break!" I broke. He says, "Break right!" There was a lot of this: "Break right!" "Break left!" And I never saw a thing. I followed him. He says "Break right!" and I'm breaking away from him. He says "Break left!" and I look back and I didn't even see him. I didn't see where he was. And here's three MiGs coming right down my ass firing their 37mm cannons. I'd never seen anything that big before. Man!

I dropped my tanks. I jacked up my power, to full power. And I pulled up into them. I almost stalled. They were going a lot faster than I was, and they shot right by me.

I dropped my nose, picked up some airspeed, and turned back towards the ground.

One of these MiGs shoots under me and I go after his ass. Well, I got up on him and I shot and hit him in the engine section. There was a big explosion. I hit him in the wing roots. He was out of power, so I came up behind him—this was my second mission, remember—and as I was overtaking him, I did a barrel roll to kind of lose a little bit of headway. I'm right over top of his canopy looking down on him. He's an oriental. He's got one of these brown leather helmets. He's looking side to side. I guess he's looking for me, and I'm right above him. So I rolled back behind him again and hit him again, and he bailed out.

I'd done a bad thing. I'd lost my leader. So I got a little counseling on that. I said, "I tell you, I was fine but after the fourth break I lost you, and I'm sorry." But, see, I got a MiG. So the wing commander, Harry Thyng, who was an ace also, came to bat for me. I didn't know this but I found out later.

We were always going up to the Yalu River and—hanging. We were getting up to 40,000ft [12,192m] and—hanging. Throttling back. Everybody else was racing around. Hell, they're all back at the base and we're still up there. So we got more contact with the enemy.

[On another mission], I was flying and Kasler got a MiG and I got tunnel vision. I saw this MiG going straight up in the air with the smoke piling on it. I'm looking at it. I looked around. Here, I'd lost everybody. I couldn't find anybody. Well, I just headed home. I was right behind them, but it was about four or five miles behind. So now my ass was really in a jam.

[Kasler] says, "Look, you lost us again. And you lost us on your second mission. What the hell's wrong with you? What's happening?" I said, "Well, I was watching that airplane and you guys turned around and you were gone." And he said, "Well, did you learn something?" And I said, "Yeah." So I didn't lose anybody after that. I stuck to 'em like glue. But I was still a little tenuous.

One of the pilots in 2nd Lt. James F. Low's squadron was 1st Lt. James H. Kasler, 15th American air ace of the Korean War. In this extraordinary glimpse into history, a youthful-looking Kasler adds his fifth aerial victory to the collection of red stars above his bunk (the second row covers probable kills). Martin Bambrick

Before Casey Colman left, he took me across the river, over into China. I hung on to him. We were racing down there into the traffic pattern at Antung. And I'm just a balloon [a new second lieutenant], you know, I'm just flying along, hanging on there, and he shoots at this airplane. There's another one trying to get into him. I'm in constant contact. I say, "You've got one right on your tail, but," I said, "he's high. He can't pull any lead on you and he can't hit you." He says, "You watch him." I say, "Well, I won't go after him because if I do, I'll lose you, so I'll just hang on to you."

So we went around [Antung] and he shot his airplane. He says, "Okay, well, I got that one." Now we're on the deck. These MiGs pulled out. They were right on the pattern. They must have been out of fuel. We got guns firing at us from Sinuiju and from Antung and we're S'ing down the Yalu River on the Mach.

When we got back to Kimpo, in the briefing room, Casey gets on the pedestal and lauds the "greatest wingman he's ever had." It embarrassed me. But he kind of knew I needed it, with some of the rumors that had been going around. He really took care of me, and then I never had any more problems after that.

Bob Love was in that flight. He was an ace. He left. Casey Colman left. And I'm flying on Bob Ronca's wing. He talked to me. He said, "Look, you know, there's some scuttlebutt around, about you leaving your leader." I said, "I understand." I said, "Don't worry. I will not leave you. You'll be right in my sights. But I've got pretty good eyes and I'll look around." He said, "Do that."

So we're flying up along the Yalu, just the two of us, we're an element. I spotted two MiGs coming across the river on the deck. I called to Bob. I said, "Bob, I've got two MiGs coming due east on the deck." He says, "Okay, you take the bounce." I said, "Wait a minute! Say that again." I knew I didn't want to hear [criticism] back at the base. He says again, "You take the bounce." I says, "Okay, drop tanks. Here we go."

We were at about 30,000ft [9,144m]. I dove down, right on the deck. I came up behind this guy. I hit him all over. I was closing. I kept firing. Debris started flying off, came back, hit my airplane, and broke my windshield. He bailed out. I took pictures of him in the chute. He had a red beard.

I thought Ronca was flying my wing. Well, he was. But he hadn't gotten a MiG. Now, he went and got the other guy. He shot the other one down. He said, "Well, he was trying to get on your tail so I shot him down." I said, "Well, we both got one." He was happy. I was happy. I had lost that stigma of leaving your leader. He explained it to everybody and that made it nice.

The MiGs stopped flying. Nothing was happening. I volunteered for alert. Nobody wanted to be on alert. I'd gotten a couple of MiGs so I was a flight leader on alert, big deal. So we went down there, four of us on alert. We were always in contact with the radar site, DENTIST. This time, they called us, they said, "We've got some action up there, we don't know what it is yet. But it's kind of circling around the Yalu River. You guys want to go up?" We said, "You want us to go up, you've got to scramble us." So they said, "Okay, you're scrambled." So we all jumped into our airplanes and flew on up there.

I was flying with Al Smiley and Dan Druen. Dan Druen was my wingman. Smiley was in D Flight and we had a fourth guy, I forget who. We were flying a foursome and we were being told, "Well, they're there." Smiley says, "Well, I'll go down to the mouth of the Yalu." I says, "Okay, I'm going to stay here." I believed the radar guys. If I couldn't see them and they could, why should I go down there to the mouth of the Yalu?

All of a sudden, we saw these short cons [contrails]. We were at 45,000. They're at 55,000. What an airplane that MiG was for flying!

I says, "Tally ho. I got 'em. They're in the cons." But I made a mistake by not making it clear that I meant short cons. Fighters normally produced long contrails: Hell, on some days we'd be up in a huge formation and the sky would be full of them. You'd have a certain contrail level, depending on temperature, and you'd stay below it for concealment. But we almost never saw short contrails and Smiley didn't get it. So Smiley says, "Where are they?" I said, "They're in the cons up here!" So he started coming back but we were right in the middle of them.

So one MiG comes diving down, I get him in my sights, he goes into a spin and bails out. It wasn't much of a hit. The next guy comes down. I got on his tail and hit him in the engine section. I rolled around him and hit him again. Dan Druen came down and made a pass at him too and said he got a "damaged" on him, which was nice. I got credit for the kill, so now I had four.

Next time was my fifth. That was a biggie. I was flying with Bob Goodrich. We were flying along the Yalu. I caught this MiG who was right underneath us. He was about 10,000ft [3,048m] below us. I said, "We've got one right below us, Bob." He says, "Okay, I gotcha." I says, "Okay, let's go down." I came down and hit him with one burst and he bailed out.

Bob said, "He bailed." I said, "I saw him." So I made ace. That was a big deal. I'd made ace on June 15, which was Father's Day. I was very close to my father.

I had some measure of success with the gunsight. Gabreski and all these other guys, they wanted to get rid of the gunsight, it wasn't worth a shit, they said. The gunsight was great if it worked. They had trouble with it. I had some success when it worked. These other guys, they would just lock it up, and use a piece of gum up there, and use tracers. A tracer is something extra that you could use and it's a good thing to have.

I went to Japan on R & R. I came back and had the toughest fight I ever had. I got on this MiG who was way, way far away from me. I was at max range. I fired a couple of times and I must have hit him because he slowed down a little bit. I finally caught him. I was flying in an A [F-86A].

This guy was going across the river. I pulled up a little bit and I lobbed these shots into him and I hit him. He pulled back around and I caught him, cut him off, and got a couple more shots into him. He turned over and he never got out of the airplane, he went right into the mountain. That was my sixth.

[Low was invited to tour 17 Air

Training Command bases in the United States lecturing on the gunsight to others].

I went back [to Korea]. It's three months later. All of my people are gone. I'm treated like a new guy. I'd had 44 missions when I left. Now, I was just locked up. I flew 40 more missions on their wing without leading a flight—and, there, I was an ace. I flew on the wing with these inexperienced captains and majors. But they forgot about my eyes! I could see at 20ft [6m] what a normal person could see at ten. So I'd go up on a mission with these guys and I'd say, "Well, we got one ahead of us there. He's at 12 o'clock, going to one." And they're straining, straining, and they can't see him. I say, "We're going to lose him." They'd say, "Ah, you take the bounce." This happened when I was flying with Murray Winslow on my seventh kill. I cut him off and knocked him down. There was nothing really great about it.

My eighth MiG was a real doozie. Now I was back to leading occasionally. This guy and I were flying. He got tunnel vision. I was going in to make a pass on this MiG and he goes ahead of me. He starts firing. I said, "Stop firing!" The guy's pulling about four or five Gs and he just wasn't making any lead. I watched him. He had his finger locked on the trigger.

Finally, he's out of ammunition. So he says, "Yellow Three, you'd better come down. I'm out of ammunition." I said, "Well, fine, you're talking to me now." So I went after the same MiG. And he was really a honcho. He was pulling Gs and racking it around. He knew how to fly. He was a good pilot.

We raced around. I fired one little burst and I knew I couldn't get him, right then. So I waited until I could get a bead on him. So I finally pulled a little lead and fired another very short burst. I finally nailed him. I got him in the engine. He's S'ing below us. We've got power. I'm flying, trying to stay behind him, watching to see what he's going to do, whether he's going to bail. And son of a gun! All of a sudden, that guy pulls straight up. He fires at me with a dead engine. These 37mm balls of fire are out ahead of me. I'm saying, "My God, I flew over this." So I rolled over on him, I finished him off, and he went into the mountain. He was really tenacious, a honcho.

1st Lt. Bill Foy, US Marine Corps, taxies out at Itazuke AB, near Fukuoka, Japan, in an FJ-2 Fury of VMF-235 Death Angels (alias the Red Noses). Commanded by Lt. Col. Donald Sapp, the squadron received its natural-metal FJ-2s not long after the Navy determined that the dash two was far from ideally suited for carrier deck operations. In addition to red trim with white stars and squadron badge beneath the canopy bow, Foy wears a typical helmet for the era, in the days before something as innocuous as a red chrome dome could attract heat-seeking infrared missiles. Bill Foy

For my last kill, ninth, I was flying Col. Royal N. Baker's airplane. He was the group commander. He had an airplane, 936, I'll never forget the number. [Baker's aircraft was F-86F-2-NA, originally F-86E-10-NA, 51-2822, *Angel Face and the Babes/The King*]. He had a gunsight in there, the new A-4 gunsight that replaced the A-1C. It was just a piece of work—of course, being a colonel's airplane.

So I'm up in MiG Alley in Baker's plane. I'm flying somebody's wing again, and I see a MiG and the other guys can't see the damn airplane. I says, "I got one! He's out at about two o'clock, there, and he's coming across." The other guys are straining, they have binoculars, and they can't see him. They hated to say it but, finally, "Well, you take the bounce."

So I says, "Okay." So the MiG pulled back to the right a little bit. And I'm out at almost max range, about 3,800–4,000ft [1,158–1,219m]. And this little gunsight went right down like it was just locked on. I put it right on him, I fired, and I hit him with the first shot. When that A-4 gunsight worked, it really worked. Everybody pissed and moaned about it. Gabreski and the guys in the 51st, they were trying to go back to the K-14 and do this and do that. They didn't like it. My squadron commander, Van Sickle, made a trip down to the 51st and they said, "Who's that balloon you've got up there? He got some MiGs." So I had some measure of success. Again, I could shoot well and I could see well. That's the reason I got so many, because I could see them before everybody else. We had captains and majors who wanted to go shoot them but they couldn't see them.

1st Lt. William H. Foy, VMF-235, NAF Atsugi, Japan, 1955, FJ-2

I first saw a newspaper article telling about the Marine Corps receiving the Fury when I was completing jet transition as a new Marine Corps pilot in Corpus Christi. That would have been around February or March 1954. A Marine major, the operations officer for our training squadron, saw some of us shiny new second lieutenants reading the article. In a very unfriendly tone of voice he told us to, "Forget it. You're not going to be flying those."

After completing jet transition in the TV-2 (T-33), I reported to El Toro [California] and was placed in a holding squadron with many other new lieutenants. When it was our turn, we would be checking out in the squadron's F9F-5 Panthers. It must have been around April when we were all summoned to a meeting where we were informed that about 40 of us would be divided between VMF-235 and VMF-451. Assigned to VMF-235, I grabbed my things and ran to my new squadron.

The two El Toro squadrons were just receiving the last of their allotted NAA FJ-2 Fury aircraft from the factory. That was to be 24 planes per squadron. We went through the normal ground school and lectures. When it became time to fly, I was picked to be the first new lieutenant to try one out on the West Coast. I have no idea whether another fresh-out-of-training pilot on the East Coast had flown an FJ-2 or not.

Although the USAF had been flying the F-86 for some time by now, the Marine Corps made much ado about this new jet of theirs. First, it was swept wing. Secondly, it had an all-movable horizontal tail. As you know, swept-wing aircraft don't take kindly to slow speeds and high sink rates. Add to that the J47 engine's very slow spool-up rate, and there could be trouble in the landing pattern. The USAF really didn't have to cope with this phenomenon because of their high pattern speeds and their diving final approach. We, like the Navy, always made slow, high angle of attack, powered-up landings. In fact, the patterns were the same we made in the old prop-driven planes.

One of my lieutenant friends had this proven to him the hard way when he landed on the golf course a couple hundred yards short of the runway. The bounce coincided with the J47 finally coming on the line, and the second bounce was on the runway. It could have been worse!

I had quite a crowd witnessing my departure with the XO (executive officer) in chase and to watch the landing. All went very well, and for the most part, few pilots had any trouble with this new plane. Without my log books I can only guess the date of my Fam 1 (first familiarization flight) but it must have been in April 1954. The model numbers for both squadrons went from 1 to 24.

VMF-235 and VMF-451 went overseas to Atsugi, Japan, in December 1954. The aircraft were sealed and taken over by transport carrier. We flew from there for one year and returned to the States the following December having left the FJ-2s there for our replacements. As nearly as I can remember, the two west coast squadrons had 13 aircraft accidents and seven fatalities during the two years I was involved with the FJ-2. A high number for peacetime flying.

The FJ-2 was not kind to our maintenance personnel. Out of an assigned 24 planes, we were lucky to start the day with 12 in commission, and regularly ended the day with around six. By today's standards they were simple aircraft, but hydraulics and electronics seemed never to stay right. I was not in maintenance but I'm sure much of the problem was with parts procurement.

As I recall, the F-86 flew with 150gal disposable drop tanks. We had specially designed 200gal tanks that were not to be disposed of except in cases of emergency. I don't think that was ever done. The tanks were aerodynamically shaped and equipped with dump valves. The internal fuel the FJ carried was pathetic. As I remember, we started up with 2,700lb of fuel, and wasted no time in taxi and run-up if we were to get airborne with 2,500lb. For that reason, we rarely flew without our drop tanks.

If we were to be back on the ground with between 500 and 800lb [226–362kg] of fuel, we could only average about 0.7hr without tanks, and 1.5hr with tanks. It takes a lot of flights to build up time that way, but two of us ended up with 400hr in the FJ-2.

I thought the FJ-2 was a very stable plane to fly. The controls were all hydraulic and nonreversible but not overly sensitive. The aerodynamic leading edge slats made slow speed flight possible. As I recall, 120 knots was a normal approach speed at the regular landing weight. Like the F-86, landings were made with the speed brakes deployed so as to be able to vary more engine RPM. FCLPs (Field Carrier Landing Practices, using an airfield marked-off to simulate a carrier deck) were flown with the canopy back (as they would have been for carrier landings) because we did not have zero-altitude ejection capability, and going in the water would probably preclude opening the canopy for egress.

In those days before all the regulations, we could jump any and all military planes in the sky. The FJ-2 matched up very well with most fighters of the day, but we were handicapped somewhat by having to hang onto the drop tanks that were usually attached. The FJ-2 performed a whole lot better at altitude without the tank's weight and drag. A turning contest at low altitude with a straight-wing jet (which were still in abundance in those days) was going to get you in a whole lot of trouble.

Climbing to 40K [40,000ft] wasn't too tough without tanks, but with tanks it was difficult. The McDonnell F2H Banshee of that era could get to 50K. So, most of our mock combat was done from 35K on down. What we really needed was more thrust. In a turning scrambling sort of fight, gobs of altitude had to be sacrificed to maintain speed, "speed" being anything above a high-speed stall. In these high-angle-of-attack turns, the slats would be trying to come out and help. If one of the four sections (the wing fold for carrier stowage had dictated four segments) came out by itself causing asymmetric lift, the plane would snap a partial roll until you relaxed the stick. Visibility from the cockpit was excellent.

Armament was four 20mm cannons. The bore was depressed 6deg as I recall from the aircraft's axis. The only explanation I ever heard for this was that it would make strafing, as in ground support, easier. In air-to-air combat we had to pull 6deg more "lead" on the target. Gunnery practice

was done with only two of the cannons firing, but it was an impressive noise as they were located right by our feet. When F-86 pilots viewed our guns, they seemed to wish that's what they had. This point can be argued, I know, but I believe we had the better firepower. Our radar-ranging APG-30 was tough to use, but we used it all the time with the gun camera, and I have a large roll of 16mm film showing pretty good tracking of the target.

In summary, the FJ-2 was a pilot's airplane, fun to fly, and didn't have any dangerous peculiarities. I personally liked the light green interior of the cockpit. It definitely was less cluttered than the F-86 cockpit layout. We just didn't have enough power with the J47 engine, but in those days not enough was the common denominator.

1st Lt. Charles Vasiliadis, 417th FBS/FBG, Hahn AB, Germany, 1954, F-86H

How many citizens of Brindisi, Italy—we'll probably never know—suffered an electrical power outage when I took it upon myself to demonstrate how a real fighter pilot flies tight pattern?

1st Lt. Charles Vasiliadis poses in front of his F-86F-30-NA Sabre (52-4728) during a gunnery deployment to Wheelus Field, Libya. Vasiliadis flew with the 417th FBS/50th FBW at Hahn AB, Germany, and was one of the first pilots overseas to convert to the F-86H model. His introduction to the F-86H in Brindisi, Italy, is the stuff of a good flying story. USAF

In January 1953, I arrived at Nellis with pilot training behind me (T-6, T-28, T-33) and orders for Korea. First, I had to learn how to fly the F-86A Sabre. Sabres and MiGs were battling each other in Korea. But at Nellis, the USAF seemed determined to kill every new F-86A student before we could give the enemy a chance to do it. At Nellis, it was not unusual to lose one F-86A and one pilot per week.

In those days, we pretty much jumped in and took off. On my second or third flight in an F-86A Sabre, I was followed out by my instructor, Brooks (Pappy) Liles, who'd gotten 4.5 MiG kills in Korea. [Capt. Brooks J. Liles was credited with one kill in World War II and four in Korea].

Our two F-86As turned at the hammerhead at runway's end, ready for takeoff, when it struck me, abruptly, that I had absolutely no idea how to close the Sabre's canopy. I had succumbed to the temptations of nearby Las Vegas last night instead of studying. I knew just enough to be dead certain that you could not fly the Sabre with the canopy open.

"RATTLER 1, what the hell's the matter with you?" Liles' voice in the radio sounded *mean*.

"Uh, one moment please, sir. Er, I mean, RATTLER 2."

Squirming, I struggled desperately to remember whether anyone had ever told me how to shut the thing. I dared not risk becoming the butt of ill-tempered joshing—perhaps for my entire career—if I had to ask Liles how to do it.

Today, I believe that divine intervention helped me find the switch. I closed the canopy, took off, and flew a training mission with Liles scrutinizing my every move. Liles had nothing further to complain about. I was a natural stick-and-rudder man.

Training in the F-86 Sabre included air-to-air gunnery (against a banner towed by a B-26 Invader) and air-to-ground bombing (with tiny, 3lb "skip" bombs and .50cal guns). I managed to continue enjoying Las Vegas and, still, to learn. I liked the Sabre—it was fleet and responsive.

What I didn't like was the number of people getting killed around me. They had a saying at Nellis, "Every man a tiger." That motto caused some unsafe, aggressive flying, and some deaths.

[Fred Newman, another pilot who went through F-86 Sabre training at Nellis during this period remembers that "we were splashing people and airplanes right and left." It wasn't that the USAF was irresponsible or that men were foolish. "It was simply that all of the standards pertaining to military flying were different in those days. This was the way it was, and no one questioned it. It was part of life, campaigning in fighters in the fifties."]

In February 1953, a ranking officer drew us instructors and students together to demand a reduction in the number of accidents that, in those days, went hand-in-glove with fighter training. For a brief period, we got the rate down. By February 7, we had had 11 accidents and four fatalities, for that month. That was an improvement.

On an early flight in the F-86A, I went supersonic. Later, at lower speed, I experienced a hydraulic failure. The stick jumped, it was hard to control, and the gauge said zero. I put down the gear by hand and landed. Soon, we were flying the F-86E model, which replaced the A. It had an irreversible flight control system with a flying tail, which replaced a hydraulically-boosted tail. It turned tighter.

In May 1953, because of progress in Panmunjom peace talks, my orders for Korea were cancelled. It was a disappointment. I wanted to shoot down MiGs. Once I completed Sabre training—survived, is perhaps the more appropriate word—I received orders to Clovis AFB, New Mexico, where the 50th FBG under Col. Wallace S. Ford was working up in factory-fresh F-86F Sabres to deploy to a newly-built airfield in Germany, Hahn. The wing's squadron's were the 10th, 81st, and 417th FBS. At Clovis, I served briefly in the 81st FBS under Lt. Col. Ed McGough before transferring to the 417th under Lt. Col. Charles E. Yeager.

We had World War II heroes and Korean War air aces working out in the F-86F, up there in the sunshine over the New Mexico desert. One of them was Capt. Robinson Risner who'd shot down eight MiGs. Everybody wanted to go up and fight Risner. He was damned good. It was difficult to defeat him.

The wing and its squadrons deployed to Europe in Fox Able 27 (phonetic for Fighters Atlantic). This was a remarkable deployment, the Sabres flying from Clovis to Alexandria AFB, Louisiana (today named England AFB), Shaw AFB, South Carolina, Dow AFB, Maine, Goose Bay Labrador, "Blue West One" in Greenland, Keflavik AB, Iceland, Prestwick, Scotland, and finally into the spanking-new base at Hahn, Germany.

At Hahn, everything was so fresh there was white dust everywhere from the lime [from construction of the aerodrome]. When you flew over Hahn, they had all these revetments. It was just absolutely gorgeous. In the states, the airplanes were always on a big ramp. But there at Hahn, we had the 417th at the departure end of Runway 06 and everything was pristine.

We went for our first gunnery meet at Wheelus Field, Libya, in the spring of 1954. We had sandstorms....

My worst peacetime incident, perhaps still remembered by some at Brindisi, occurred because my wing was slated to convert to the F-86H model. Brindisi was the Italian port where the new Sabre versions arrived via sea. The F-86H was a fantastic airplane. It was 1,000lb [454kg] heavier than the F model but whereas the F-86F had a 4,700lb [2,132kg] thrust engine, the H had 9,300lb [4,218 kg] and sometimes it got over 10,000lb [4,536kg] of thrust.

I remember one time I got the damned airplane up to 63,000ft [19,202m]. I wanted to see how high I could go. I got up higher than anybody had been in an F-86H and I said to myself, "You dumb shit! If you lose pressurization, you'll be dead!"

The 10th FBS got the F-86Hs first and the 417th was to follow. Around Christmas 1955, Bobbie Gall was the F-86H acceptance pilot down at Brindisi, Italy. They needed somebody from the 417th to go down and I was a bachelor, so I volunteered. So they checked me out, locally, in IFR conditions. After just one ride to qualify in the F-86H—the manual requires seven missions to transition from the F to the H model—I went down to Brindisi. My ops officer, Jim Yealy, had warned me. "Vas," he said, "this airplane doesn't have a leading-edge slat on it, it's a hard wing, so whatever you do, remember you cannot fly it around on the edge of a stall like you can in the F model."

At Brindisi, I'm supposed to be the expert, making an acceptance flight of this new F-86H that has just been unloaded from the boat.

So my first flight in the F-86H, I take off, I fly the mission according to the acceptance card, and come back and land. I make a big, safe traffic pattern and come in and land. I says, "Air Force jet 617, turning base, gear down, indicators checked, pressure up, full stop." And a voice comes from the tower. "You call that a traffic pattern?"

I don't know when I've been put down like that. My pride was hurt. After all, I'm a Sabre pilot! And this voice is inferring that I am too stupid to know how a real fighter pilot flies a tight pattern!

Sabre pilot and MiG killer Lt. Henry A. (Hank) Crescibene went to work for Republic and moved to Brindisi, Italy, to help the Italian Air Force transition to the F-84F Thunderstreak. First encountered when Karl Dittmer painted his Sabre in Korea, Crescibene re-enters our narrative as the challenger who prompted 1st Lt. Charles Vasiliadis to demonstrate a tight pattern at the Brindisi airfield in a newly arrived F-86H Sabre. Karl Dittmer

So I decide to show this smart-ass I can fly a better pattern. "Air Force jet 617, on the go." I took off and cobbed that F-86H and it accelerated. I kept it right inside the runway, came right around, and hit that final. I think we were supposed to break at about 300 knots. I must have been going 570, 580 knots. I hit that break, dropped everything, and high-speed stalled it, right around, turned on base. "Gear down, indicators checked, pressure up." And all around the pattern, I was going, "Up yours!" thumbing my nose at the guy who'd criticized my earlier, safe pattern. I thought I was going to kill myself, but it was a question of honor.

What it was, there was this Republic test pilot, Hank Crescibene—whom I got to know later on—who was up in the traffic path because he was checking out the Italian base commander in the F-84F. He's up there, nothing to do, so he criticizes my pattern. It's like he's impugning my manhood. And he flew F-86s in those great air battles with MiGs that I'd missed.

He and I didn't know each other then—but Crescibene's remarks about flying a tight pattern stuck in my mind longer than Yealy's warning did.

Next day, I take off, request a low pass, and come right down. I went right over where the F-84Fs were parked and knocked him off the wing of one. The repercussion from my airplane sent Crescibene falling to the ground from the wing of his parked jet. After I landed, he was livid. I said, "Don't bug me, little man." I said to myself, "I'm going to show him how a fighter pilot flies an airplane over here, okay?"

Meantime, an Italian lieutenant had come up to me and asked me to "put on a show" in the F-86H Sabre. He begged me, "Give the boys something they can appreciate." These were the same Italian pilots who were learning about the F-84F from Crescibene. I said to him, "You tell your boys, if they want an air show, they came to the right man."

Next time I flew, I came beating up the runway just as low as I could get. You wouldn't dare go any lower. After I land, the Italian lieutenant says, "Good air show!" He says, "That was very low."

My next attempt at being a real fighter pilot was less successful. I went over Brindisi harbor. I came back. It was late. It was about 4:30 in the afternoon. I said to myself, "I'm really going to come down on this inactive runway between the Italian F-84Fs and the American F-86Hs and do a real number on 'em." And as I'm inching my way down, all of a sudden, out of a corner of my eye, I see a telephone wire—boom.

I pulled back on the stick. If I'd stayed lower, I'd have flown underneath it. Maybe the tail would have hit it. But I pulled up, and I momentarily caught 23,000 volts right across the nose of the aircraft. It put indentations on the air intake. Then, when the wire snapped, it ricocheted off my right wing and put a dent in the right wing. I was so low, the people watching couldn't see me any more. The next thing they see is sparks.

I pulled a cloverleaf, came down, landed. All I could see was eyeballs and gaping mouths. I figured I had just unintentionally done my "going out of the Air Force air show." When I got out of the airplane, the Italian F-84F wing commander came up to me livid, trembling. He was pissed off at me for beating up his aerodrome. He said, "This is not a fighter pilot, this is a suicide pilot." I said to him, "I don't have to listen to your dribbling mouth because I have real problems of my own about my career now," and I taxied on to park without talking to him.

There followed communications between the Italian Air Force, the American Embassy, and the Pentagon. The general idea was, "Get that crazy Greek for beating up our airfield in his F-86H." I laugh when I tell the story today. At the time, I knew I'd lose my wings.

The next day, Black Jack Randall comes down from Hahn in a T-33 to haul my ass out of there. We got back up in our T-33 to Hahn AB and the tower called, "573, is Lieutenant Vasiliadis aboard?"

"Yes he is."

"Please advise the lieutenant that the wing commander's car will transport him directly up to wing headquarters." Colonel Ford had now been replaced by Col. Fred J. Ascani, former head of flight test activity at Edwards AFB, California, and a long-time Sabre pilot.

First, I had the humiliation of being greeted by Jim Yealy who had counseled me about cooling it in the F-86H. Together, we went to see the wing commander.

Ascani knew from a well-established record of good performance that I was, in fact, a good pilot and a serious officer. I was about to take off my wings and give them to Ascani and tell him it's about time I got out of this Air Force and went back home and became a lawyer, like my mother wanted me to. But he treated me so kindly, so humanely, and made me feel like such a dumb shit, and then he said he'd go to bat for me. I was determined to shape up after that. We completed our transition to the F-86H and I flew it thereafter.

Cdr. J. Richard (Dick) Powell, VF-142, FJ-3M

I made my first flight in a NAA FJ-3 Fury on 27 March 1956, at the time the only Fury that had been delivered to his squadron, VF-142, then known as the Fighting Falcons.

Later, I flew the FJ-3M version, one of the first warplanes equipped with AAM-N-7 Sidewinder heat-seeking missiles. FJ-3Ms were simply existing FJ-3s with missile capability added. I made a ten-month cruise aboard USS *Hornet* (CVA-12) in the Fury, and eventually logged a couple of hundred hours with 50–60 carrier landings.

The FJ-3 had the 6-3 wing. This made it very maneuverable. About the only aircraft we couldn't outfight was the F-86H. But our guys, when they flew well, learned how to build up energy vertically and to outsmart the other guy and get into position to shoot him.

On 9 October 1956, I had to bail out of an FJ-3M after I learned that my ejection seat wasn't working! The following is the tale of this mishap.

I took off from NAS Miramar, near San Diego, California, in an FJ-3M Fury (BuNo. 139233, coded A-202) belonging to VF-142. It was my second flight that day. My handwritten remarks of the day's earlier, first flight have survived:

"I returned to the squadron ready room and read the bulletin board, eyeing with satisfaction the picture of a voluptuous and scantily-clad blonde accompanied by some esoteric free verse on how she disapproved of midair collisions. This was in keeping with statistics and [with] a rather impressive poster received the previous week from the Naval Safety Center, decrying the practice with the slogan, 'A midair can ruin your whole day!'

"How true, and how little I appreciated, then, the moments of terror, defying statistical probabilities, I would undergo within hours...."

Four FJ-3M Furys under my command were to engage an air-to-air banner towed by a fifth FJ-3M (with one of the first four providing escort).

We taxied to the warm-up apron and performed the various aircraft systems checks so conducive to long life of both aircraft and pilot.

PRIME Tow [the fifth, target-tow FJ-3M Fury] was on the duty runway calling for takeoff, which was granted from the tower. Halfway down the 8,000ft [2,438m] runway he was airborne in a steep rate of climb holding down his airspeed as he got the tow off the deck. Good tow! Banner straight! PRIME Four, the Fury escorting the tow aircraft, BuNo. 139254, coded A-207, piloted by Ens. Rex D. Nelick, rolled down the runway and joined PRIME Tow, who completed his 180deg turn to climb eastward towards the gunnery range.

"Miramar Tower, this is PRIME One with three for takeoff," I said into my oxygen mask. I launched with my trio of FJ-3Ms, close behind the banner-tow FJ-3M and its escort, Ensign Nelick. Minutes later, the banner-tow pilot reported problems retracting his flaps. The tow-plane pilot reported that he would continue climbing to 20,000ft (6,096m) to check his fuel flow to determine whether he'd have sufficient fuel to continue the flight with his flaps locked in the down position.

East of Escondido, California, at 30,000ft (9,144m), I got a call from TOMAHAWK Green, leader of a two-plane flight of USAF F-100 Super Sabres. The Air Force wanted to fight. The Super Sabres belonged to the 34th Fighter Day Squadron from George AFB at nearby Victorville.

I spoke to TOMAHAWK Green. Both flight leaders agreed to meet over Riverside for what's known today as DACT (dissimilar air combat training).

Five minutes later, our flights tally ho'ed each other. I turned into the flight of F-100s with my wingman and told my section leader to yo-yo up to cover his section. At this time all aircraft were making heavy contrails that attracted several other aircraft. The sky was rapidly becoming overcrowded.

The tow pilot jettisoned his banner. The tow escort, Ensign Nelick, turned to a northerly heading and climbed to join my three FJ-3Ms.

Ensign Nelick heard much talking on the tactical frequency about F-100s. He observed many contrails over nearby March AFB. He assumed that the contrails were made by the aircraft he wished to join and headed in their direction. At about 25,000ft (7,620m), he saw two aircraft and followed them for a short time.

When he was sure that the aircraft were not from his flight, Ensign Nelick reversed his bank and departed in a steep climbing turn. He then saw two F-100s above and ahead, so he turned in their direction. The F-100s were in a left turn and Ensign Nelick was in a climbing left turn in pursuit.

As the tow-escort pilot entered the area, mock combat had begun between the F-100s and my flight. Ensign Nelick sighted the F-100s and entered a left climbing turn toward them. The accident report, covering what happened next, contains a sentence that shines with brilliance for its insights:

"The stage was set for a midair collision when two aircraft try to occupy the same position in the sky...."

Ensign Nelick began a 180deg turn apparently too close on another aircraft—that's me, in FJ-3M number 202. That's when everything went wrong. As the accident report later described it:

"Ensign Nelick in 207 collided with Lt. Powell in 202. On impact both pilots felt severe jolts, and the aircraft entered uncontrolled spins."

It was a hell of a thud, like you're in a steel drum and somebody hits you with a super baseball bat.

Nelick, hitting me the way he did, had overlooked the obvious principle that two objects can't occupy the same place at the same time. To quote the report again: "Upon impact in the air the left wing of 207 and the right wing of 202 were severely damaged causing loss of control of both aircraft. Parts of two wings and the drop tanks that were installed were torn off when the two aircraft collided and fell to the ground."

Caught in a traumatic midair emergency, both of us struggled desperately to get out of our aircraft. Even in 1956, the Fury's RAPEC ejection seat was deemed reliable. But Nelick and I encountered uncommon difficulty.

I positioned myself in the ejection seat, pulled my curtain to eye level, hesitated, and pulled the curtain all the way down. The canopy jettisoned when the curtain came to eye level, just as it was supposed to. Next, the seat was supposed to blast me into space, separating me from the crippled FJ-3M and enabling my parachute to deploy. But none of this happened!

When the curtain came all the way out, the seat did not eject. My oxygen mask was ripped off by the powerful blast of air that came with the canopy departing, but I was still strapped inside my Fury.

For Ensign Nelick in the other Fury, things started out worse but got better. Nelick pulled his face curtain to eject from his spinning FJ-3M but the canopy would not jettison. He pulled the curtain several times and nothing happened. Nelick then pulled the emergency canopy jettison handle on the left side of the instrument panel. He found the handle extremely difficult to pull. Desperate, he grabbed it with both hands and yanked, hard. The canopy flew loose. Nelick pulled the ejection curtain and his seat fired.

He was the lucky one.

I literally climbed out of my FJ-3M Fury as it plummeted earthward. At some time during my efforts to get my seat to fire, I realized that there were negative Gs on the aircraft and that all I would have to do to free myself was to release my safety belt. When my final effort to fire the seat failed, I unbuckled.

I kicked hard with my feet and was thrown clear of the tumbling FJ-3M. My parachute opened at 30,000ft (9,144m). Almost immediately, I lost consciousness due to anoxia. An observer on the ground reported later that it took my parachute 23min to lower me to the ground!

Ensign Nelick's chute opened at much lower altitude, and he reached the ground first. Both FJ-3M Furys hit the ground—one of them within a few feet of a farmhouse—burned, and exploded. Another typical day in naval aviation? Well, not exactly. Nor was the mishap caused by any flaw in the FJ-3 or FJ-3M.

I liked the Fury. It was light to the touch but was a tough airplane. I was impressed that the axial-flow engine offered far better performance and fewer mechanical hang-ups than the centrifugal-flow turbojets used until then by most Navy fighters, including the Cougar.

For NAA, it was no small feat to turn out an aircraft that measured up against a product of the Grumman Iron Works, the Navy's prime supplier of carrier-based fighters. My main criticism: The Fury's APG-30 gun fire-control radar was the same shitty piece of equipment we had in the F9F-6.

We used the guns when we went out to El Centro. We had damn few jams. The guns were farther apart than those on the F9F-6 but tighter, with a nicer pattern, converging at 1,000ft [304m]. Had we ever been called to fly the FJ-3 Fury in combat, we would have undoubtedly done well.

And the bottom line? The US Navy in 1956 said that an FJ-3M Fury cost exactly $384,000. Not a bad price for a tactical jet aircraft.

Once the decision was made to introduce a second Sabre wing to the USAF arsenal in Korea, the 51st FIW, Checkertails, shifted from the F-80C Shooting Star to the F-86E Sabre almost overnight. The 51st introduced the yellow bands on fuselage and wings that became standard for Sabres in all units. The checkers consisted of black squares against the natural metal of the vertical tail. These F-86E Sabres of the 39th FIS/51st FIW receive maintenance attention on the pierced steel planking (PSP) hardstand at Suwon.
via Douglas E. Slowiak

CHAPTER SIX

F-86 Sabre at War (Part II)

Col. Harrison R. Thyng, commander of the 4th FIW, viewed the Korean conflict as a very bitter and hard-fought air war. All of the cards were stacked in favor of the enemy. Thyng said that his personal feelings were difficult to describe when his pilots were prohibited from striking the enemy across the Yalu.

"It was a modern-day fight that paralleled knightly warfare in the Middle Ages," Thyng commented. "You patrolled the Yalu River and watched the enemy forming at Antung—3mi [4.8km] away." It was often like a joust, with both opponents setting up, eyeing each other, and converging. Thyng was certain his "young Sir Galahads" could prevail if only personnel, supply, and maintenance headaches could be cured.

Thyng's allegory on King Arthur was well intended, but it overlooked the plain truth that war along the Yalu was grim and dirty. It was no fun to be high over the Yalu on a freezing day, MiG cannon shells slamming into your aircraft. It was hard to handle a parachute with a broken arm and scramble on the cold, wet ground, pursued by communist soldiers with burp guns and grenades. Pilots who ejected were cornered and caught, beaten, humiliated, and starved by their communist captors. In the entire war, only one man was captured and escaped. More frequently, a pilot was trapped inside a crippled Sabre as it spun out of control, pinned by G forces or a frozen canopy, unable to get out at all while the world came rushing upward....

If the situation was to improve, Thyng needed more than aspirin. He needed help. Most importantly, more Sabres had to be brought into Korea.

With the ADC enjoying first claim on sparse resources, even finding more Sabres wasn't going to be easy. Getting them to Korea would be harder. No matter what happened, the Americans would remain outnumbered, but perhaps by just a little less.

After Colonel Thyng's unorthodox wake-up call, Chief of Staff Gen. Hoyt S. Vandenberg continued to be reticent about shipping more Sabres to Korea for about a month. Then, on 22 October 1951, the chief of staff issued a controversial order to the ADC. Defying the long-held wisdom that the Soviet threat to North America was more important than Americans dying on an obscure Asian peninsula, Vandenberg ordered ADC to send 75 F-86A and E Sabres with pilots and crew chiefs immediately to Alameda, California, to be loaded aboard an escort carrier for transit to Japan. One Pentagon officer put into rather gruff terms the significance of the chief's decision. "I don't give a damn how many tempers flare up in ADC," he said. "When our guys have to go into MiG Alley to fight, I want them to have a lot of friends flying wing."

Vandenberg also acted personally to bring about changes in the way Sabres in Korea were being supplied and supported. One measure was the consolidation of off-site depot maintenance at Tsuiki, Japan.

Getting enough Sabres to Korea, finally, involved a kind of horse trade. Vandenberg instructed Gen. O. P. Weyland to give an equal number of F-80 pilots and crew chiefs to ADC. For once, the beleaguered combatants in Korea got the better half of a deal.

The way was paved to equip the 51st FIW at Suwon with Sabres. Initially, the 51st would have two squadrons, the 16th and 25th. Already in Korea, the 4th FIW was to get its third squadron, the 335th, into action. The number of Sabre squadrons committed to the air-to-air duels over MiG Alley was to increase from two to five. Later on, when the 51st could accom-

Maj. George A. Davis was the ranking American ace, as well as one of the most experienced F-86 Sabre pilots in the 4th FIW. He seemed certain to remain the top ace and continue adding to his score of 14 aerial victories. Instead, in a raging battle on 10 February 1952, Davis attacked a MiG formation in a bold move that cost his life and made him—posthumously—the only F-86 Sabre pilot to be awarded the Medal of Honor. USAF via Larry Davis

modate a third squadron, there would be six squadrons in the air-to-air phase of the war.

The men who rounded up airplanes for the 51st felt they had carte blanche to choose any Sabre at any base they visited. No hangar queens for these would-be MiG killers. The 51st apparently never took on any F-86A models, for there were now plenty of F-86Es available with the all-flying tail, the first of several innovations with a chance to put the Sabre on a par with the MiG-15.

At Alameda, Sabres for the 51st were weatherproofed and loaded aboard two carriers, to be despatched in early November.

Getting the 4th FIW to Korea had been difficult enough. No real plans existed for this second wing of Sabres. The move was made anyway. Bill Rogers was a mechanic with an ADC squadron at Victorville AFB, California (later named George AFB). "In October 1951, approximately 25 of us crew chiefs, 25 pilots, and 25 airplanes were sent to Korea (along with others from different bases in the United States) to convert the 51st FIW, already in Korea, from F-80s to F-86s."

51st FIW

"After going from Alameda, California, to Japan on the baby aircraft carrier USS *Cape Esperance* (CVE-88) [as well as USS *Sitkoh Bay* (CVE-86)]," Rogers recalled, "We processed the planes in Japan and sent them on to K-13 Suwon in Korea. I believe that the 51st flew its first combat missions in the F-86 on 8 December 1951." Rogers became a member of the 25th FS or Assam Dragons, part of the 51st. This second Sabre wing had World War II ace Col. Francis S. Gabreski (who'd come down from the 4th) as wing commander and Lt. Col. George L. Jones as group commander.

The war did not wait for a second wing to get its Sabres into operation. On 4 November, Capt. William F. Gass, a Marine flying on an exchange tour with the 336th FIS/4th FIW, dueled two MiG-15s and followed one of them into a violent Lufbery turn. The enemy pilot abruptly went into a flat spin and ejected. This made Gass the first Marine to claim credit for a MiG.

On 27 November 1951, pilots from the 4th shot down four MiGs. One was credited to Maj. Richard D. Creighton who became the war's fourth American ace.

On 30 November 1951, 31 Sabres led by Col. Benjamin S. Preston, the 4th Group's commander, came upon an unusual enemy formation of 12 twin-engine Tupolev Tu-2 bombers, 16 Lavochkin La-9 propeller-driven fighters, and 16 MiG-15s. This may have been a premature attempt to resurrect the North Korean Air Force. UN forces had detected attempts to open the airfield at Uiju south of the Yalu River and had intercepted some communications in Korean rather than Chinese. Whatever the case, this gaggle of enemy aircraft found two flights of Sabres swarming down on them, firing—and missing. When the Sabres re-engaged, an La-9 went down, then a Tu-2.

In the fray was Maj. George A. Davis. Commander of the 334th FIS, Davis was a natural leader and key figure in the Sabre story. He had been one of the small cadre of pilots at March Field who had engineered the transition from F-80B to F-86A by the 1st Fighter Group in 1948. He was easygoing, well-liked, and, even then, they were also saying that Davis seemed certain to become the war's ace of aces.

On this day, Davis added to an existing kill by claiming three Tu-2s, then picking off an unwary MiG—to become the war's fifth American ace. Maj. Winton W. (Bones) Marshall destroyed one Tu-2 and one La-9 to become the sixth jet ace.

On 1 December 1951, Col. Gabreski's 51st FIW began Sabre operations from Kimpo. According to member Kenneth F. Rhodes, "We made the transition from F-80C to F-86E so fast, the engines never shut down." The 51st wing never operated the F-86A model.

The group commander, Lt. Col. George Jones, recognized immediately that the 51st needed distinctive markings on its aircraft. It always happens this way: In peacetime, the USAF experiments with ways to camouflage its planes to make them harder to see. In war, the aircraft must be painted to make them easier to see, lest Americans shoot at each other. To prevent their Sabres from being mistaken for MiGs, the 4th FIW had been flying with forward-slanting black-and-white stripes on the center fuselage, not dissimilar to the Normandy invasion stripes worn by American warplanes during World War II. Jones didn't want to copy the other wing's stripes, so he set forth to design something else.

Capt. Ed Matczak, group materiel officer and budding artist, used grease pencil to draw a picture of an F-86 with a rearward-slanting yellow band on the fuselage and yellow bands on wing and tail. The yellow bands looked far more attractive than the rival 4th's paint job. The conversation that created the standard Sabre markings of the war was concluded with alacrity.

Matczak: "How's this?"

Jones: "That's it."

Matczak's yellow bands not only

looked better, but also made it even easier for the good guys to distinguish a Sabre from a MiG.

Col. Walker H. (Bud) Mahurin, the World War II ace who joined the 51st later on, claimed that the large yellow stripes bordered in black were designed to set the 51st apart from the 4th, and to increase flagging morale (along with squadron-colored neck scarves bearing squadron insignia for the pilots). Later on, the 51st also adopted black-and-white squares on the tail (which were more often black against natural metal), and thus became known as the Checkertails. This was not a new idea. The original Assam Dragons had flown P-40

With a new wing adding Sabres to the fray along MiG Alley, there had to be more signs. The 51st FIW operated from Suwon with the three squadrons represented on this signboard, the 16th, 25th, and 39th.

Not clear is the purpose of the likenesses of animals. For example, while this signboard includes a picture of a pussycat, the 39th FIS was actually known as the Cobras. Robert F. Dorr

2nd Lt. Bernard Vise taxies past mud and muck at K-13 Suwon AB in his F-86E-1-NA Sabre (50-598), My Best Bett. *The blue fin cap color above the black checkers on the tail identifies Vise's Sabre as belonging to the 16th FIS/51st FIW at Suwon. A red band indicated the wing's 25th squadron, a yellow band the 39th. Vise's tour of duty coincided with a second wing tank shortage that hampered Sabre operations, although NAA-built tanks are in evidence here.* Curvin Miller

F-86 Sabre pilots of the 4th FIW at Kimpo (left to right): 2nd Lt. Michael E. DeArmond became a POW after being shot down while flying an F-86E Sabre nicknamed Eric's Reply, *normally flown by British exchange officer Paddy Harbison. 1st Lt. Billy B. Dobbs, according to a squadron mate, shot down five MiG-15s but was credited with four and was later killed in a T-33 mishap. Maj. Zane S. Amel, commander of the 335th FIS / 4th FIW, also lost his life in a post-Korea mishap. 1st Lt. Robert W. Smith was viewed by fellow airmen as an excellent fighter pilot. Capt. Philip E. Colman had five kills in China during World War II and racked up four MiGs in Korea. 2nd Lt. Coy L. Austin, says a wingman, was "mild-mannered and quiet but could fly with the best of them."* USAF via Paddy Harbison

Warhawks and P-51B Mustangs in India and China, painting checkertails on the latter.

But the yellow bands did not remain theirs for long. Matczak's yellow bands were adopted by the depot at Tsuiki, and before long both fighter wings were flying yellow-banded fighters. The 4th's invasion stripes were abandoned. Eventually, most F-86 units adopted the yellow-and-black fuselage bands, at least for a time, among them squadrons in Europe.

As for flagging morale, the F-86E was a giant step forward. By now, the F-86E with the all-flying tail was becoming standard, and pilots praised the way the E model could maneuver with the MiG.

But a classified report from the period listed all the obstacles fighter pilots were up against. F-86E Sabres, the report said, were "almost invariably outnumbered" by "extreme odds." MiG Alley itself, where the fighting took place, was "at the outer range of the F-86E combat radius" and "is over enemy territory at all times."

And no matter how worthy the F-86E, it could not fully satisfy the demands of hard-working crew chiefs. S/Sgt. Daniel Walker, crew chief for 51st pilot Capt. Iven C. Kincheloe, noticed that the aileron actuators leaked (a glitch peculiar to the F-86E model)

and that, when the worst happened, all of the hydraulic fluid in the airplane gushed out. When the aft section of the Sabre had to be removed for engine work, the spiral disconnects were difficult to loosen or tighten properly. The canopy seal was never right.

Men like Dan Walker had to cope with a difficult supply situation that was partly responsible for Colonel Thyng's complaint to the Pentagon. Even if maintenance and supply problems had been more effectively handled, it had long been clear that the 4th FIW, alone, could not handle hundreds of MiGs. Though new Sabres were constantly arriving, the aircraft-out-of-commission rate spiraled rapidly upward. Forty-five percent of the Sabres in Korea had to be listed as out of commission in January 1952, 16.6 percent for want of parts and 25.9 percent due to maintenance problems. With two Sabre wings flying combat, the need for external fuel tanks jumped 500 percent in four months, and supply levels of the tanks were nearly exhausted in January. Many Sabre pilots had to fly combat patrols with only one wing tank, reducing patrol time to compensate for reduced fuel yet often just barely making it home with a dead-stick landing.

Heavy Fighting

In January 1952, MiG bandit trains crossing the Yalu routinely numbered 100 or more aircraft, seizing advantage of their high-altitude capability by flying at 50,000ft (15,240m) and jockeying into position to bounce the Americans at Mach 0.9. The 4th FIW still had mostly older F-86A models and, by a tiny margin, these were faster than the newer, more maneuverable F-86Es, All of the wing's flight leaders, however, flew E models. This meant the 4th had real difficulty getting high enough and fast enough to take away the enemy's advantage in those critical first moments of a fight. In contrast, the 51st Wing had factory-fresh F-86Es and could swarm into MiG Alley fast enough (perhaps a few miles per hour slower than the A model but no slower than the enemy) and nearly as high as the MiGs.

In several engagements, 51st pilots caught the MiGs from behind, broke up their ragged formations, and shot them down. The score for January: 31 MiGs downed, five Sabres lost. All but a half dozen of the MiG kills were racked up by the new guys in the 51st.

Men who fought those great air battles over the Yalu have tried, in the years since, to portray a difference between the 4th and 51st Wings. In numerous interviews with members of both outfits, a portrait has emerged of some 4th pilots as MiG happy, willing to take risks to score aerial victories. The fliers in the 51st, on the other hand, are sketched as more serious and machinelike in their approach to warfare. No general statement can apply to all. But it is clear that some pilots were willing to take enormous risk to get MiG kills. Only those who were there are entitled to draw the thin line between valor and foolhardiness.

On 10 February 1952, Maj. George A. Davis—the leading ace of the war and among the most seasoned of fighter pilots—attacked a MiG formation at 32,000ft (9,753m) near the Yalu, just in time to prevent the MiGs from bouncing some Allied bombers. Davis wracked his F-86E Sabre (51-2725) around in a tight turn to close on the MiGs and quickly achieved his 13th and 14th MiG kills. Within seconds, however, a MiG pulled behind him and shot him down. With Davis' loss, the USAF was deprived of one of its finest air combat tacticians and a potential future leader. For his gallantry in pressing the fight to the enemy, Davis posthumously became the only Sabre pilot awarded the Medal of Honor.

Sabres downed 17 MiG-15s in February 1952 with but two losses (in-

In 1948-1949, Sq. Ldr. William (Paddy) Harbison was an exchange officer with the 71st FS / 1st FG, at March Field, California, and became the first Briton to fly the Sabre operationally. On 21 January 1950, his brother Eric Harbison of the RAF's No. 14 Squadron was killed in a gunnery mishap with a Vampire F.Mk5 near Sylt. When Paddy was sent to do further exchange duty with the 4th FIW in Korea, Eric's Reply *was an F-86E Sabre. Though the British pilot received credit for one MiG-15 damaged in combat, the Sabre assigned to him was shot down with 2nd Lt. Michael E. DeArmond on board. DeArmond was released by the communist side after the armistice.*
USAF via Paddy Harbison

This pair of F-86F-10-NA Sabres (51-12963, 51-12954) are among the first two F models to arrive in Korea and are being flown by 4th FIW pilots Karl Dittmer and Clifford D. Jolley. While no evidence of it is visible in this portrait, these Sabres were equipped with rocket-assisted takeoff (RATO) bottles in the lower fuselage, intended to provide a burst of speed to improve closure rates with the MiG-15. Karl Dittmer

cluding Davis). During heavy fighting in March 1952, Sabre pilots were credited with 39 MiG kills and sustained just three losses. In April, the score was 44 MiGs, four F-86s. One of the sporadic attempts by the other side to move aircraft to a location south of the Yalu was countered on 22 April 1952 when Maj. Elmer W. Harris and Kincheloe shot up the base at Sinuiju, destroying two Yak-9 propeller-driven fighters. (Aircraft destroyed on the ground did not count as kills.)

Throughout the war, Sabre pilots crossed the forbidden Yalu to engage MiGs on their own turf, ignoring rules, politics, and direct orders telling them to stay out of Chinese air space. At the 51st FIW, Gabreski, Jones, Mahurin, Maj. William Whisner, and others adopted a hot-pursuit policy, flying what they called Maple Special incursions into China when circumstance gave them a shot at a fleeing MiG pilot. These border crossings were kept secret from most other pilots. Kincheloe found out by accident, then had to be included.

These cross-border missions were an invitation to trouble. Lt. Bill Ginther came back from a mission with revealing gun-camera film. He had attacked a MiG over Manchuria and, trying to escape, the MiG pilot had dived to earth, pulling out just in time to pass along the runway at the crowded Antung airfield. Ginther began firing at the MiG while flying so low that the gun camera film, as Mahurin described it, showed "row after row of MiGs lined up on either side of the runway," so that "it appeared that the F-86 was flying even below the tops of the MiG tails." While enemy technicians stood on the MiGs watching, Ginther shot down his MiG, got out of the place, coaxed his Sabre home—and burned his film.

The number of Sabre air aces kept going up. They included Whisner, commander of the 25th FIS/51st FIW, who became the seventh jet ace (and his wing's first) on 23 February 1952. Gabreski became the eighth on 1 April, Capt. Robert H. Moore the ninth on 3 April, Kincheloe the tenth on 6 April; Capt. Robert J. Love 11th on 21 April, and Maj. William H. Wescott, the war's twelfth Sabre ace on 26 April 1952.

Gabreski—then and today, America's top living ace—got his fifth kill in an F-86E Sabre (51-2746) belonging to the 25th FIS/51st FIW, which Bill Wescott had named *Lady Frances* and the crew chief had dubbed *Michigan Center* (the nickname assigned by a pilot appeared on the left nose; nicknames assigned by crew chief and armorer appeared on the right nose, so that some Sabres had three names). Wescott got his fifth kill in the same airplane. The strapping Kincheloe, who was 6ft 2in (1.88m) with silver-blond hair and had the build of a football linebacker, became the first ace to get all of his MiG kills while flying the same airframe (51-2731), diligently nursed by crew chief Dan Walker.

This RF-86A Sabre (48-217) is one of the Project Ashtray airplanes converted in Japan for photo-reconnaissance missions in the Korean War and belongs to Col. Edward S. Chickering's 45th Reconnaissance Squadron, 67th Reconnaissance Wing at Kimpo. Nicknames on the right side of a Sabre were usually applied separately by crew chief and armorer, hence the two appellations Every Man a Tiger *and* Honeybucket. *A nickname given to the aircraft by its pilot would have appeared on the left side.* via Robert Esposito

More Losses

The USAF lost another fine leader, this time temporarily, when Bud Mahurin was shot down on 13 May 1952. Mahurin—who had transferred to Kimpo to command the 4th Fighter Group under the 4th FIW's Harry Thyng—was shot down by antiaircraft fire. The loss occurred during an early attempt to transform the Sabre into a fighter-bomber by slinging two 1,000lb (454kg) bombs beneath its inboard pylons. Later attempts were to be more successful. Mahurin became a prisoner of war (POW). Accused of signing propaganda statements under enemy duress, Mahurin had gone into the war (in his own words) "a fun-loving, gung-ho professional aviator." He was to emerge frustrated, hardened, and bitterly anticommunist.

In May 1952, 27 MiGs were claimed in exchange for air-to-air losses of five F-86s. Four more men became aces: Capt. Robert T. Latshaw (13th ace) and Maj. Donald E. Adams (14th) on 3 May, 1st Lt. James H. Kasler (15th) on 15 May, and the soon-to-depart 4th FIW commander Colonel Thyng (16th) on 20 May.

Although battle lines on the ground in Korea had long since stabilized (which did not mean that men were not dying in what seemed in many respects a bitter re-enactment of World War I trench fighting), General Weyland wanted to do more than maintain stability in the sky. Having two Sabres wings instead of one, and the F-86E instead of the F-86A, had improved things markedly, but the Americans had a few more steps to take if they were to finally take the edge away from the MiG.

Apart from larger fears that the situation in Korea could spread—there was always the danger of tensions between Nationalist and communist China boiling over—Weyland wanted to attain complete supremacy in the air. Weyland wanted not merely to do well against the enemy's MiG force but to defeat it.

A directive that went to American airmen in Korea on 10 July 1952 recognized three factors. The first was that the communists had amassed in the Far East large air forces that could be offensively employed against UN forces any time the enemy chose to use them that way. The second was that major sources of enemy supply remained off limits to UN air attack while the enemy's supply pipeline from his sanctuary to his front lines was measured in scores of miles rather than (as with the Americans) many thousands. Moreover, enemy supply requirements were low. Merely attacking the front end of his supply line on Korean soil alone was unlikely to prevent the enemy from maintaining supplies adequate to continue the fight. Third—an important factor in sorting out how to use resources—friendly forces in a stabilized ground situation did not require great amounts of close air support. The point of this directive was that the number-one priority in Korea was the struggle for command of the air—the campaign between the Sabre and the MiG.

Weyland knew that he had an ace up his sleeve—the F-86F version of the Sabre, which was soon to reach the combat zone. Until now, Weyland knew, production of American warplanes had not kept up with the war's demands. In February 1952, the Pentagon had informed the brass in Korea that the USAF had purchased 60 F-86E-6 Sabres from the Canadian manufacturer, Canadair. There were now enough aircraft to transfer the 39th FIS to Suwon; together with the 16th and 25th FIS, these belatedly brought the 51st Wing up to full strength of three squadrons.

The 39th FIS—the sixth and final Sabre squadron committed to the air-to-air campaign along the Yalu—began in July 1952 to receive the new, much-improved F-86F Sabre. Early F-

An F-86 Sabre of the 335th FIS/4th FIW heads for MiG Alley from Kimpo in 1952. The 335th FIS was nicknamed the Chiefs, and the squadron badge is readily apparent here. Karl Dittmer

86Fs retained the all-flying tail, which was so successful in maneuvering against the MiGs, but also retained leading-edge wing slats. The slats were a boon to low-speed performance, making the Sabre easier to land and to fly in the airfield pattern, but they hindered performance in combat—and worse. "Sometimes," remembers RAF pilot Paddy Harbison who flew an exchange tour with the 4th Wing, "when you were pulling Gs, the slats would pop out and deprive you of speed." Flight tests in the United States had already shown how to make the Sabre, finally, superior to the MiG-15 in all respects. The answer was to replace the slatted wing with a hard wing.

The 6-3 Wing

Col. John W. Mitchell took command of the 51st Wing on 13 June 1952, replacing Gabreski. Weeks later, a development came that may have seemed only of middling importance at the time. In fact, it was the most important event since Sabre pilots began to gain the advantage on their adversary. In August 1952, the 51st FIW flew its first combat missions with three F-86F Sabres with solid leading wing edges.

The hard wing on late F-86Fs (replacing the leading-edge slats found on previous Sabres, including early F-86Fs), when combined with the all-flying tail, gave the Sabre a pair of secret weapons. Steps were taken to retrofit all F-86Fs with the new solid wing.

The new wing was also known as the 6-3 wing because it replaced the four leading edge slats with a smooth, unbroken leading surface that was extended 6in (15.24cm) at the wing root and 3in (7.62cm) at the wing tip. To improve the flow of air over this redesigned wing, a 6in (15.24cm) barrier fence was added at the 70 percent mark on the span.

For the first time, the Sabre now had the performance to outfight the MiG-15 in every regime. The hard-wing F-86F could operate at 52,000ft (15,849m), improved climb rate, tighter turn, and speed in level flight at least 10 knots faster than the F-86E.

Even while the USAF zeroed-in on the key to defeating the MiG in the air, efforts to employ the Sabre in a very different capacity as a fighter-bomber continued to produce mixed results. Weyland felt he had no choice but to request still more F-86s to carry bombs to the enemy. On 18 July 1952, plans were established to equip the 8th FBW, now flying F-80C Shooting Stars, and the 18th FBW (with an attached squadron of the SAAF), now flying F-51D Mustangs, with new F-86F Sabres modified as fighter-bombers. Target for beginning of the transition: November 1952. For the first time, UN fighter-bombers would be able to take on MiGs if some expansion of the conflict made this necessary.

Fledgling Ace

The 4th Wing's 2nd Lt. James F. Low became the 17th, and most junior, American air ace with his fifth MiG kill on 15 June 1952. This achievement by a butter-bar lieutenant was mind-boggling: Dad Low became an ace barely six months out of flight school. Low turned inexperience to his advantage. Unlike older pilots who had to change, Low had no trouble learning how to use the A-1CM automatic ranging gunsight that was replacing the Mark 18 sight on F-86E Sabres but was deemed finicky and unreliable by pilots more comfortable with the earlier version.

Fellow Sabre pilot Capt. James A. Horowitz's novel *The Hunters*, written under the pseudonym James Salter (to which Horowitz changed his name after he became a figure in American letters), immortalizes a defiant, risk-taking junior fighter jock. Both Low and Salter acknowledge that this fighter jock is, in thin disguise, James F. Low. A young Robert Wagner played the upstart in the film.

While Jim Low was on a tour of the United States to tell USAF pilots about the gunsight, Lt. Col. Donald

Rodewald was sent to Korea to troubleshoot gunsight problems. Rodewald found that in the combat zone there was no test equipment, no spare parts, and a paucity of qualified people to keep the sights working properly. Very simply, the gunsight was effective but was cantankerous and had not been well designed for the crude maintenance environment, and extremes of heat and cold found in Korea.

The 18th air ace, Capt. Clifford D. Jolley, also of the 4th Wing, got his fifth MiG on 8 August 1952.

On 4 September 1952, a prolonged duel in which the Sabres were vastly outnumbered, F-86 pilots shot down 13 MiGs and sustained four losses. It was during this raging battle, with MiGs flitting back and forth across the Yalu River, that one Sabre pilot radioed to his buddies, "I need a little help. I'm up here alone and I've got 50 MiGs cornered." Maj. Frederick C. (Boots) Blesse shot down his fourth and fifth MiG-15s to become the 19th jet ace of the Korean War. In another intense battle on 21 September, Capt. Robinson Risner became the 20th ace.

Within days, Blesse became the leading Sabre ace when he brought his score to eight MiG-15s and one Lavochkin La-9. But he suffered the setback of having to eject into the Yellow Sea when he ran low on fuel amid a battle. A Grumman SA-16A Albatross amphibian rescued him.

September 1952 was a good month. Sabre pilots of the 4th and 51st Wings were credited with 61 MiG kills and seven probable kills, while four Sabres were lost in air-to-air combat.

In the fall of 1952, the 4th FIW's 334th squadron carried out a high-risk experiment. Spanking-new F-86F Sabres (among the first in Korea) were fitted with solid-fuel rockets, to be fired for brief periods to improve closure rates with the MiG-15 (Chapter 5). These rockets, sometimes inaccurately referred to by those who flew with them as jet assisted takeoff (JATO) bottles did not change the external appearance of the F-86F but added weight and center-of-gravity problems. Two MiG kills were achieved using rocket boost (by ace Jolley) but an F-86F piloted by Capt. Troy G. Cope was lost in combat. The rocket-boost scheme was not popular with pilots.

Jolley recalled that, "only four of us were selected to fly these aircraft because they demanded a little extra 'feel.' They were tail-heavy and started porpoising at 35,000ft (10,668m). I was able to catch the last two MiGs I destroyed with this gimmic, but without it, I might have been just as successful; because of the heavy tail mushout I got on a split-S to initiate the attack." The JATO scheme was quickly dropped.

By the time he ended his 11-month tenure as commander of the 4th FIW on 2 October 1952, Col. Harrison R. Thyng could rightly feel that he had been instrumental in turning the tide. It is possible that no one noticed. Headlines, Hollywood hype, and glory were being heaped on younger Sabre pilots like Kincheloe, Low, and Capt. Dolphin D. Overton III. Harry Thyng was an ace in two wars, a leader willing to accept risk to help his men, and the premier American fighter-wing commander of his era. Only partly due to the colonel's efforts—it was widely believed that the 4th enjoyed preference in pilot assignments over the 51st—Harry Thyng's 4th FIW in October 1952 was probably the finest fighter unit ever put into the field by any nation's air arm. The press, at the time, ignored Thyng almost completely.

While a mission was up, crew chiefs and armorers watched and waited to learn what was happening up in MiG Alley. A privileged few were able to listen in to radio traffic while Sabres and MiGs tangled with each other. The rest waited, and when the Sabres returned they looked for black char marks on the nose that showed that the guns had been fired. A considerable group of 4th FIW groundlings convenes around air ace Capt. Clifford D. Jolley's Sabre as Jolley returns with battle damage for the second time. Karl Dittmer

In the late months of 1952, an incredible 30 MiGs went down during dogfights without being fired at. Sabre pilots found themselves observing a series of abrupt, uncontrollable spins from which the Chinese pilots were unable to recover. Whatever caused these spins, the MiG pilots got better at it. In early 1953, American pilots observed 24 MiGs going into spins but only five enemy pilots ejected or died, the others recovered. No good explanation has ever emerged for this apparently temporary problem with the MiG-15.

While the Sabre continued to battle the MiG, Pentagon planners kept

1st Lt. Richard B. Keener arrived at Kimpo in January 1953 to join the 335th FIS/4th FIW at the height of Korean fighting. By now, F-86F Sabres had supplanted F-86A and F-86E models although the 6-3 hard wing associated with the F-86F-30 had not yet replaced the leading-edge slats shown here. Just about ready to fly, Keener is doing a walk-around check of his F-86 on the steel-mat hardstand. Richard B. Keener

running into delays in their plans to deploy Republic RF-84F Thunderflash aircraft to Korea for the reconnaissance mission. As a stopgap measure awaiting the RF-84F, six F-86A Sabres were locally modified with a camera mounted parallel to the longitudinal axis of the Sabre with a mirror arrangement to assure vertical coverage. Known as Project Ashtray airplanes, the photo-modified RF-86A Sabres had the speed to operate in MiG Alley with minimal escort, but the aircraft was never deemed particularly successful in its eye-in-the-sky role. The 67th Reconnaissance Wing at Kimpo under Col. Edward S. Chickering assigned five of the RF-86A Sabres to its 45th Reconnaissance Squadron, where they flew in company with Lockheed RF-80A Shooting Stars.

Enemy Strength

By January 1953, the communist air armada confronting UN forces in Korea totaled 1,485 aircraft, including 950 MiG-15s, 165 propeller-driven fighters, 100 Ilyushin Il-28 twin-jet bombers, and 270 other types. Gen. Glenn O. Barcus, now the top airman in theater, was concerned about the possibility of an enemy air offensive backed by the Il-28 bombers, two of which had made a provocative flyby along the Yalu on 17 December 1952, within eyesight of Sabre pilots.

The 4th Wing was now commanded by Col. James K. Johnson, the 51st by Col. John Mitchell. The two F-86 Sabre wings were constantly challenged in their thrust-and-parry campaigning along MiG Alley. And more Americans were gaining ace status. Col. Royal N. Baker, 4th Group commander, became the 21st jet ace on 17 November 1952 and eventually claimed 12 MiGs and one La-9. Capt. Leonard W. (Bill) Lilleyof the 334th FIS/4th FIW got his fifth MiG on 18 November 1952 to become the 22nd ace. On 22 November, Capt. Cecil G. Foster of the 51st Wing became the 23rd. On 24 January 1953, Capts. Dolphin D. Overton III and Harold E. Fischer, Jr., both of the 51st, became jet aces 24 and 25. On his last four Sabre missions in his combat tour, Overton racked up five kills to set a record for achieving ace status in the shortest time. On 30 January, Lt. Raymond J. Kinsey of the 4th Wing shot down the first Tu-2 prop-driven bomber to be spotted by the Americans in more than a year.

Both sides were constantly changing tactics in the continuing duels along the Yalu. Lt. Col. Robert P. Baldwin, who commanded the 51st Group from January to August 1953, stressed air discipline to his flight leaders and repeatedly pounded on the theme of flight integrity. Baldwin likened MiG Alley combat to hounds chasing the fox. In a heavy dogfight, it was easy for aircraft to become scattered in all directions, and an individual pilot could become a sitting duck. Baldwin insisted that pilots never fight in any unit smaller than a pair. He also looked for talent wherever he could find it. Baldwin recalls:

"A classic example was the assignment of this ROTC second lieutenant from Cal-Tech. He was not a rated officer and was the picture of a scientist. I asked him when he arrived what his assignment and duties were. He said he was merely assigned to the 51st FIW to help out in any way he could. I assigned him as operations analyst. His job was to watch out for patterns or trends.

"Within two or three weeks [of Baldwin's arrival], we found ourselves badly outnumbered by the enemy in aerial engagements. We would jump three to four MiGs and very quickly they would be reinforced by four more, and then four more, and so forth. The young second lieutenant came up with the problem and the solution. He determined that the MiGs were coming up on set paths like trains, four MiGs to every 3min. The 'railway' stretched from Antung south to the Chong-Chong River and back across the Suiho Reservoir [on the Yalu] and the MiGs went in both directions. We immediately changed tactics. We laid out a racetrack oval pattern across the track he had plotted. We also went to six-ship flights. We had six F-86s engaging their four MiG-15s, then six more F-86s arriving to take on their four reinforcement MiGs. It was a turkey shoot for about two weeks."

One of the shooters was Lt. Col. Edwin L. Heller, commander of the 16th FIS/51st FIW, who flew an F-86E Sabre nicknamed *Hell-er Bust X* (51-2756), and who scored his third and fourth MiG kills on 22 January 1952. Typical of mature, sensible leaders, Heller was well liked because he supported the troops. When he found a junior pilot behaving arrogantly toward his crew chief, S/Sgt. Clio Morales, Heller made sure the crew chief had the support he needed. The 16th's commander was already a five-kill ace from World War II, but before he could repeat the accomplishment in Korea he was shot down and taken prisoner on a hapless day when he was flying somebody else's airplane, leaving *Hell-er Bust X* with no owner.

On 16 February 1953, 1st Lt. Joseph McConnell, Jr., of Heller's 16th FIS/51st FIW shot down his fifth MiG but, because of delayed confirmation, became the 27th ace of the war. Capt. Manuel J. (Pete) Fernandez, Jr., of the 334th FIS/4th FIW was recognized as the 26th ace when he claimed his fifth and sixth kills on 18 February. Colonel Baker's 13 kills made him the leading ace of the conflict and it might have seemed heresy to suggest that youngsters like McConnell or Fernandez might challenge him. But they were going to.

Sabre pilots continued to chase MiGs across the Yalu in violation of the rules. A history of the period tells us that "[i]n the heat of combat in the latter part of February 1953, some Sabre pilots possibly pursued fleeing MiGs across the Yalu for short distances." In fact, it was happening regularly. Kincheloe got one of his kills in the neighborhood of Mukden, about 60mi (97km) north of the forbidden line. Thirty-four MiG-15s fell to the Sabres in March, with just two air combat losses.

Though some pilots were still uncertain that the Sabre could perform as a fighter-bomber, the decision to slot the F-86F into this additional role went forward. Except for bomb shackles, a modification of its gunsight, and special 200gal external fuel tanks, the F-86F fighter-bomber was the same

Seen at Itazuke AB near Fukuoka, Japan, during a 1953 ferry flight to Okinawa, this factory-fresh, hard-wing F-86F-30-NA Sabre (52-4818) was being flown by a Korean pilot, even though some time was to elapse before South Korea's air force acquired Sabres. The markings and yellow bands are standard (although a yellow band or other identifying color is noticeably missing from the vertical tail), so neither the photographer nor the author can identify a unit for this aircraft.
Richard B. Keener

At Suwon, where the 51st FIW mounted its missions to MiG Alley, Sabres display the black-on-aluminum checkertails worn by wing airplanes and the red fin cap color of the 25th FIS. This F-86E-10-NA Sabre (51-2832), Karens Kart, *belongs to squadron commander Lt. Col. Al Kelly and is crewed by A/3C R. E. Wright, both of whose names appear on the nose. In 1952, the USAF replaced Army-style enlisted ranks, such as private first class, corporal, and so on, with its own terminology, namely airman third class, airman second class, and so on.* Curvin Miller

aircraft as the F-86F dogfighter. The 18th FBW, located at the new K-55 Osan AB 45mi (72km) south of Seoul made a squadron-by-squadron conversion from the F-51D Mustang to the F-86F. This wing had the 12th and 67th squadrons as well as the wing's No. 2 Cheetah Squadron of the SAAF. The wing was commanded by Col. Frank S. Perego who had been one of the early Sabre pilots at March Field before the conflict. On 27 March 1953, the wing's Maj. James P. Hagerstrom flamed his fifth MiG to become the war's 28th ace and the war's only ace from the 18th FIS.

On 28 March 1953, Col. James Johnson (4th Wing commander) became the 29th ace and, the next day, Lt. Col. George Jones (4th Group commander) became the 30th. Also in March, Fernandez accounted for four more MiG-15s, capping his fighting frenzy with two kills on the same day on 21 March—raising his total to ten and putting him within reach of Colonel Baker's front-runner status. In this very different American era, one USAF public affairs weenie went on record with concern that an emerging hero happened to be Hispanic.

Ace Contest

Fernandez was being challenged for the top ace slot by 1st Lt. Joseph McConnell. On 12 April 1953, McConnell claimed his eighth MiG but was also shot down. He was plucked from the Yellow Sea by a 3rd Air Rescue Group H-19 helicopter. By 24 April 1953, now promoted to captain, McConnell had also become a double ace with ten kills.

With the 4th and 51st FIWs flying the Sabre on air-superiority missions and the 18th using it as a fighter-bomber, a fourth USAF wing now joined the armada in South Korea. The 8th FBW at K-13 Suwon AB (across the field from the 51st) began converting from the F-80C Shooting Star to the F-86F Sabre. The 8th FBW, which consisted of the 35th, 36th, and 80th squadrons, achieved the transition gradually with relative ease, but the shift to the Sabre was taking longer than Gen. Glenn Barcus wanted. The 8th FBW flew its first Sabre combat mission on 7 April 1953.

In the spring of 1953, the 4th FIW played host to Project Gunval, which brought ten F-86F Sabres, equipped with four 20mm cannons rather than the usual six .50cal machine guns, to Korea for combat evaluation. The Gunval exercise was not conclusive enough to justify modifying additional Sabres to cannon armament. In fact, the F-86F reached parity with the MiG-15 for other reasons, namely its higher-thrust engine and the solid wings. Because most squadrons now were equipped with F-86F models, Colonel Johnson was able to say to a group of his pilots in March 1953 that they now had a fighter that was "practically equal" to the MiG-15, with the caveat that the Sabre had to be maintained in top condition by all-important ground personnel.

In April 1953, a MiG pilot shot down the 51st FIW's Capt. Harold Fischer who was, by now, a ten-kill double ace. Fischer became separated from his wingman and crossed the Yalu into Manchuria before he was downed and taken prisoner. By the end of the month, Captain Fernandez had downed his 11th MiG-15 to remain one kill ahead of Captain McConnell, but still two victories behind the total of 13 attained by Colonel Baker.

While escorting fighter-bombers on 10 May 1953, Fernandez shot down one MiG and shared credit for another. Added to a pair of additional kills in May, Fernandez now had 14.5 aerial victories and was the top-scoring American ace. But in a remarkably aggressive performance, McConnell claimed three MiGs early in May and shot down three more on 18 May 1953 to raise his tally to an unbeatable 16 MiG kills. This was to remain the record for the war and was to make McConnell the ace of aces in the Korean conflict.

Also amid heavy fighting on 18 May 1953, Lt. Col. George I. Ruddell, commander of the 39th FIS/51st FIW and pilot of an F-86F called *MiG Mad Mavis* (51-12940), destroyed his fifth MiG to become the 31st jet ace of the war.

On 26 May 1953, Maj. James Jabara, who had returned for a second tour of duty in the combat zone (again with the 334th FIS/4th FIW), was leading a flight of four Sabres when he sighted 16 MiGs crossing the Yalu near Uiju. Jabara led his flight into the center of the MiGs, scattered them, and then pounced on a pair of MiGs that hadn't gotten out of the way fast enough. Jabara quickly forced one MiG into a fatal spin and shot down another, the eighth and ninth aerial victories for the war's original American ace.

With the capabilities of the F-86F, American pilots—despite the obvious limitations of politics and geography—now commanded the air and gave up nothing to the MiGs. No longer could the MiG-15 fly higher or seize the initiative. In June 1953, virtually all air-to-air engagements were initiated not by the Chinese but by the Americans. Most of the fighting took place below 40,000ft (12,192m) where the F-86F was most lethal. In June 1953, a month of fighting that shattered all previous records, Sabres shot down 77 MiG-15s, including a record 16 in a single day on 30 June.

The 4th Wing's Lt. Col. Vermont Garrison, at the decrepit age (for a fighter pilot) of 37, became the war's oldest (and its 32nd) air ace when he scored a MiG kill on 5 June 1953. Capts. Lonnie R. Moore and Ralph S. Parr became the 33rd and 34th aces on 18 June 1953, and Lt. Col. Robert Baldwin, 51st Group commander, became the 35th ace on 22 June 1953. On 30 June 1953, Lt. Henry Buttelmann, a mere 23 years of age, became the war's youngest (and 36th) American ace. Also by the end of June 1953, Major Jabara had run his kill tally up to 14, putting him within two MiGs of Captain McConnell's top-ranking score and within one-half kill of Captain Fernandez as the war's second-ranking ace.

Bad weather and reticence by the MiGs prevented more F-86F Sabre pilots from immediately capitalizing on the many aerial victories of June 1953. The weather was exceedingly marginal on 11 July 1953 when Maj. John F. Bolt, a Marine Corps officer serving an exchange tour with the 51st Wing, shot down his fifth and sixth MiGs to become the 37th American ace of the war. July—the final month of the war,

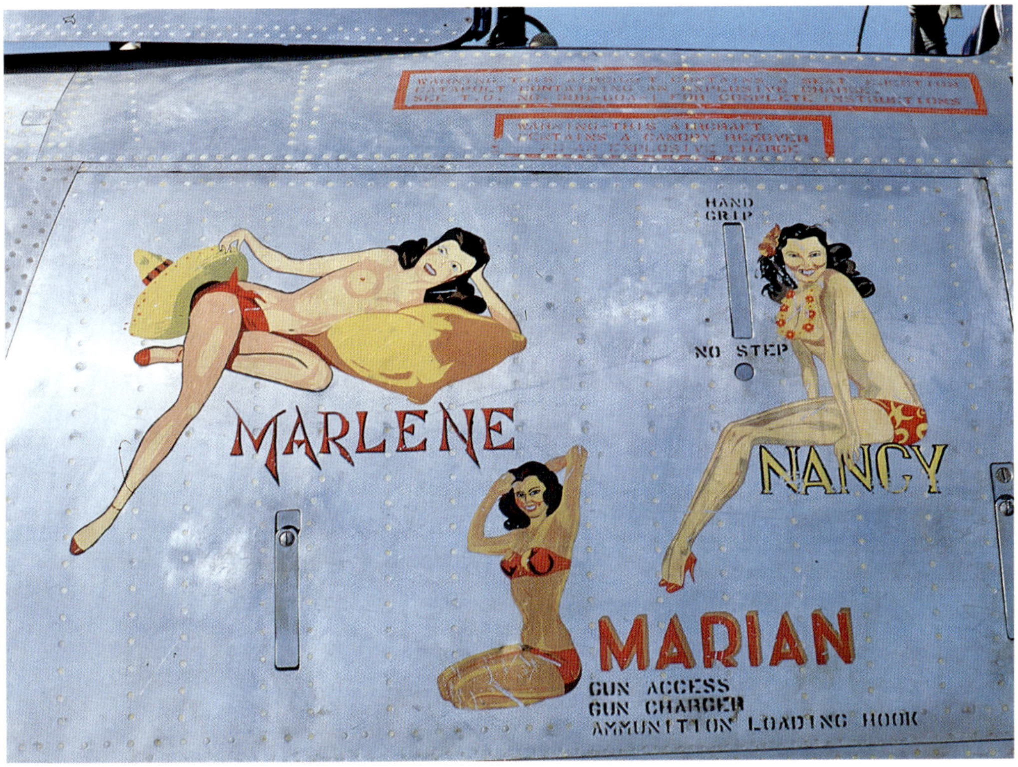

Marlene, Marian, and Nancy *make up a bevy, and an extraordinary collection of nose art, on this F-86E-10-NA Sabre (51-2864) belonging to the 39th FIS/51st FIW at Suwon. The Sabre named for a trio of ladies also was credited with two MiG kills.* Curvin Miller

though no one knew it at the beginning—started out more quietly and took a disastrous turn on 20 July 1953 when MiGs shot down two F-86Fs without sustaining a loss.

As July 1953 unfolded, two 4th Wing pilots, Capt. Clyde A. Curtin and Maj. Stephen L. Bettinger, became the 39th and 40th American air aces. Bettinger himself was shot down and taken prisoner. His wingman reported his victory but two witnesses were required to confirm a claim, so Bettinger was not confirmed as an ace until released from captivity on 2 October 1953. Of the 40 Americans who attained ace status in Korea, only one did not fly Sabres—the only US Navy ace, Lt. Guy Bordelon, pilot of an F4U-5NL Corsair, racked up five propeller-driven Bedcheck Charlies. Before the truce was signed on 27 July 1953, Major Jabara toted up his 15th kill to pass Fernandez and become the war's second-ranking MiG killer and, with McConnell, one of just two triple aces.

Closing Actions

On 22 July 1953, Lt. Sam P. Young of the 51st Wing racked up the final MiG kill of the Korean War. Just hours before the truce was signed on 27 July 1953, Capt. Ralph Parr shot down an Il-12 twin-engine transport, the war's final kill. Fifth Air Force aircraft withdrew from their last strikes against enemy targets in North Korea at 10pm on 27 July 1953 and the final phase of the air war in Korea ended, replaced by an Armistice Agreement signed by the opposing armies but never by any government.

In the Korean War, the USAF lost 971 aircraft, including 58 Sabres downed in air-to-air combat. Most aircraft losses (671) were caused by the enemy's intense and accurate ground fire with a substantial number (206) being claimed by other causes. The communist side's figures are not available, but according to American numbers the other side lost 600 MiGs in air-to-air combat, with another 143 listed as probably destroyed. Many years after the war, a revisionist study by the USAF, code named Sabre Measure Charlie, downgraded the overall kill ratio from more than 10:1 to a new figure of 7:1—still the best achievement in any sustained fighter campaign.

A study by the Rand Corporation concluded that the F-86 Sabre and the MiG-15 were evenly matched below 35,000ft (10,668m) with the MiG superior at higher altitudes. This was perhaps true for the entire 1950–1953 period, but by the end of the war, when the hard-wing F-86F in use, it was no longer a match. In July 1953, no fighter aircraft in the world could take on the F-86F Sabre without being at a disadvantage.

It was over. Yet, it was not over.

In February 1955, Jack Q. Kimball of the 335th FIS/4th FIW led a flight of 12 F-86Fs escorting an RB-45C Tornado reconnaissance aircraft over the North China Sea. Eight MiG-15s attacked the formation. Kimball's flight shot down two of the MiGs and chased the remaining six back north, with no losses. The two MiG kills were toted up by Lt. Charles (Fish) Salmon and Capt. George Williams.

And still, it was not over.

Lt. James McInerney was a member of Lt. Col. Bob Dawson's 35th FBS/8th FBW on 10 May 1955. Having redeployed from K-13 Suwon AB in September 1954, the squadron was now operating out of K-8 Kunsan AB conducting the coastal patrols provided for in the truce agreement.

"Our mission," McInerney remembers, "was to fly up the west coast of Korea, make a left hand procedural turn at the Manchurian border, and turn south. We had eight F-86s. Twelve MiG-15s were flying to the right (east) of us, paralleling our course about 5,000ft [1,524m]. I don't know where the MiGs came from. Radar tracked 92 MiGs at one time or another during the action. Some were seen taking off from Sinuiju.

"The MiGs rolled in at the most opportune time for us and the worst time for them. We'd started our turn. All we needed to do was tighten up the turn. Our worst problem was drop tanks flying off when their intentions became known to us. As I tightened up, hanging in with Dawson, a couple

Stud/Honest John, *alias F-86E-10-NA Sabre (51-2747) was the Sabre flown by Col. Walker (Bud) Mahurin, the World War II ace who commanded the 4th Fighter Group and was shot down on 13 May 1952 while flying another Sabre. This photo was taken after Mahurin became a POW; the black teardrop shape painted beneath the canopy covers up Mahurin's Korean War tally of three and one-half MiGs destroyed, one probable MiG kill, and one MiG damaged.* via Norman Taylor

Liza Gal/El Diablo *is the F-86E-10-NA Sabre (51-2800) flown by Capt. Chuck Owens of the 4th FIW. At the time this portrait was snapped, Owens had four MiG kills plus four probables. Owens later was credited with an additional one-half of an aerial victory (shared with another pilot), and thus fell short of becoming an ace.* via Norman Taylor

of guys overshot. My wingman Hal Pedersen overshot. We reversed. I started plinking the guy. Flashes came out of his left wing root and he started trailing dark smoke."

It was to turn out, on later count, that McInerney fired 896 rounds at the MiG-15. "We chased him up north. We had picked up some lore that was called the right of hot pursuit." In this tense, postwar period, once fired upon American fighter pilots were free to carry the fight across any border that might get in their way.

In the middle of this melee—McInerney chasing and firing at a MiG-15—a flight of straight-wing MiGs, apparently MiG-9s, flew by the Sabres in trail. "They crossed a T in front of us. Pete called, 'MiG at 12 high.' It was their flight leader. I saw a straight-wing MiG coming straight down on us with big cannon flashes. He did a barrel roll around us and went under. Pedersen broke off.

"As for the MiG-15 that I was chasing, the pilot punched out. I saw in front of me what appeared to be Mukden, but wasn't sure. I headed south as fast as I could. My altimeter said 400ft [121m]. I was alone and completely afraid." McInerney saw the other side carrying out air-sea rescue activities as he crossed the water. "When I got safe, I climbed to altitude, shut it down, and got into a flameout pattern for Kimpo."

Americans often forget that Armistice negotiations continue today at Panmunjom. When this volume went to press in 1993, most of the Cold War was over but Korea remained a volatile trouble spot where a million men faced each other across 2mi (4km) of ground. Sabres were eventually replaced by more advanced fighters, though they soldiered on with South Korea's air arm until the late 1980s—but the Korean War has never been resolved.

As for Jim McInerney, he made it to Kimpo—barely. At the controls of his F-86F (52-4417), McInerney had achieved the last MiG kill of the Korean era. It was the final aerial victory by an American pilot flying an F-86 Sabre.

Lt. Col. George I. Ruddell, commander of the 39th FIS/51st FIW and pilot of this F-86F-10-NA Sabre MiG Mad Mavis *(51-12940), grins at a press camera as he returns to Suwon on 18 May 1953 after shooting down his fifth MiG-15 to become the 31st American jet ace of the war. Ruddell eventually added eight MiGs to his World War II score of 2.5 aerial victories.* via Douglas E. Slowiak

Sabre Squadrons in the Korean War

4th FIW (K-14 Kimpo AB, Korea): 334th FIS, 335th FIS, and 336th FIS.

8th FBW (K-13 Suwon AB, Korea): 35th FBS, 36th FBS, and 80th FBS.

18th FBW (K-55 Osan AB, Korea) 12th FBS, 67th FBS, and No. 2 Squadron, SAAF Cheetahs.

51st FIW (K-13 Suwon AB, Korea): 16th FIS, 25th FIS, and 39th FIS.

APPENDIX 1

F-86 Serial Numbers

NAA F-86s

Designation	**S/n**	**Quantity**
XP-86	45-59597/59599	3
Subtotal		3
F-86A-1-NA	47-0605/0637	33
F-86A-5-NA	48-0129/0316	186
YF-93A	48-0316/0317	2
F-86A-5-NA	49-1007/1068	62
F-86J	49-1069	1
F-86A-5-NA	49-1070/1339	270
Subtotal		554
YF-86D	50/0577/0578	2
F-86D-1-NA	50/455/0491	37
F-86D-5-NA	50-0492/0517	26
F-86D-10-NA	50-0518/0553	36
F-86D-15-NA	50-0554/0576	23
	50-0704/0734	31
F-86D-20-NA	51-2944/3131	188
F-86D-25-NA	51-5857/5944	88
F-86D-30-NA	51-5945/6144	200
F-86D-35-NA	51-6145/6262	118
	51-8274/8505	232
F-86D-40-NA	52-3598/3897	300
F-86D-45-NA	52-3898/4197	300
F-86D-50-NA	52-4198/4304	107
	52-9983/10176	194
F-86D-55-NA	53-0557/0781	225
F-86D-60-NA	53-0782/1071	290
	53-3675/3710	36
	53-4018/4090	73
Subtotal		2,506
F-86E-1-NA	50-0579/0638	60
F-86E-5-NA	50-0639/0689	51
F-86E-6-CAN	52-2833/2892	(60)*
F-86E-10-NA	51-2718/2849	132
F-86E-15-NA	51-12977/13069	93†
Subtotal		336
F-86F-1-NA	51-2850/2927	78
F-86F-5-NA	51-2928/2943	16
F-86F-10-NA	51-12936/12969	34
F-86F-15-NA	51-12970/12976	7
F-86F-20-NH	51-13070/13169	100
F-86F-25-NH	51-13170/13510	341
	52-5272/5530	259
F-86F-30-NA	52-4305/5163	859
F-86F-35-NA	52-5164/5271	108
F-86F-35-NA	53-1072/1228	157
F-86F-40-NA	55-3816/4030	215
	55-4983/5047	65
Subtotal		2,239
F-86H-1-NA	52-1975/1976	2
F-86H-1-NH	52-1977/2089	113
F-86H-5-NH	52-2090/2124	35
	52-5729/5753	25
F-86H-10-NH	53-1229/1528	300
Subtotal		475
YF-86K	52-3630	(1)‡
	52-3804	(1)‡
F-86K	54-1231/1350	120
Total of NAA built F-86s:		6,233

NAA FJs

Designation	**S/n**	**Quantity**
XFJ-1	39053/39055	3
FJ-1	120342/120371	30
Subtotal		33
XFJ-2B	133756	1
XFJ-2	133754/133755	2
FJ-2	131927/132126	200
Subtotal		203
FJ-3/3M	135774/136162	389
	139210/139278	69
	141364/141443	80
Subtotal		538
FJ-4	139279/139280	2
	139281/139323	43
	139424/139530	107
FJ-4B	139531/139555	25
	141444/141489	46
	143493/143643	151
FJ-4F	(139282, 139284)§	(2)
Subtotal		374
Total of NAA-built FJs:		1,148
Total of NAA-built F-86s and FJs:		7,381

Canadair CL-13

Mark	**RCAF S/n**	**Quantity**
CL-13 Sabre Mark 1	19101	1
CL-13 Sabre Mark 2	19102/19199	98
CL-13 Sabre Mark 3	19200	1
CL-13 Sabre Mark 2	19201/19452	252
CL-13 Sabre Mark 4	19453/19890	438
CL-13A Sabre Mark 5	23001/23370	370
CL-13B Sabre Mark 6	23371/23752	
CL-13B Sabre Mark 6		655
Total of Canadair-built aircraft:		1,815

Commonwealth

Designation	Mark	S/n	Quantity
CA-26		A94-101	1
CA-27	30	A94-901/921	21
	31	A94-922/942	21
	32	A94-943/990	48
		A94-351/371	21
Total of Commonwealth-built aircraft:			112

Fiat

Designation	S/n	Quantity
F-86K	53-8273/8322	50
	55-4811/4936	126
	56-4116/4160	45
Total of Fiat-built aircraft:		221

Mitsubishi

Designation	S/n	Quantity
F-86F-40	55-5048/5117	70
F-86F-40	56-2773/2882	110
F-86F-40	57-6338/6457	120
Total of Mitsubishi-built aircraft:		300
Total of F-86 Sabres:		8,681
Total of F-86s and FJs:		9,829

*Included in Canadair CL-13 Sabre Mark 2 total
†F-86F aircraft with F-86E engine
‡Included in F-86D total
§Included in FJ-4 to al

APPENDIX 2

Korean War Aces

In Order of Achieving Ace Status

	Name	Date
1.	Capt. James Jabara	20 May 1951
2.	Capt. Richard S. Becker	9 Sept. 1951
3.	Capt. Ralph D. Gibson	9 Sept. 1951
4.	Maj. Richard D. Creighton	27 Nov. 1951
5.	Maj. George A. Davis, Jr.	30 Nov. 1951
6.	Maj. Winton W. Marshall	30 Nov. 1951
7.	Maj. William Whisner	23 Feb. 1952
8.	Col. Francis S. Gabreski	1 Apr. 1952
9.	Capt. Robert H. Moore	3 Apr. 1952
10.	Capt. Iven C. Kincheloe, Jr.	6 Apr. 1952
11.	Capt. Robert J. Love	21 Apr. 1952
12.	Maj. William H. Wescott	26 Apr. 1952
13.	Capt. Robert T. Latshaw	3 May 1952
14.	Maj. Donald E. Adams	3 May 1952
15.	Lt. James H. Kasler	15 May 1952
16.	Col. Harrison R. Thyng	20 May 1952
17.	2nd Lt. James F. Low	15 June 1952
18.	Capt. Clifford D. Jolley	8 Aug. 1952
19.	Maj. Frederick C. Blesse	4 Sept. 1952
20.	Capt. Robinson Risner	21 Sept. 1952
21.	Col. Royal N. Baker	17 Nov. 1952
22.	Capt. Leonard W. Lilley	18 Nov. 1952
23.	Capt. Cecil G. Foster	22 Nov. 1952
24.	Capt. Dolphin D. Overton III	24 Jan. 1953
25.	Capt. Harold E. Fischer, Jr.	24 Jan. 1953
26.	Capt. Manuel J. Fernandez, Jr.	18 Feb. 1953
27.	Capt. Joseph McConnell, Jr.	16 Feb. 1953
28.	Maj. James P. Hagerstrom	27 Mar. 1953
29.	Col. James K. Johnson	28 Mar. 1953
30.	Lt. Col. George L. Jones	29 Mar. 1953
31.	Lt. Col. George I. Ruddell	18 May 1953
32.	Lt. Col. Vermont Garrison	5 June 1953
33.	Capt. Lonnie R. Moore	18 June 1953
34.	Capt. Ralph S. Parr, Jr.	18 June 1953
35.	Col. Robert P. Baldwin	22 June 1953
36.	1st Lt. Henry Buttelmann	30 June 1953
37.	Maj. John F. Bolt	11 July 1953
38.	Lt. Guy Bordelon	16 July 1953
39.	Capt. Clyde A. Curtin	14 July 1953
40.	Maj. Stephen L. Bettinger	20 July 1953

(All except Bordelon Flew F-86s)

In Order of Number of Kills

Name	Enemy Aircraft Destroyed—Air-to-Air: World War II	Korea	Date of 5th Victory
Capt. Joseph McConnell, Jr., USAF	—	16	16 Feb., 1953
Maj. James Jabara, USAF	3.5	15	20 May, 1951
Capt. Manuel J. Fernandez, USAF	—	14.5	18 Feb., 1953
Maj. George A. Davis, Jr., USAF	7	14	30 Nov., 1951
Col. Royal N. Baker, USAF	3.5	13	17 Nov., 1952
Maj. Frederick C. Blesse, USAF	—	10	4 Sept., 1952
Capt. Harold E. Fischer, USAF	—	10	24 Jan., 1953
Col. James K. Johnson, USAF	1	10	28 Mar., 1953
Lt. Col. Vermont Garrison, USAF	11	10	5 June, 1953
Capt. Lonnie R. Moore, USAF	—	10	18 June, 1953
Capt. Ralph S. Parr, Jr., USAF	—	10	18 June, 1953
2nd Lt. James F. Low, USAF	—	9	15 June, 1952
Capt. Cecil G. Foster, USAF	—	9	22 Nov., 1952
Maj. James P. Hagerstrom, USAF	6	8.5	27 Mar., 1953
Capt. Robinson Risner, USAF	—	8	21 Sept., 1952
Lt. Col. George I. Ruddell, USAF	—	8	18 May, 1953
Capt. Clifford D. Jolley, USAF	—	7	8 Aug., 1952
Capt. Leonard W. Lilley, USAF	—	7	18 Nov., 1952
1st Lt. Henry Buttelmann, USAF	—	7	30 June, 1953
Maj. Winton W. Marshall, USAF	—	6.5	30 Nov., 1951
Col. Francis S. Gabreski, USAF	31	6.5	1 Apr., 1952
Maj. Donald E. Adams, USAF	4	6.5	3 May, 1952
Lt. Col. George L. Jones, USAF	—	6.5	29 Mar., 1953
Capt. Robert J. Love, USAF	—	6	21 Apr., 1952
Maj. John F. Bolt, USMC	6	6	11 July, 1953
1st Lt. James H. Kasler, USAF	—	6	15 May, 1952
Maj. William T. Whisner, USAF	15.5	5.5	23 Feb., 1952
Capt. Richard S. Becker, USAF	—	5	9 Sept., 1951
Capt. Ralph D. Gibson, USAF	—	5	9 Sept., 1951
Maj. Richard D. Creighton, USAF	2	5	27 Nov., 1951
Capt. Robert H. Moore, USAF	—	5	3 Apr., 1952
Capt. Iven C. Kincheloe, Jr., USAF	—	5	6 Apr., 1952
Maj. William H. Wescott, USAF	—	5	26 Apr., 1952
Capt. Robert T. Latshaw, Jr., USAF	—	5	3 May, 1952
Col. Harrison R. Thyng, USAF	9	5	20 May, 1952
Capt. Dolphin D. Overton, III, USAF	—	5	24 Jan., 1953
Col. Robert P. Baldwin, USAF	—	5	22 June, 1953
Capt. Clyde A. Curtin, USAF	—	5	14 July, 1953
Lt. Guy Bordelon	—	5	16 July, 1953
Maj. Stephen L. Bettinger, USAF	1	5	20 July, 1953

APPENDIX 3

Sources

This book is an attempt at a general history of the design, development, and operational and combat use of the F-86 Sabre.

Because this is history, every attempt is made to use terms and expressions for the period covered. Military ranks, assignments, and nomenclature are given for the time covered.

Many who flew F-86 Sabres in combat in Korea went on to reach other high and low points in their lives. Where these pilots' lives are part of the Sabre story, they appear in this narrative. I have resisted the urge to tell readers about F-86 Sabre pilots who later withstood captivity in North Vietnam, were elected to Congress, pinned on general's stars, or walked on the Moon. No man knew, while flying the F-86, what would happen to him years later.

James Salter's novel *The Hunters* can be found today only in a public library (with difficulty), so I must apologize to anyone under forty who may not appreciate how profoundly Salter influenced my generation. Salter created the finest work ever to appear in print—*ever*—about men who fly and fight.

No one could write about the North American F-86 Sabre without incurring a debt to Ray Wagner, Larry Davis, Larry Milberry, and Warren Thompson. Wagner's 1963 Sabre book, out of print for a quarter century, remains one of the finest single-aircraft-type books. Davis has been researching the Sabre since he learned to read, which happened in 1949, and has published several important contributions. Milberry gave us the definitive history of the Canadair Sabre, a work more comprehensive than any volume the size of this one could be. Although I interviewed dozens of Sabre personnel in producing this volume, Thompson has interviewed hundreds.

This book, at least, contains a number of firsts. Some of the information on foreign air forces, like many of the photos on these pages, has not appeared before. James F. Low is controversial and has never previously permitted an interview. James McInerney has not previously described the Sabre's final American kill in 1955.

Thousands of facts appear on these pages. Any errors are the sole responsibility of this author. But this book would have been impossible without help.

Among the fraternity: Hal Andrews, Mike Bennett, Mark Berent, Warren M. Bodie, Walter Boyne, Victor Chun, David P. Crawley, Duncan Curtis, Ed Davies, Larry Davis, Jim Dunn, Robert Esposito, Peter R. Foster, John Fry, Jerry Geer, Dan Hagedorn, Joseph G. Handelman, Tom Hildreth, Albert Norman Kalow, Gerhard Lang, Bob Louden, Sam McGowan, David W. Menard, Peter B. Mersky, David Ostrowski, Steve Pace, Neville C. Parkins, Kevin L. Patrick, Norman Polmar, C. M. Reed, Douglas E. Slowiak, Jelle Sjoerdsma, Jim Sullivan, Norman Taylor, Chris Tompkins, Nick Veronico, and L. J. Vosloo.

The following were interviewed; Martin J. Bambrick, Jr. (335th FIS/4th FIW), James Brickel (49th FIS), Guy Larry Brown (VMF-232), Harry D. Brown (25th FIS/51st FIW), Joseph A. Buebe (Kimpo), Ralph Burr (VF-53), Earl J. Cheney (16th FIS/51st FIW), Philip E. Colman (335th FIS/4th FIW), Karl Dittmer (335th FIS/4th FIW), William H. Foy (VMF-235), Curtis E. Francom (334th FIS/4th FIW), Rowland G. (Doc) Freeman (VA-144), James J. Hagenback (71st FS/1st FG), William (Paddy) Harbison (71st FIS/1st FG; 4th FIW), Dean Houck (Fasron-12), Clem Koselke (16th FIS, 51st FIW), Leonard W. Lilley (334th FIS/4th FIW), James F. Low (335th FIS/4th FIW), James E. McInerney, Jr. (35th FBS/8th FBW), Roger Monroe (Wright-Patterson AFB), Clio Moralez (16th FIS, 51st FIW), James R. (Dick) Powell (VF-142), Don Primeau (VF-62), John V. Seliga (VMF-122), Eric G. Smith (335th FIS/4th FIW), Johnnie M. Vance (VMF-122), Charles Vasiliadis (417th FBS/50th FBW), Mary Stearns Wass (NAA/Hahn).

The following shared their experiences via correspondence or by telephone: Gordon Beem (4th FIW), Syd Burrows (No. 434 Sq., RCAF), R. Y. Costain (Flight Systems), Larry Counts (Flight Systems), Michael E. DeArmond (335th FIS/4th FIW), Donald O. Griffith (335th FIS/4th FIW), Richard B. Keener (335th FIS/4th FIW), Tom Mackin (NAA/Selfridge), Riggs Monfort (16th FIS/51st FIW), George Nelson, Jr. (VMF-312), Phillip A. Norton (51st FIW), John D. Nossick (16th FIS/51st FIW), Robin Olds (94th FS/1st FG), Tab Riley (CF-43), Francis X. Rozinski (VMF-312), James Salter (335th FIS/4th FIW), R. A. Stevens (Suwon AB), Walter C. Stewart, Jr. (VMA-212), Richard I. Sudhoff (West Coast Island Defense Unit), W. D. Taylor (4th FIW), Dean Tracy (1st FG), Fred C. Wise (NAA/Inglewood), Charles E. Yeager (417th FBS/50th FBW).

Special thanks are due to Bruce Potts of Australia's *Flightpath* magazine, Colonel Peter J. (Monster) Wilkins of the South African Air Force, Tim Parker, Greg Field, and Barbara Harold.

The views expressed in this book are mine and do not necessarily reflect those of the United States Air Force.

Robert F. Dorr
Oakton, Virginia

APPENDIX 4

Bibliography

Allward, Maurice. *F-86 Sabre.* New York: Charles Scribner's Sons/London: Ian Allan, 1978.

Anderson, Colonel Clarence E. (Bud), with Joseph P. Hamelin. *To Fly and Fight: Memoirs of a Triple Ace.* New York: St. Martins Press, 1990.

"Answers from Our First Jet Ace," *Newsweek,* 25 June 1951, p. 52.

Blair, Morgan M. (Mac), "Evolution of the F-86." Paper delivered at Evolution of Aircraft Wing Design Symposium, American Institute of Aeronautics and Astronautics, 18 March 1980.

Childerhose, R. J. *The F-86 Sabre.* Dallas, Texas: Len Morgan Books, 1965.

Chilstrom, Ken (ed). *Test Flying at Old Wright Field: By the "Wright Stuff" Pilots and Engineers.* Omaha, Nebraska: Westchester House, 1991.

Davis, Larry. *F-86 Sabre in Action.* Warren, Michigan: Squadron/Signal, 1978.

———. *F-86 Sabre in Action.* Carrollton, Texas: Squadron/Signal, 1992.

———. *MiG Alley.* Carrollton, Texas: Squadron/Signal, 1978.

———. *Air War Over Korea: A Pictorial Record.* Carrollton, Texas: Squadron/Signal, 1982.

Futrell, Robert Frank. *The United States Air Force in Korea 1950-1953.* Washington: Office of Air Force History, 1983.

Harbison, Squadron Leader William, and Flight Lieutenant R. Knight. *The F-86 versus the MiG-15.* Report for the [British] Royal Air Force. Kimpo: 1952.

Mahurin, Colonel Walker (Bud). *Honest John.* New York: Van Rees, 1962.

Mason, Francis K. *The North American FJ Fury.* London: Profile Publications, 1965.

Mesko, Jim. *FJ Fury in Action.* Carrollton, Texas: Squadron/Signal, 1990.

Salter, James. *The Hunters.* New York: W. W. Norton, 1962.

Shacklady, Edward. *The North American F-86A Sabre.* London: Profile Publications, 1965.

Sickinger, Peter. *Canadair CL-13A Sabre Mk.5.* Arnsberg: Impressum, 1992.

Stanaway, John. *Cobra in the Clouds: Combat History of the 39th Fighter Squadron 1940–1980.* Temple City, California: Historical Aviation Album, 1982.

Wache, Siegfried. *Canadair Sabre CL.13B Mark 6.* Arnsberg: Impressum, 1992.

———. *North American (Fiat) F-86K Sabre.* Arnsberg: Impressum, 1980.

Wilson, Stewart. *Meteor, Sabre and Mirage in Australian Service.* Sydney: Aerospace Publications, 1989.

Index